Indian Madhyamaka Buddhism
After Nagarjuna

Other Books

by

Richard H. Jones

_____

Science and Mysticism

Mysticism Examined

Reductionism

Mysticism and Morality

Curing the Philosopher's Disease

Piercing the Veil

Time Travel and Harry Potter

Nagarjuna: Buddhism Most Important Philosopher

For the Glory of God . . .: Christianity and Modern Science

One Nation Under God?

INDIAN MADHYAMAKA BUDDHIST PHILOSOPHY AFTER NAGARJUNA

Volume 1

———

*Plain English
Translations and Summaries
of the Essential Works of
Aryadeva, Rahulabhadra,
Buddhapalita, and Bhavaviveka*

———

Translated and Summarized
by
Richard H. Jones

Jackson Square Books
New York
2011

Distributed by www.createspace.com

Printed in the United States of America

Library of Congress Cataloging-in-Publication Data

Indian Madhyamaka Buddhism after Nagarjuna / translations with commentaries by Richard H. Jones
Includes bibliographical references and index.
ISBN-13: 978-1460969892
ISBN-10: 1460969898
1. Mādhyamika (Buddhism) — Early works to 1800. I. Jones, Richard H. 1951-

Contents

Abbreviations

CS — Aryadeva's *The Four Hundred Verses* (*Catuh-shataka-shastra-karikanama*)

HVNP — Aryadeva's *Hand Treatise* (*Hasta-vala-nama-prakarana*)

MAS — Bhavaviveka's *Summary of the Meaning of the Middle Way* (*Madhyamaka-artha-samgraha*)

MHK — Bhavaviveka's *Verses on the Heart of the Middle Way* (*Madhyamaka-hrdaya-karikas*)

MK — Nagarjuna's *Fundamental Verses of the Middle Way* (*Mula-madhyamaka-karikas*)

MKV — Buddhapalita's Commentary on Nagarjuna's *Fundamental Verses on the Middle Way* (*Mula-Madhyamaka-karika-vritti*)

R — Nagarjuna's *Jewel Garland of Advice* (*Ratnavali*)

SS — Aryadeva's *One Hundred Verses* (*Shataka-shastra*)

SSK — Nagarjuna's *Seventy Verses on Emptiness* (*Shunyata-saptati-karikas*)

VP — Nagarjuna's *Pulverizing the Categories* (*Vaidalya-prakarana*)

VV — Nagarjuna's *Overturning the Objections* (*Vigraha-vyavartanti*)

YS — Nagarjuna's *Sixty Verses on Argument* (*Yukti-shashtikas*)

Preface

This book is the first of two companion volumes to my *Nagarjuna: Buddhism's Most Important Philosopher* (Jones 2010). It presumes that the reader is familiar with the earlier book and will contain no independent discussion of Nagarjuna. Rather, it presents the developments of the Madhyamaka tradition in India after Nagarjuna. The texts selected for inclusion here begin with authors alive during Nagarjuna's lifetime (Aryadeva and perhaps Rahulabhadra) and continue with the most prominent authors of the next few centuries (Buddhapalita and Bhavaviveka). The next volume will contain selections of the works of the most prominent authors in the culmination of Indian Madhyamaka thought: Chandrakirti and Shantideva.

As with the earlier book, the translations from Sanskrit here are attempts to make the works understandable to members of the general public who are interested in philosophy. They are not literal translations designed for scholars in Buddhist studies. The basic texts, unlike their commentaries, were pithy because they were designed to be chanted and memorized (and they are still chanted and memorized today). Many texts were also not written down for a long time, and so they were intentionally kept short and rhythmic to make transmission easier. Longer texts with more explanations would have been helpful for us today, but the works were never meant to be understood independently of a teacher or a tradition's commentary — it was understood that there would be a teacher there explaining the lines more fully. Extensive commentaries were usually only recorded later. The texts often repeat the same word or a variation of it more than once in a verse or a passage to make memorization easier. Mostly the basic texts are in one standardized form: verses of four lines of eight syllables each. But this means making the number of syllables fit the meter count, and that leads to problems for understanding the text: some lines are very condensed thoughts, while others contain some extra words thrown only in to keep the meter correct. Sometimes there is no verb in a line but only nouns and ancillary words. That the listeners would share a common philosophical background and thus already know the meaning of many of the technical words also made it less necessary for the authors to expand their thoughts. In many lines, a pronoun is used to refer to a word in a previous verse or to something that the listener has been told but that the translator must now supply — sometimes even a pronoun is omitted.

The objective here is to glean the philosophical content of the works and present it in an intelligible fashion for the reader today — if some of the original author's style is preserved, so much the better, but that is not the goal. As with the earlier book, the basic works have been reformatted here from a series of verses into sentences and paragraphs grouped as the subject-matter dictates. This makes the texts much easier to follow and understand. Changing the grammar and syntax (e.g., changing a passive voice to active) also helps clarify the meaning. Translations that attempt to follow rigidly the form and word order of the works end up stilted. For many translations, the reader still has to be able to look at the original Sanskrit in order to understand what the translator is saying — and in that case, what is the point of the translation at all? Attempts to modernize the works — e.g., translating a word that means "unreasonable" or "unacceptable" as "illogical" or "logically contradictory" or "logically impossible" — have been resisted because of the danger that they distort the original works and mislead the modern reader. (One concession has been to change the experiential flavor of verbs denoting "is not found' or "it not seen" to the bare ontological claim "does not exist.") Certainly, overtly reading in contemporary philosophy and science into premodern texts has been avoided.

But if something can be said in one language, it should be translatable into another, even if the translation must be longer to make what was being said in the original intelligible in another language. What Ludwig Wittgenstein said in the preface to his *Tractatus LogicoPhilosophicus* should apply to translations too: "What can be said at all can be said clearly." (Most people who are not professional philosophers focus on the second half of the sentence: ". . . and what one cannot speak of, one must be silent.") These texts were never deliberately obscure or "mystical" or "esoteric" — they were meant to be of practical value to practicing Buddhists. The problem raised by the philosophical issue of whether all translations are indeterminate can be mitigated in practice if a wide enough sampling of an author's or a tradition's thought is studied. Like any translator, I hope I have succeeded in not imposing my own ideas or reasoning on these authors when making sense out of a passage, but all translations of necessity involve some interpretation, and translators cannot help but look at a past thinker through the lens of their own knowledge and presuppositions when trying to understand a text. (I have added brief material in parentheses in the translations to help explain my understanding.) Moreover, the original author's ideas are not always clear. Many passages remain hard to understand and open to different readings, even after more of his works and later commentaries have been consulted. No matter how many texts are consulted, translators faces the danger that they are forcing a text to make sense to themselves, no matter what the original author said. Am I unconsciously rewriting, say, Aryadeva's arguments to make them better (or at least more modern) than they really are? In rendering the verses into English, am I reading in what I think the text *should* say? In simplifying a work, am I cleaning up the arguments or inadvertently changing them? The more one moves away from a literal translation, the greater the danger of making the text say what the translator thinks it should say. But the most any translator can do is give his or her best effort to retain the original author's intent.

* * *

I. Texts

Aryadeva
(ca. Second or Third Century)

Aryadeva was a direct student of Nagarjuna and is considered by Buddhists as the co-founder of the Middle Way (Madhyamaka) school. This would place in the later second or third century C.E. Aryadeva probably wrote between 225 and 250 C.E. (Lang 1986: 8). If the various legends preserved in Tibetan and Chinese texts are to be believed (see Sonam 2008: 10-15), he was the natural or supernatural son of a king of Sri Lanka who, like the Buddha, renounced his royalty. He traveled to South India where he encountered Nagarjuna and became his student. Both were at a time at the famous monastery at Nalanda. He succeeded Nagarjuna and did much to preserve the Madhyamaka school. He was a formidable advocate in India's formal philosophical debates, winning both by his reasoning and (if the legends are true) also by magical deeds if the debater first used magic to defeat him. His texts directly address both Buddhist and Hindu opponents, unlike the works most likely composed by Nagarjuna.

Whether Aryadeva wrote the first work presented here — the *"Hand Treatise"* — has been questioned. Chinese Buddhists attribute it to Dignaga, who is associated with the Yogachara school (see Lang 1986: 15; Potter 2003: 318). But since verse 4 of the text criticizes the Yogachara position that only external objects, not the mind, are illusory, it is more likely that a Madhyamaka Buddhist wrote this work (Tola & Dragonetti 1995: 5). Even if Aryadeva was not the author, it is still worth including here since it gives a concise summary of the Madhyamaka point of view in fairly nontechnical terms — e.g., it does not include the word "emptiness" — that makes it more accessible to the general public. It employs the distinction between ultimate truth and conventional truth, although this is not unique to the Madhyamaka school (Thomas & Ui 1918: 272). It asserts the universal conditionedness of things, the nonexistence of self-existence, and the illusory character of the world; it also shows the Madhyamaka method of analyzing an opponent's position without arguing positively for one's own and without appealing to religious texts as authority or invoking any experiences other than our ordinary experience of the world (Tola & Dragonetti 1995: xxiii). It also introduced the rope/snake analogy made famous centuries later by Hindu Vedanta Advaitins into India's philosophical literature. (This assumes the tract is in fact by Aryadeva and is not a much later work.)

The *Hand Treatise* also has a commentary attached to the text that is presumably by the author himself. This is also translated here following the text. Each verse has four lines and in the case of verses 1 and 3 the commentary is broken up into two parts, one each for two lines of the verse. Some versions of the text, including the reconstruction utilized here, have seven verses. But the title — the *"Treatise Named 'Hair in the Hand'"* — seems to mean something about the treatise being a doctrinal summary short enough to fit in the hand or being as clear as a hair held in the palm of the hand to be examined. A six-verse version fits this title better: the first five verses may represent the five fingers of a hand and the concluding verse would then represent making a clenched fist from the five fingers.

The translation here is from the reconstructed Sanskrit from the Tibetan of the text and commentary in Thomas & Ui 1918: 275-287, although I am not always confident that it must be following the original text.

The second text, the *Four Hundred Verses on Yogic Deeds*, is Aryadeva's most important work. The work consists of sixteen chapters of twenty-five verses each. It is very possible that the teaching had to be cut or expanded to fit this form. Only about a third is available in the original Sanskrit, although all of it is preserved in Tibetan and Chinese. Modern scholars have reconstructed the Sanskrit from the Tibetan. Translations from Tibetan (Lang 1986, Berzin 2007, Sonam 2008) have also been consulted. In Tibetan, the text is written in a "very tense style" with each verse consisting of four lines of seven syllables each — in many instances, some of the seven syllables only serve to preserve the meter and do not affect the meaning (Sonam 2008: 20). This opens the text to different understandings.

The first half of the text could be presented as a dialog between Aryadeva and a king, although the king's questions are not presented in the text itself, as with Nagarjuna's *Jewel Garland of Advice*. The second half, which is more philosophical in nature, also appears to be a dialog between Aryadeva but now with various Hindu and Buddhist opponents. The text does not supply his opponents' statements, but possible claims and questions are reconstructed here and presented in italics. Some verses in both halves have been augmented by material in parentheses to make their meaning clearer. Any translation reflects the translator's understanding, and such comments flesh out mine.

The last text, the *One Hundred Verses*, is attributed to Aryadeva, but in style it is quite different from the *Four Hundred Verses* and may well be by another author. Nevertheless, it still represents early Madhyamaka thought. It too no longer exists in Sanskrit. At some point the text consisted of one hundred verses each with four lines of eight syllables, but such a version no longer exists. The summary here is based on the translation by Giuseppe Tucci (1929) from a Chinese translation and the summary by Karen Lang (1999b). Material from its traditional commentary by another Buddhist is also summarized here and placed in brackets (with my explanations again in parentheses). The numbers are not to the original verses, but have been added to the opponent's remarks for purposes of reference.

* * *

The Hand Treatise
(Hasta-vala-nama-prakarana)
With its
Traditional Commentary

Homage to the noble Bodhisattva Manjushri!

Some people consider the merely conventional three realms (the world created by desire, and the formed and formless realms created through meditation) as self-existent and do not grasp the ultimate truth. This treatise has been composed in order that, by discriminating the true nature of reality, the correct knowledge may arise in those people.

[1ab] Consider a rope perceived as a snake: when the rope is seen clearly, the conceptualization of a snake is seen to be without reality.
Here the treatise says that in a place that is lit only by a dim light there arises a cognition with certainty "This is a snake." This false cognition arises

on seeing something sharing a common feature with the form of a rope but not grasping the rope's own form. When the rope's own form is ascertained with certainty, the knowledge results that there was no such object as a snake. Because of this, that false cognition of a snake is recognized as an erroneous cognition corresponding to no object in reality, since it was merely a product of fancy.

[1cd] When that rope's parts are seen, then the cognition of that rope as a snake is also seen to be erroneous.

If the rope is also examined by dividing it into its parts, the existence of the rope as a separate entity itself is not perceived. Since this "rope as a separate (self-existent) entity" is not perceived, the perception of the rope as a separate (self-existent) entity too is, like the conceptualization of a "snake," erroneous and nothing else,

In addition, just as the cognition of the rope is erroneous, so also is the cognition of the parts: (self existence) is not perceived when the parts are examined in the same manner by dividing them into their parts and in turn into their fractions and particles. Since the self-existence of the parts is not perceived, the conceptualization that has the form of the perception of these parts of the rope, like the conceptualization of "a rope," is also merely erroneous.

[2] If the own-form of all other dependent things is examined carefully, all objects within the scope of worldly cognition are found to be dependent upon something else.

When the rope and its parts are examined through the separation of their parts and so forth, their self-existence is not perceived. The conception of the rope itself and the parts themselves is, like the conception of the snake, erroneous. In the same way, when the parts and so forth of any objects of worldly cognition whatsoever — pots, cups, and so forth — are examined, all are found to be dependent upon something else. And when all the things are completely divided up to the last parts, any thing — the pot and so forth — is seen to be merely dependent upon a convention. What is dependent upon something else does not exist from the point of view of what is real.

[3ab] Since anything without parts cannot be conceived, the last part is equivalent to being nonexistent.

What is the last part of all dependent things — the substance of the particles, which is only one without parts — is without reality since it cannot be perceived or imagined. It is like a garland of (nonexistent) sky-flowers or a rabbit's horn.

But precisely because the substance of parts, if it indeed exists at all, has an unimaginable defining characteristic, you may ask how can it be known that it is not one in nature? Because, even supposing that it exists, it has different spatial parts. (That is, if it is one, it cannot be divided into parts.) For example, the substances of such (observable) things as a pot, cloth, or cart, which do exist, are seen to have different spatial parts — east and west, top and bottom, and so forth. If the substance of (unobservable) particles also happens to exist, it undoubtedly must be admitted that it too has different spatial parts — east and west, and so forth. Having different parts, the substance of the particle cannot be shown to be one. Since various divisions of the substances are seen, its oneness does not exist. Even though the substance of the particle cannot be perceived, let this claim of the oneness of a particle's substance be given up.

[3cd] Thus, a wise man does not conceive what is merely an error as real from the ultimate point of view.

Because the three realms are merely erroneous, a wise man — one who desires to attain the ultimate good — must not consider them as real from the ultimate point of view.

You may claim "Even if it is maintained that it is true that those external objects — the pot and so forth — are imagined out of nothing, since entities have an inconceivable form, still the erroneous *cognition itself* that has the form of perceiving those objects exists. The erroneous cognition exists in the same way as, for example, the perception of a magical creation or a mirage exists, even though the magical creation and mirage themselves do not exist." We answer this as follows in the next verse.

[4] Since those things that appear in an erroneous cognition are not real, they are not as they appear in that cognition. That cognition is of the same nature as those things — i.e., an appearance without reality.

The error indeed is an erroneous cognition of a substantive form (i.e., seeing the object as real). But the form itself does not possess substance. The object of the cognition also is not real. Since the content of the cognition is an erroneous form, the cognition itself is of the same nature and is not real.

You may ask, how is this known? Because in the world, too, if a cause does not exist, neither does the effect. (That is, if the cause [the content of the illusion] is not real, neither is the effect [the resulting mental state].) If a seed does not generate a sprout, we do not see such a thing as the existence of the sprout. Thus, we declare the example of a magical illusion not to be a valid counterexample. (The magician [the cause] does not exist, and so neither does his creation — both are illusions, and neither is real.)

[5] *Whosoever with a subtle mind conceives all things as merely dependent, that intelligent one easily abandons desires and other attachments, just as the one who knows that there is no snake but only a rope abandons the fear of the snake.*

In the three realms, which as explained above are merely dependent phenomena, one who with a subtle mind perceives with certainty that objects are without substance and are merely conventional designations abandons the thought of observable objects such as pots. In the same way, for such a person the fear produced in him by the thought "(What is actually) a rope is a snake" no longer exists once there is certainty, gained through the examination of the characteristics of the rope, that it is only a rope. In the same way, that person also by examining thoroughly the things that cause desire and so forth easily and quickly removes the nets of the mental afflictions such as desire.

[6] *In pondering worldly things, one should act as worldly people do. One who desires to abandon the mental afflictions (hatred, greed, and desire) must investigate things from the ultimate point of view.*

Worldly people, who conceive things as "a pot" and so forth as real, impose conventional designations on them — "This a pot," "This is a cloth," "This is a cart." In the same way, one should act in the previously accepted ways according to conventions. Afterwards, those who wish to abandon the mental afflictions, such as desire, must thoroughly investigate things from the ultimate point of view as has been explained. Having thoroughly investigated things in that way, the nets of impurities — desire and so forth — do not arise again.

Notes

Prologue. The three realms are merely conventionally designated (*vyavahara-matra*). What is needed is to discriminate the "proper nature" of everything — their "*svabhava*" in the nontechnical sense of what is properly the nature of something.

Verse 1. Unlike Nagarjuna's works, this text employs the famous rope/snake example to illustrate what is real and what is an illusion. This example is more associated with the Hindu Advaita Vedantins who came along five centuries later. Shankara's teacher Gaudapada used the example and he may have had a Buddhist for a teacher. Advaitins utilize it to distinguish the phenomenal world from the transcendental reality *Brahman/atman*, but the distinction in Buddhism applies only within the phenomenal world to what is real there and what is not.

Also note the *experiential* nature of an illusion — it is visual, not mere an erroneous thought or judgment. Knowledge and the root-error (*vidya* and *avidya*) in Indian philosophy in general is of this nature.

Aryadeva uses "own-form (*sva-rupa*)" here and throughout the text. If he discussed instead "*self-existence* (*sva-bhava*)" (which he also uses), it would fit the Madhyamaka picture more clearly. This may be an instance of the author using more common terms and ideas for his audience, but the commentary of verse 2 does not equate the two concepts.

Verse 2. Here the distinction between worldly knowledge (*samvriti-jnana*) and the point of view of what is ultimately real in the world is important. All that we observe are collections of parts — a pot, a cloth, a cart. All are designated by conventions we contrive for our convenience (Tola &Dragonetti 1995: 14 n. 41).

We should not use "*ultimate reality*" when discussing "reality from the ultimate point of view (*paramarthatas*)" — to Westerners, it gives the connotation of "God." The Madhyamikas are not discussing any transcendental reality, or any source of the phenomenal world, but how the phenomenal world is when it is free of our conceptualizations. The phenomenal world free of our projections is how things are "from the ultimate point of view." It is no more than the world around us seen properly. It is not a matter of "degrees of reality" or one reality being dependent on a transcendental source. Rather, it is a matter of *two different perspectives on the same thing*: phenomenal reality with self-existent parts and without any self-existence.

Verse 3ab. The position being refuted here is that of the Hindu Vaishe-shikas' theory of indivisible particles. Only what is without parts can be changeless and thus real. Note that the *substances* of observable objects (e.g., pots and carts) — *dravyas* — are said to exist because they can be seen. Thus, *dravya* is not merely the smallest bits of matter in the Western sense of "atoms" or their parts. (See the *Four Hundred Verses* 16.13.) The standard criticism of the atomic theory is this: if the alleged atom has no parts it cannot combine to form larger wholes; and if it has parts, then it is not an atom (Potter 2003: 318).

According to the text, anything, including observable objects, are divisible into parts, and so none are self-existence but the products of causes and conditions. If we analyze parts into smaller and smaller parts, we do not end up with nothing, but with something that is "equivalent" to nothing because it cannot be conceptualized. That is, what does not exist or its equivalent cannot be expressed because there is no object of consciousness to conceptualize. In the second half of the verse, the author speaks of an "inconceivable form (*achintya-rupa*)."

Verse 3cd. The word translated here as "error (*branta*)" has the connotations of "wandering about with a confused mind" rather than a direct perceptual illusion.

Verse 4. The claim is that to make a perception or any cognition (*vijnana*), consciousness contains both the sensory-sensation and the form; if the sensation is illusory, then the consciousness is too (Thomas & Ui 1918: 282 n. 1). Aryadeva's response is that since the alleged cognition is not a true cognition of anything, it likewise is an error to think the cognition itself is real. But Aryadeva's point does not follow at all: the dream is real even if the content of the dream (e.g., a tiger attacking you) is not. The state of consciousness itself exists, even if the content of this state does not correspond to anything external. All Aryadeva or any Buddhist has to argue is that the state of consciousness is impermanent and dependently arisen too, as he does in the *Four Hundred Verses* 16.24. To the Yogacharins, the mind is real but the external objects are not. Aryadeva responds that the state of consciousness is in the same ontological category as external objects: impermanent and dependently arisen. This is not ontological nihilism: Arya-deva is not claiming that either consciousness and external objects do not exist in the conventional sense or that ultimately there is no reality — the "way things really are" is simply impermanent and conditioned. Things are not "nonexistent" (*asat*) only in the sense of being totally non-existent, nor are they "real" (*sat*) in the sense of being permanent and unchanging. They are an "*illusion*" in that they arise dependently upon other things and are impermanent and empty of anything that would give them self-existence, but something is still there.

Aryadeva says that the error is seeing the form (*rupa*) as having substance (*dravya*) when form in fact does not. If we read *svabhava* ("self-existence") for *dravya*, the text would have a standard Madhyamaka claim.

Verse 5. Aryadeva now expands his analysis of the rope to all things that arise. All things are merely conventional (*vyavahara-matra*) and without substance (*dravya*). The three mental afflictions are hatred, greed, and desire. (See CS, chapter 6). (The commentary is amended to read "(What is actually) a rope is a snake" from the Sanskrit that translates "a rope is a snake" since no one thinks "That rope is a snake" — if we think "That rope ...," then we have identified the object as a rope to begin with and know it is not a snake. It is misidentifying what is there that is the problem.)

Verse 6. Here is an explicit mention of the doctrine of the "two truths." Note that the conventional point of view must also be utilized — it is not dismissed. That is, even the enlightened, who see things from the ultimate point of view, must use conventional terminology to lead others to enlightenment (MK 24.10).

"Impose (*adhyaropa*)" means the process by which the mind, deluded by error, attributes to reality a nature that does not belong to it (Tola & Dragonetti 1995: 17 n. 60). Here Nagarjuna might have used another term — "*prapancha*." This is the reification of our concepts — i.e., projecting our conceptual distinctions onto reality. They are the alleged objective counterparts, as it were, to our subjective creations. (See Jones 2010: 149-150, 169.) To Yogacharins, not only are such objectifications are mind-only, but the entire phenomenal realm is mind-only. Madhyamikas believe there is something there to be projected upon. In this way, Madhyamaka Buddhism is more "realistic" in contrast to the Yogachara's "idealism." (This becomes more prominent in Bhavaviveka's works.)

* * *

Four Hundred Verses on Yogic Deeds (*Catuh-shataka-shastra-karikanama*)

Homage to the most excellent ones who possess great compassion!

1. *Rejecting Belief in Permanence*

[1] What could be more improper from our ordinary point of view than if someone who is subject to the Lord of Death — the ruler of the three realms (the world created by desire, and the "formed" and "formless" realms resulting from meditation), and who is not subject to death — were to sleep soundly like the conquerors of death (the enlightened)? [2] For we are born only to die; we arise dependently (upon causes and conditions) and are liable to being reborn. It appears that death is inevitable and continued life is not. [3] You see your past as brief and your future rebirths as not. But whether you consider them equal or unequal in length, the thought is like a cry of fear! [4] Because death is common to others, you do not fear it. Does envy cause you to suffer when someone else is harmed?

[5] Sickness can be cured and the ails of aging can be treated. Thus, you need not fear them. Nevertheless, there is no cure for the final ordeal. Thus, you obviously should fear it. [6] Death is common to all — we are all like cattle about to be slaughtered. And when you see others die, why do you not fear the Lord of Death? [7] If you think "I am eternal" because the time of your death is uncertain, still the Lord of Death will strike at some moment.

[8] You may look toward future rewards in this life while ignoring the fact that your life is waning — what kind person would say you are wise when you put yourself at stake? [9] Why do you pawn yourself to a karmic debt that will have to be paid off later by doing destructive deeds now? Instead, you need to be completely free of clinging to yourself, as are the wise. [10] What we call the "life" of anyone is nothing but (a series of) moments of consciousness. Ordinary people do not perceive this; thus, it is rare to know oneself. [11] You like a long life, but you dislike the symptoms of old age. Amazing! Your conduct could seem right only to ordinary people like yourself.

[12] Why do you grieve the death of your son and others when you should be grieving about your own certain death? When the mourner is himself a victim, why should he not be criticized by the wise? [13] When someone without requesting your permission becomes your son, then it is not wrong when he also dies without requesting your permission. [14] Because of delusion, you do not notice your son's appearance, but his indication to depart is clearly demonstrated by his old age.

[15] To a father, his son is adorable, but the son does not love his father in the same way. Because of such attachment, worldly people go to lower rebirths; hence, a better rebirth is difficult to attain. [16] When your son is disobedient, no one would call him adorable. And when he is obedient, your attachment is produced. It is merely like a business transaction!

[17] The suffering caused by parting from a loved one quickly wanes from people's hearts. See the impermanence of love! This end of suffering demonstrates that. [18] You hurt yourself in following the social customs for someone's death, even when you know the futility of it. This is hypocritical and unwise (since it does not even relieve suffering). [19] People of this world, already brimming with suffering, wander from one rebirth to the next. Why add suffering to people who already suffer?

[20] If meeting brings joy, why is parting not also a joy? Do not meeting and parting come one with the other? [21] Since the past has no beginning and the future no end, why are you concerned with the short time of being together and not with the time you are separated, even though it is much longer?

[22] Time, in segments starting with moments, is indeed an enemy. Thus, never having a longing for what is in fact an enemy.

[23] You fool! From fear of separation from your family you do not renounce your householder life and leave home (to take up the religious life). But the separation from home that the wise ones freely perform will be still be done to you by the Lord of Death. [24] You may think "I will retreat into the forest after I have completed the householder's duties" — but (this means that) whatever you do as a householder must be given up, and so what is the value in having done it in the first place?

[25] Anyone who by reflection has gained the conviction "I am going to die" has completely abandoned all attachment — what fear then can he have even of the Lord of Death?

2. *Rejecting Belief in the Pleasurable*

[1] The body is seen like an enemy, yet you must take care of it (but you should not value it). By living a long disciplined life, great merit is created. [2] Our suffering is produced from our bodies, and our happiness from other sources — so why are you devoted to your body, the container of all your suffering? [3] Pleasure does not come to human beings as much as pain does — so how can you think that the pain is negligible? [4] Ordinary people are bent on securing pleasure, but those who are happy are rare to find. Thus, it seems as if suffering is pursuing beings who are decaying. [5] Pain can be had at will, but what pleasure is there to be had at will? Why are you devoted to what is rare but do not fear what is plentiful?

[6] The body that experiences pleasure becomes the vessel of suffering. Being devoted to the body and being devoted to a foe — these two seem the same! [7] The body will not itself become pleasurable, no matter how long you try. It is unreasonable to say that its own nature can be overcome by something else. [8] For the privileged, suffering is mental; for others, it is physical. Every day, day after day, both types of suffering afflict the world.

[9] Pleasure is controlled by our own conceptualizations, and our conceptualizations are governed by pain. Thus, there is nothing anywhere more powerful than pain. [10] Pain increases with the passage of time. Thus, pleasure is experienced as something alien to the body. [11] Many causes of pain are experienced — illnesses and others — but the causes of pleasure do not seem as extensive. [12] When pleasure intensifies, its opposite (pain) is experienced. But when pain intensifies, its opposite is never experienced. [13] We see the conditions of pleasure simultaneously with its opposite. But the conditions of pain are never seen simultaneously with its opposite.

[14] When you have spent, are spending, and will spend time undergoing the process of dying, in no way is it proper to say that the process of dying is pleasurable. [15] When hunger and so forth constantly afflict embodied beings, in no way is it proper to say that being afflicted is pleasurable. [16] Although each element lacks power of its own, the body is formed by the combination of the four elements (earth, water, fire, and air), and in no way is it proper to say that the combining of conflicting elements is pleasurable. (That is, the elements composing the body are themselves in a state of constantly conflicting with each other and cannot bring pleasure.) [17] Because there is no permanent cure for cold and so forth, in no way is it proper to say that the breaking down of the body is pleasurable. [18] Because

there is no action done without exertion, in no way is it proper to say that performing action is pleasurable.

[19] In this life and the next, one should constantly guard against doing what leads to bad rebirths for the sake of momentary pleasure. For in no way is it proper to say that a low rebirth is pleasurable.

[20] For human beings, there is never any pure pleasure even in riding horses and so forth. What was not intended at first (i.e., pain) only increases; so what is the purpose? [21] Just as some people become happy when they vomit into a golden pot, so some think that alleviating pain is pleasure. [22] Whatever you do to end the pain that already exists only begins another pain. Thus, consider what the Sage (the Buddha) said: "Arising and ceasing, both are suffering." [23] If ordinary people do not see pain, it is because it is covered by a veneer of pleasure. But there is no pleasure that can in reality overshadow pain. [24] Ordinary people must be taught "By mistaking pain for pleasure, you are not free from attachment." Thus, the buddhas have said that this is worst delusion of all.

[25] What is impermanent is constantly being harmed, and what is being harmed cannot be pleasurable. Thus, all that is impermanent is said to be suffering.

3. Rejecting Belief in Purity

[1] There is no end to craving for things, regardless of the amount of time you spend, because one is never satisfied. Your exertion to satisfy your body will have no effect — it is as useless as a bad doctor's treatments. [2] Just as the craving for dirt cannot be stopped in earthworms that devote themselves to eating dirt, so craving for sensual pleasure only increases in those who devote themselves to indulging their cravings.

[3] There is no difference in the least in sexual intercourse with different women since all women are composed of what is impure. Since the appearance of a woman of superior beauty is also enjoyed by others, of what use is she to you? [4] Whoever sees her imagines himself satisfied with her. You fool! Even such beings as dogs share this, so why are you attracted? [5] This woman, whose every limb is beautiful to you, was previously enjoyed by everyone. So do not be so astonished that you too find her beautiful.

[6] If you see those women with good qualities as attractive and the reverse for the opposite, which is truly attractive? For neither quality exists

alone. [7] A fool's desire does not arise solely for a woman with good qualities — how can reason prevent those who become involved with women without reason? [8] A woman will remain with you as long as she does not know another man. Thus, she must constantly be kept from opportunity, as with a bad disease.

[9] An old man does not desire what he did as a young man. So why wouldn't the enlightened be thoroughly disgusted with the follies of youth? [10] Those without desire have no sensual pleasure, and those who are not foolish also do not have it. Indeed, what kind of sensual pleasure can someone have whose mind constantly turns away from desire? [11] You cannot have sex constantly with the woman to match your fondness for her. Thus, what is the use of holding on to the possessive thought "This is mine and no one else's"?

[12] If desire itself were pleasurable, there would no need for women. But pleasure, unlike desire, is not something that should be rejected. [13] Even with sex with a woman, pleasure arises from something else (i.e., one's imagination). What sensible person would claim that it is caused by his lover alone? [14] Those who are free of attachment see the infatuated as suffering like a leper, blinded by a longing to scratch, scratching his sores and oblivious to the harm his longing caused. [15] During a famine, those without a protector, tormented by hunger, bear whatever abuse occurs to them in order to get food — that is how the infatuated act when they are around women.

[16] Through arrogant pride, some people develop attachment even to their latrines! And some people who are infatuated with a particular woman will show jealousy. [17] It is reasonable that delusion and anger occur about what is impure, but it is completely unreasonable that desire for it occurs. [18] If a pot of filth is objectionable to most people, why would one not object to that from which the filth comes (i.e., the human body)? [19] Even clean things are rendered unclean by contact with the human body. What intelligent person would say that the human body is pure?

[20] Anyone who lived inside the filthy enclosure of the womb and who could not survive without the filthy liquid is like a filthy worm who feeds on filth but develops arrogance only out of stupidity. [21] No method will purify the inside of the body. The efforts you make to clean the outside of the body will not clean the inside.

[22] If, like leprosy, containing urine were not common to all, those who contain urine would be avoided like lepers. [23] Just as some who lack

a nose (through the effects of leprosy) delight in an artificial nose, so a desire to make your body attractive by adding flowers and so forth is considered a remedy for the body's impurity.

[24] It is improper to call "pure" that toward which one develops freedom from desire. There is no real thing that is the cause for desire.

[25] In sum, impermanence, impurity, suffering, and lack of self — all four can be in one thing (i.e., the body).

4. *Rejecting Belief in a Self*

[1] Oh king, what wise person would have arrogant pride, thinking "I" or "mine"? For all entities are the same in serving all embodied beings. [2] As a servant of the people, supported by one-sixth of your subject's harvest and so forth, why are you so arrogant? Whatever you do depends on you being under the people's power. [3] When those under a king's care receive what they are owed for their work (i.e., their wages), they think he is a donor. So too, after he has given what ought to be given, the king vainly thinks "I am a donor!"

[4] The wise consider yours as a situation of suffering, but you regard it wrongly. Living by working for others, what can cause you pleasure? [5] A king is the protector of his people, but he must also be protected by them. Why take pride because of one? Why have you not abandoned pride because of the other? [6] Among all the castes, everyone takes pride in their work. It is difficult to find anyone who makes a living without attachment. If you incur as your share one-sixth of the demerit their pride generates, a good rebirth will be rare for you. [7] Anyone who acts at the insistence of others is known on earth as a fool. And there is no one else equal to you in being dependent of the will of others.

[8] You claim "Protection of the people depends on me," and you take payment from the people. But in carrying out your duties, you commit evil deeds (e.g., killing). Who equals you in the lack of kindness? [9] If evil-doers should not receive your kindness, then no ordinary person should receive your protection (since they too do wrong).

[10] Where can't we find rationalizations for doing things that make us happy? But the reasons (such as scriptural authority for killing an animal) do not destroy the demerit resulting from an action. [11] If providing his people proper protection is a ruler's religious duty, and so justifies acts of

cruelty, then why isn't the work of artisans who make weapons also not considered righteous?

[12] If a king protects his people out of a sense of attachment to them, he should be denounced, just as wise ones denounce craving for existence as the mother of all those in the world.

[13] Only a fool acquires a kingship. And since fools have no mercy, a king, even though he is a protector, does not follow his religious duty. [14] Some seers say the actions of a king following his duty do not produce demerit, but not all such acts are performed by the wise — even among seers, there are the inferior, the middling, and the superior.

[15] In the former cosmic ages, virtuous rulers protected the people like their children. But today in the dark age (the Kali Yuga), through the law of this time of discord, the world is made into a hunting ground. [16] If a king incurs not karmic harm by seizing an opportunity to attack his enemies, then others such as thieves also would not incur karmic harm in the first place.

[17] Giving up all one owns for liquor and so on is not considered an offering. So, why is it considered an offering to give up one's life in battle?

[18] Oh king, as the protector of the world, you have no protector yourself. Without any protector yourself to guide you, your actions are reckless and do not lead to release. Who then would be happy to be a king? [19] Fame, even long after you are dead, contributes nothing to your advantage. Your cruelty as a king may even enhance your fame, but it will be of no advantage to you at all — if it did, then why do those who cook dogs alive not enjoy great fame?

[20] Since sovereignty over others is a product of past karmic deeds, it cannot be said that any person of any caste will not be the recipient of a kingship in some future life. [21] Castes are determined in this world for all means of livelihood. Thus, no inherent distinction between sentient beings due to caste is found (since all people are in some caste based on past karmic actions). [22] A long time has past since the four ancestral classes were first drawn up, and women's minds are fickle (and so they sometimes bear children outside their class). Thus, there is no certain line of descent of the warrior class. [23] Even a member of the lowest class can become a warrior through actions. I wonder if a member of the lowest class cannot even become a brahmin priest through his acts.

[24] A king cannot distribute his karmic misfortune as he can distribute his material wealth. Indeed, what wise person ever destroys his own future

for the sake of someone else's? [25] Once the wise have seen others who are endowed with equal or greater power than themselves, the pride caused by power does not remain in their hearts (and so should it be with kings).

5. *The Actions of a Bodhisattva*

[1] No action of the buddhas lacks a reason — even their breathing arises only for the sake of sentient beings. [2] Just as the name "Lord of Death" terrifies ordinary people, so does the name "the Omniscient One" terrifies the Lord of Death. [3] The Sage can see what should be done and what should not be done, what should be said and what should not be said. Thus, what reason is there to say that the Omniscient One is not all-knowing?

[4] If one does not understand that intention generates an action, one will not see the merit or demerit even in such actions as "moving." Thus, the mind is established as chief in all actions. [5] Since the purpose of a bodhisattva is solely to benefit others, every act by a bodhisattva incurs only good merit, whether such acts would be wholesome or not when done by others, because the acts are controlled by their mind. [6] The merit that is generated by bodhisattvas, who have the intention to become a fully-enlightened buddha, far exceeds the merit that would make every person on earth a ruler of all the world. [7] Someone may build a reliquary made of precious gems as high as the universe itself, but it is said that more merit is generated in training others to develop the intention to become a fully-enlightened buddha.

[8] A spiritual teacher who wishes to benefit a student must pay attention to him. Because the student does not know what will benefit him, he is called "one who must be taught." [9] Just as a doctor is not disturbed by a patient who rages at him while possessed by a demon, so a sage sees the disturbing mental afflictions as the enemy, not the student who possesses them. [10] At first, the teacher should teach whatever is dear to the student, for someone who is disinclined to hear is not a good vessel for the final teaching.

[11] Like a mother especially anxious for a sick child, so a bodhisattva is especially compassionate toward those who are not wise. [12] Those with knowledge and skillful means become students of some and teachers of others, instructing those who do not understand. [13] Just as it is a rare

disease that a skilled doctor cannot cure, so it is very rare for a bodhisattva who has acquired the power to train to find an untrainable student.

[14] If a someone within a bodhisattva's sphere of influence does not receive encouragement and goes to a bad rebirth, that bodhisattva will be blamed by others with intelligence. [15] How can one who does not accept that sympathy for those oppressed by mental afflictions is good, later give to the helpless out of compassion?

[16] Bodhisattvas remain as long as the universe endures in order to help all beings caught in the cycle of rebirths. If those who are indifferent to bodhisattvas bring ruin upon themselves, so much worse is it for those who are hostile to bodhisattvas! [17] Bodhisattvas who have in all rebirths the five extrasensory abilities for helping all sentient beings may assume inferior forms, like those of animals, but it is very difficult to help in this way.

[18] The Buddha, the one who has traversed the path, has said that the merit that is constantly being accumulated by bodhisattvas for eons through their skillful means is immeasurable even by the omniscient.

[19] The word "giving" indicates death, the Buddhist doctrine, and other rebirths. Thus, the word is always of interest to bodhisattvas.

[20] If one thinks that generous giving now will result in receiving something of great value in return in the future (i.e., a good rebirth), then this giving and receiving will be criticized as being only like business transactions for profit.

[21] For a bodhisattva, even previously committed evil acts do not have negative karmic effects. One cannot say that a bodhisattva who possesses good karma is unable to benefit others. [22] Even while voluntarily remaining in the realm of rebirth, there can be no harm done in this realm to a bodhisattva with a powerful mind. For such a being, worldly existence and nirvana are not different. [23] Why shouldn't a bodhisattva, who, from having control over his mind at all times, is able to take any rebirth he wishes, not become the ruler of the world?

[24] Even in this world, among excellent things some things appear greater. Thus, realize that the Buddha's inconceivable power certainly exists. [25] Just as the ignorant fear the extremely profound teaching of emptiness, so do the week fear the marvelous teaching of the bodhisattvas' deeds.

6. *Ridding Yourself of Mental Afflictions*

[1] Desire increases because of pleasure, and anger increases because of pain. Why aren't those with pleasure ascetics? Why are ascetics the ones with pain? [2] The activity associated with desire is acquisition. The activity associated with anger is discord. The activity of confusion causes both of these to flare up, like the wind does for the elements. [3] Desire is painful because of the separation from what you desire. Anger is painful because of your lack of power. Confusion is painful because of your lack of understanding of the nature of reality. Because of these three mental afflictions — desire, anger, and delusion — you do not understand these pains.

[4] Just as one sees that there is no connection between phlegm and bile, so does one see that there is no connection between desire and anger. [5] Desire should be treated like a servant, since strict control is its antidote. Anger should be treated like a lord, since deference is its antidote. [6] Throughout the day, all three arise: when one wakes up in the morning, delusion arises; later, anger arises at work; lastly, desire arises after work.

[7] Desire, although an enemy, appears as a friend. Thus, you may not fear it. But shouldn't people especially rid themselves of a harmful friend? [8] Desire arises in two ways: from habits (i.e., repeated causes) and from new circumstances (i.e., new encounters with an object of desire). The latter is easy to deal with; the former is not.

[9] While anger remains strong, it definitely generates much demerit. But by understanding the distinctions of the mental afflictions, the afflictions will cease. [10] Just as our tactile sense pervades our body, so is delusion present in all the mental afflictions. Thus, by the destruction of delusion, all the mental afflictions will also be destroyed. [11] When dependent arising is seen, delusion does not occur. Thus, every effort will be made here to explain this very subject.

[12] Characteristics such as these are seen in people who desire: liking to dance, being extravagant in giving and receiving, being greedy, and being fastidious in their appearance. [13] The buddhas said to those who desire: "Fine food, clothing, and dwellings are all things to be avoided, and you should always remain close to a spiritual teacher."

[14] Through anger, one who is powerless only makes himself look ugly. But one who has the power to harm and is without mercy is said to be worse.

[15] It is said that hearing harsh words brings the evil that one had previously done to an end (i.e., hearing this is the karmic effect of evil that

one had previously done). Only the confused and unwise do not want to purify themselves. [16] And even the harsh words you hear are not harmful by their own nature. The harm done to you by the harsh words you hear comes only from your own imagination — it is fantasy to think that it comes from something else.

[17] Just as it is said that an abusive person should be punished, why then shouldn't those who speak kindly be rewarded?

[18] If your faults are known to others even though you have not mentioned them, then it is wrong to be angry with someone who has spoken the truth about them. How much more so with someone who is mistaken! [19] Even from an inferior, there is no escape from harsh words. Thus, you should view the unpleasant words as isolated and trivial.

[20] Harming others in return for the harm they did to you is not of the slightest benefit to you. Your respect for a person whose anger does not benefit you is only an addiction to your mistaken idea. [21] Through patience, enormous merit is acquired effortlessly. Who is as foolish as one who impedes this by anger? [22] In particular, anger does not arise toward those who are more powerful than you. So why do you admire someone whose anger oppresses the weak? [23] Patience should be cultivated toward the source of anger. It is foolish to fear a source that can lead to accumulating wholesome qualities. [24] Who can put can end to all slights before going to the next life? Thus, you should think that enduring disparagement is better than generating karmic demerits.

[25] Mental afflictions can never remain in the mind of one who understands that nothing abides in consciousness. (See Chapter 15.)

7. Ridding Yourself of Attachment to Sensual Pleasures

[1] There is no end to this ocean of suffering of the cycle of rebirth. Why, oh foolish one, are you not afraid of drowning in it?

[2] Youth has fallen behind and then in the next life it is ahead again. Though it seems to last, in this world youth, old age, and death are in a competitive race. [3] For the unenlightened in the cycle of rebirths, there is never a life of your own choosing according to your will-power. Always being under the power of something else (i.e., karma), what intelligent person would not be afraid? [4] The future has no end, and in the past you have always been an ordinary being. So act now so that it will not again be like it

was in the past. [5] The coming together of a listener, teachings to be heard, and someone to explain the teachings is rare. Thus, in short, the cycle of rebirth has an end if these three conditions come together but does not if they do not.

[6] Most people cling to a destructive direction of action. Thus, most ordinary people definitely go to bad rebirths. [7] On earth, one experiences the ripening fruit of negative deeds as only injurious. Thus, the wise see the cycle of existence as similar to a slaughterhouse.

[8] If "insane" means "one's mind is not under control," what wise person would say that those who remain in the cycle of rebirths is not insane? [9] One sees that the pain of walking ceases when one stops walking. Thus, the intelligent person directs his mind toward ending all karmic action. [10] When a single effect's original cause is not seen, and one sees the extensive effects of even a single negative act, who would not be afraid? [11] Not all ends will necessarily be achieved, and those that are achieved definitely come to an end. So why exhaust yourself for their sake? [12] Action is undertaken only with effort, but the result disintegrates effortlessly. Even though this is true, you still are not at all free from attachment to actions!

[13] There is no pleasure in the present related to what is past or to what is in the future. And the present passes — why then do you exert yourself for pleasure? [14] The wise feel the same fear for even a rebirth in a heaven as for one in one of the hells. It is rare indeed for them not to fear any rebirth anywhere. [15] If the foolish ever clearly perceived the suffering of the cycle of rebirths, then at that moment their mind would completely cease.

[16] A being without pride is rare, and the proud have no compassion. Thus, it is said that it is very rare to go from a bright rebirth to a brighter rebirth.

[17] It is said that whoever renounces sense-objects in this life will obtain the pleasures of better sense-objects in heaven — for what reason would this distorted teaching be held? [18] When you receive luxurious objects as a result of karmic merit, you must constantly protect them from others. How can something that must be constantly protected from others really be your own?

[19] The social requirements of religious duty conform to whatever is the established custom of a given society. Thus, it seems that custom is even stronger than religious duty.

[20] Attractive objects are acquired by wholesome acts. Yet even such objects are denounced by the wise. By giving them up, one will be happy. Why acquire what is better to reject?

[21] For anyone who has no need for worldly power, the requirements of religious duty are meaningless, and people call anyone who strives for worldly power a fool. [22] If you crave the requirements after seeing the fruits that will come from them in the future, why are you not afraid when you see an end to those fruits?

[23] Merit is in all respects like the wages of a worker. How could those who do not want even a wholesome reward (i.e., a better rebirth) do what is not wholesome? (Merit only achieves more auspicious rebirths; nirvana results from knowing reality as it really is and cannot be achieved by any amount of merit.) [24] Those who see the world as like illusory beings or like a collection of mechanical devices quite clearly attain the highest state.

[25] For those who do not enjoy any objects encountered in the cycle of rebirths, it is altogether impossible to take pleasure here in this world.

8. *Training the Student*

[1] Just as friendship between people who disagree does not last long, so desire for things does not last long once all their faults are recognized. [2] Desire has no object — some are attracted to an object; others repelled by it; others feel confused. [3] Apart from our conceptualizations the existence of desire and so forth is not found. What intelligent person would believe that something is real that is only a conceptual construct? (That is, desirability and repulsion are not objective features of the object itself but are only our subjective reactions based on our conceptualizations.)

Objection: Since men and women are bound together by mutual desire, we cannot give up desire.

Reply: [4] A real bond between a man and a woman is not found, since the separation of that which is bound together is impossible and yet separation in this case is seen. (Only a permanent bond would be real.)

[5] Those with little merit do not know enough even to raise a doubt about this teaching. Merely entertaining the prospect that it might be true shatters the cycle of rebirths. [6] The Sage said that this teaching will increase its benefits until liberation from the cycle of rebirths, and so someone who has no respect for the teaching clearly is not intelligent. [7]

The buddhas have declared that one who views what is not empty as empty and thinks "Nirvana is mine!" has not in fact attained nirvana because his view is wrong. (That is, we need genuine experiential knowledge.)

[8] Where there is a teaching related to the world, engagement is proclaimed. Where there is a teaching related to the ultimate status of things, disengagement is proclaimed.

[9] You may be afraid, thinking "Nothing exists — why do anything?" But if there is something that can be done, this teaching of emptiness does not lead to the withdrawal from all action. [10] Being attached to your own position and disliking another's position, you will not attain nirvana. There is no tranquility for one who lives in oppositions (of metaphysical views).

[11] Not acting (i.e., not committing any deeds having karmic effects) brings about nirvana. Action (with karmic consequences) brings about rebirth again. Thus, nirvana is easy to attain when one is free of doubts; the latter is not. [12] How can anyone who has no fear of this world take an interest in stilling the mind? To leave the cycle of rebirths behind is as difficult as leaving home. [13] Some who are tormented by pain are seen longing for death. But because of their confused state of mind, they do not attain the highest state.

[14] Giving is recommended to people of the lowest ability, proper conduct to those of middling ability, and stilling the mind to those of the highest ability. Thus, always do what is highest! [15] First, turn away from unwholesome acts. Next, turn away from the notion of a "self." Finally, turn away from seeing all things as self-existent. Anyone who knows this is wise. [16] Whoever sees one thing as it really is sees how all things really are. The emptiness of one thing is precisely the emptiness of all.

[17] The buddhas recommend attachment to religious requirements for those who desire a higher rebirth. Such attachment is disparaged for those who seek liberation. Of what need is there to mention any other attachment? [18] Those who desire merit should not always speak of emptiness. Doesn't medicine turn into poison in the wrong cases? [19] Just as foreigners are unable to comprehend an alien language, so ordinary people cannot comprehend the truth without reference to worldly matters. [20] The buddhas have mentioned what is real, and what is unreal, and what is both real and unreal, and what is neither real nor unreal. Indeed, does not everything called "medicine" depend on the illnesses being treated?

[21] If you see reality correctly, the highest state is attained. If you see a little of reality, a good rebirth is attained. Thus, the wise constantly direct

their mind toward contemplating one's inner nature. [22] Through realizing how reality truly is, one attains nirvana — even if not in this life, inevitably in the next life without effort, just like when karma ripens in the next life.

[23] It is extremely rare for all actions to bring about their intended results. It is not that nirvana is absent in this world, but the coming together of the conditions for liberation (e.g., meeting a spiritual teacher) is rare.

[24] After hearing that the body lacks good qualities, attachment does last long. By means of this path, won't all disturbing attitudes be exhausted?

[25] Just as the end but not the beginning of a seed is seen, so a beginningless cycle of rebirth can come to an end. A new birth does not arise once its causes are incomplete.

9. Refuting the Permanence of Things

[1] Everything arises as an effect. Thus, nothing is permanent. There are no buddhas other than the sages who see entities as they really are.

Objection from the Hindu Vaisheshikas: The smallest bits of matter are not caused, and there are permanent things (e.g., the mind and space) that are not a product or a cause.

Reply: [2] Nothing is found anywhere at any time that is not dependent (i.e., does not arise dependently upon causes and conditions). Thus, there is nothing anywhere at any time that is permanent.

The self is attracted to things. Thus, the self exists and is permanent.

Reply: [3] There is no entity without a cause. And nothing permanent has a cause. Thus, the ones who know the that-ness of reality say that establishment without a cause is certainly not established.

If we cannot see that something is produced, then it is permanent.

Reply: [4] Seeing that the produced is impermanent, one may think the unproduced is permanent. If so, since we see only produced things, then there are no permanent things.

Treatises on knowledge say that space is permanent and self-existent.

Reply: [5] Space and so forth are conceived as permanent by ordinary people. The bright do not see real things even on a conventional level.

Space is permanent because it is omnipresent and partless.

Reply: [6] What is named a region of space (e.g., the eastern direction) is not present in all regions of space. Thus, there clearly are parts in what possesses different regions.

Time is permanent.

Reply: [7] That in which the activity or inactivity of an entity is perceived (i.e, the continuum of time) depends on something else. Thus, it is also an effect.

Causes are permanent.

Reply: [8] Any cause that does not have an effect cannot have the property of being "a cause." Thus, it follows that causes are effects. (That is, gaining the property of being a "cause" depends on there being an effect; thus, being "a cause" is *caused by* that effect.) [9] When a cause becomes the cause of something else, it undergoes change. Anything that undergoes change cannot be called "permanent." [10] An entity whose cause is permanent is produced by something that has not come into being. Whatever arises by itself has no cause. [11] How can something that is produced by a permanent cause be impermanent? A cause and effect that have dissimilar characteristics is never seen.

Vaisheshikas: The smallest particles of the four elements are permanent and partless but are activated to form larger entities by the force of karma; thereby, the universe and entities within it are produced.

Reply: [12] Particles have parts that are causes and parts that are not. (That is, in combining to form objects, some of the sides of the particles meet and some do not; only the sides that meet bond and thus are causes of the larger whole.) Thus, a particles has both causal and noncausal parts. How can that which is complex be permanent? (Only what is partless can be permanent.) [13] The spherical shape of the parts is not present in the effect (i.e., compound whole). Thus, full contact of the particles does not occur. [14] The space occupied by one particle cannot be occupied by another. Thus, one cannot hold that the cause (the particles) and the effect (a visible, compound object) are equal in dimension. (Thus, there is no total interpenetration of particles.) [15] Whatever has an eastern side has an eastern region. Thus, one cannot assert that particles that have different regions are the ultimate (partless) particles. [16] In moving forward, a space is left behind. (But partless particles allegedly do not take up a new space or vacate any space; thus, a particle is not partless.) A particle without these two effects is not something that moves. (And therefore, a partless particle could not move to form compound entities.)

Partless particles can be perceived by yogic powers.

Reply: [17] That which is partless has no front, middle, or rear; thus, it is invisible. By what means could the invisible be seen?

Particles must exist because without them visible, compound entities could not exist, and the particles must be permanent because they have no cause. They produce the effect of making compound objects without giving up their identity.

Reply: [18] An effect destroys its cause, and thus the cause is not permanent. Or, alternatively, where the cause exists, the effect does not. (That is, the cause is permanent and thus does not change and so cannot bring about an effect). [19] A permanent entity that shows resistance is not seen anywhere. (No entity can resist changes and effects from other entities.) Thus, the buddhas never say that particles are permanent.

Objection from Vaibhashika/Sarvastivada Buddhists: The buddhas do say that uncompounded entities are permanent. The third "noble truth" means that there is a way to end something — i.e., suffering.

Reply: [20] If liberation were different from being bound to the cycle of existence, what is bound, and the means of liberation, then it could not arise from the bound state, and thus it could not be called "liberation" (from anything). (That is, if liberation were a separate, self-existent entity, it could not be related to our present state.) [21] In the state of nirvana without any residue, the bodily aggregates do not exist and thus the conventional person could not exist. With the bodily substratum extinguished, what nirvana is there for one to see? (That is, there is no conventional self in addition to the aggregates, as these Buddhists believe.)

Objection from the Hindu Samkhyas: Liberation is the separation of the conscious self from unconscious matter.

Reply: [22] What would be the point of consciousness for someone free from existence at the time of liberation? And to exist without consciousness is clearly the same as not existing at all. [23] If a self existed at liberation, there would be the potential for consciousness. If a self did not exist at that time, there would not even be a thought about future becoming. [24] Certainly, those who are liberated have nothing else. Thus, it is said that it is best to get rid of (the idea of) a self.

Objection, leading to the next chapter: [25] The conventional point of view is preferable, and the ultimate point of view is not. For on the worldly level, things have some existence, but none do from the ultimate point of view.

10. *Refuting the Existence of a Self*

[1] Since an inner self cannot be male, female, or neuter, it is only out of ignorance that you think of your "self" as male. [2] When all of the elements constituting a body are not male, female, or neuter, how can what relies on these be male, female, or neuter?

[3] Your "self" is not my "self," and thus there is no (one universal) self since this cannot be ascertained. Doesn't the conception of a "self" arise (only) in relation to impermanent entities?

Objection: There must be something that is reborn through karmic acts or attains freedom; thus, there must be a self.

Reply: [4] A human being, like the body, undergoes changes from one rebirth to another. Thus, it is not possible for you to claim that the self is distinct from the body and is permanent.

An inner self moves the outer body.

Reply: [5] What is called "moving" cannot arise from an intangible entity (since the nonphysical cannot affect the physical). The conventional self thus is not the agent for the body's movement. [6] If the self is permanent (and so cannot be harmed), why advocate nonviolence and wonder about its conditions? A diamond never has to be protected from a woodworm!

The self must be permanent because it has memories of previous rebirths. It could not have memories of what was something else.

Reply: [7] If you claim the self is permanent because of the memory of past rebirths, we reply: how can you claim that the body is impermanent when you see a scar from a wound inflicted earlier? (That is, an impermanent entity can carry the effect of earlier events.)

Vaisheshikas: The self is connected to qualities (e.g., knowing and pleasure).

Reply: [8] If the self comes to be a knower by being connected to knowing, then the eternal self itself is not that knowing and is not permanent but changes. [9] The conventional self that has such qualities as pleasure is seen to vary in accordance with those qualities. Thus, the self cannot properly be permanent while it experiences those qualities.

Samkhyas: The self has consciousness by its nature. It is not connected to consciousness — it is consciousness.

Reply: [10] If consciousness is permanent, any cause is superfluous. If fire is permanent, it cannot rely on fuel.

To be conscious requires having means (e.g., senses).

Reply: [11] Unlike with an action, if there is a self-existent entity, it would not fluctuate until its destruction. Thus, it is impossible that the self continues to exist and cognition do not.

Even if there is no consciousness prior to actually experiencing sense-objects, still its potential exists because the person exists.

Reply: [12] Sometimes one sees the base of intentions and sometimes one sees the acts resulting from intention. Thus, the human being undergoes change, like iron sometimes being melted.

Vaisheshikas: Only part of the self has a mind, a part the size of a particle; that part is in contact with sense-objects; the self itself is permanent and pervasive like space.

Reply: [13] If merely the part of the self with mind is conscious while the person is vast like space, then it would seem that the person's nature itself is not to be conscious. [14] If the self is in everyone, why doesn't someone else think "I" in relation to me rather than himself? Certainly it is unacceptable to say that it is obstructed by itself.

Samkhyas: The activity of three nonconscious qualities — the bright, the dull, and the passionate — constructs the manifest, material world.

Reply: [15] There is no difference at all between the insane and those for whom qualities are the creator and yet are unconscious! [16] What could be more unreasonable than for qualities to know how to construct such things as houses and yet not be able to experience them consciously?

Vaisheshikas: The self is the only doer of deeds and is also the only experiencer of their results.

Reply: [17] What is active cannot be unchanging (since its very acts change it), and what is all-pervasive cannot act (since it has no place to move). A lack of action is tantamount to nonexistence. (That is, if, alternatively, the self does not do anything, then it is the same as if it did not exist.) Thus, why do you not rejoice in the doctrine that there is no real self?

[18] Some see the self as all-pervading. Some see it as the size of a person's body. Some see it as minute. But those with insight see that no self exists. [19] How can what is permanent be harmed? (For a harm would be a change and the real is changeless.) Why should there be liberation for what cannot be harmed? Thus, the idea of liberation is unreasonable for anyone whose "self" is permanent. (That is, such a self could not experience the suffering that motivates the quest for liberation, and so there is no reason to undertake such a quest.) [20] If there actually existed a self-existent self, it

would be unreasonable to say "There is no such self," and it would indeed be an error to claim that one who knows reality attains nirvana.

There is no self in the cycle of rebirths, but a liberated self is self-existent.

Reply: [21] If a self exists at liberation, it could not have been nonexistent before. For whatever is seen concerning something when it has no relation to anything else is its true nature.

If there is no self to maintain continuity, compound things would cease as soon as they were created.

Reply: [22] If impermanent entities had no continuity, how could there be grass and so on? If this claim were true, delusion would not arise in anyone (since it would disappear the moment it arose)! [23] Even if a self exists, still the body is seen to arise from other something else (i.e., causes and conditions), to continue by means of other causes, and then to disintegrate by other causes. [24] Just as a seed arising from causes and conditions causes a sprout, so all impermanent entities arise from other impermanent entities. [25] Since entities arise and continue, they are not annihilated. And since they cease, permanence is not found.

11. *Refuting the Notion of Self-Existent Time*

Objection from Abhidharma Buddhists: The past and present are called "past" and "present" because of their relation to the future.

Reply: [1] The pot that has not yet come into existence does not exist now. Nor does the pot that has already passed away exist in the future. And if the present and the past pots did in fact already exist in the future, the future would not exist. (That is, the future would not be *future* since it *already would exist*; there would no time that had not yet come to be.)

Part of the past pot has not yet come into existence; thus, the past pot is not altogether nonexistent when the future pot appears.

Reply: [2] How can something that has already disintegrated (i.e., the past pot) still exist as part of what has not yet come into existence? How can what is future in nature ever pass away?

Objection: [3a] A future entity remains future in nature.

Reply: [3b] Such an entity is present now and so cannot be "future in nature." (That is, it exists now because its nature exists now.)

Objection from the Buddhist Sarvastivadins: [4a] The future exists, the past exists, and the present exists.

Reply: [4b] Then what does not exist? How can anyone assert impermanence for what exists at all times? [5] If the past has passed from the past
(into the present and future), how can it be the past? If the past has not
passed from the past, how can it be the past (since it is still functioning and
thus not ended)? [6] If the future pot is produced, isn't it present now? If it
is unproduced, isn't the future permanent? (That is, if the future pot is
unproduced, it would never change and be permanent.)

Objection: [7a] The future is impermanent because, although it is not
yet produced, it does disintegrate.

Reply: [7b] Since the past does not disintegrate (because what is gone
can no longer disintegrate), why is it not considered permanent? [8] If the
past and present are not impermanent, then the third that is different from
these (i.e., the future) is also not impermanent.

*Future things exist because they are produced later when the right causes
and conditions arise. What does not exist (e.g., a barren woman's child)
cannot be produced later.*

Reply: [9] If something that will be produced later exists already, then
the fatalists' position (of determinism) is not erroneous. [10] It is unreasonable to say that something that will come to occur later exists previously. If
what already exists were to arise later, what has already been produced
would arise again.

The future exists because future things can be seen with yogic powers.

Reply: [11] If future thing are perceivable before they are produced, why
aren't nonexistent things (e.g., a rabbit's horns) also perceivable? Indeed, the
future is not remote for someone for whom it already exists. [12] If wholesome conduct is already done even though it has not been undertaken yet,
then yogic discipline is not needed. But if even the slightest thing still must
be done, then there is no possibility of the effect preexisting in the cause. [13]
Indeed, if the impermanent exists, how can there be a preexisting effect? In
this world, what has a beginning and an end is called "impermanent." (If
there is no permanent cause, no effect or anything else could preexist in it.)

*Sautrantikas: Future conventional entities do not have any existence at
all; they are totally nonexistent, like a rabbit's horns.*

Reply: [14] If so, (then future emotional afflictions would not arise), like
those who are already liberated, and liberation would occur without effort.
So too, passion would arise without attachment. [15] For both those who
maintain that effects preexist and those who maintain that the future effect
is totally nonexistent, the support pillars in a building a house are useless.

(That is, if the effects [pillars for supporting a house] already exist in the cause [the house], there is no need for them and they would not be produced; if they do not exist in the cause, they cannot support the house because they are unrelated to it.)

Samkhyas: Effects are real because they are transformations of the causes.

Reply: [16] The transformation of things is not perceived even by the mind. Nevertheless, the unlearned imagine that the present truly exists.

Time exists because the conventional entities that form the basis for imputing the existence of time exist.

Reply: [17] How can an entity having no duration truly exist? How could an impermanent entity continue to exist? If something could continue as it existed at first, it could not grow old in the end. [18] Moreover, just as one moment of consciousness cannot apprehend two moments of an entity's existence, so two moments of consciousness cannot apprehend the same moment of an entity's existence.

Duration has self-existence because it is a characteristic of time.

Reply: [19] If time has duration, then duration is not a characteristic of time itself. Or if there is no duration, then without duration nothing ends. (That is, if there is nothing persisting, there is nothing to come to an end.)

Duration exists because there are impermanent things that endure.

Reply: [20] If impermanence is separate from an entity, then the entity itself is not impermanent. If impermanence and the entity are one, then how could the entity abide even for a moment since it is impermanent?

Entities continue to exist because endurance is stronger than impermanence.

Reply: [21] If impermanence is weaker than endurance, then why should there reversal be seen? (That is, we see that enduring entities end up decaying and thus are impermanent.) [22] If impermanence is not weaker, then it would be present in all entities. Either nothing would endure, or nothing would be impermanent. [23] If impermanence were itself permanent, endurance could not always persist. Or, an entity that was permanent later becomes impermanent (which is impossible since what is permanent cannot change). [24] If entities both endure and are impermanent at the same time, then either it is wrong that things are impermanent or that things endure.

Time exists or otherwise it would be impossible to remember past lives.

Reply: [25] Things that have disappeared do not reappear, and past consciousness also does not reappear. Thus, what is known as "remembering" is in fact deceptive since it arises in relation to a false object. (That is, memory is defective or misconceived since both its object and the cognition itself of that object are past and are not in fact arising anew in the memory.)

12. Refuting Wrong Views

[1] An impartial, intelligent, and interested listener is called a proper vessel (for this teaching). The good qualities of a teacher do not change, nor do those of a listener. [2] The Buddha spoke of the (suffering inherent in the) cycle of existence and its causes. He also spoke of peace and the method to attaining peace. But worldly people, who cannot comprehend this teaching at all, attribute the fault (that some fail to understand) to the Sage.

[3] You Samkhyas and Vaisheshikas are truly amazing! You agree that by giving up mental afflictions one attains nirvana. What reason is there for you to dislike the teaching that puts an end to all mental afflictions? [4] How can those who do not know the method for renunciation effectuate renunciation? It is for this reason that the Sage said "Peace is not found in any other system."

If the Buddha is truly omniscient, he must have knowledge of hidden things. But how can we be sure he has such knowledge?

Reply: [5] Whoever doubts what the Buddha said about hidden matters should come to understand his teaching on emptiness — relying on that, one can develop confidence that the Buddha had knowledge in these matters too. [6] Those teachers who have difficulty seeing the world as it really is are confused about other matters. Those who follow such teachers will be misled for a very long time. [7] Those who attain nirvana by themselves (without a teacher) do something that is extremely difficult to do. But the mind of the mediocre, even when following a teacher, cannot proceed to nirvana.

Why are some people afraid of the doctrine of emptiness?

Reply: [8] When something is not seen, fear does not even begin. On the other hand, when something is seen, fear completely vanishes. Thus, it can be said with certainty that fear arises only in those who know a little. (Here, fear arises in those who know only a little of the doctrine of emptiness.)

[9] Assuredly, fools are familiar only with matters that keep them in the cycle of rebirths. Because of their unfamiliarity with the doctrine of emptiness, they fear what would extricate them from the cycle. [10] Anyone who

is shrouded in delusion and creates an impediment to the truth will not even go to a rebirth attained by good qualities — what is the point of speaking about liberation (to them)? [11] Lapses in ethical conduct are better than lapses from the correct view of reality. Higher rebirths are gained through ethical conduct, but one attains the highest state through the correct view. [12] For the mediocre, a conception of an "I" is better than to teach them the doctrine of selflessness. For the latter doctrine would lead the unwise to bad rebirths (because of their misunderstanding), while the extraordinary attain the state of peace through it. [13] Selflessness is said to be the unrivaled doorway to peace, the destroyer of all wrong views, and the field of all buddhas. [14] The mere mention of this doctrine terrifies the unreceptive. Indeed, what thing that is powerful is not seen to frighten the weak?

If this doctrine destroys all wrong views, shouldn't it be taught even to the unreceptive?

Reply: [15] The doctrine was not taught by the buddhas for the sake of academic debate! Nevertheless, it destroys others' contentions, just as fire destroys fuel. [16] Whoever understands this doctrine will not relish another. Thus, this doctrine seems to me to be the threshold leading to the destruction (of all wrong views). [17] How could those who abide in the thought "In reality, there is no self" rejoice in existing or be frightened by nonexistence?

[18] After seeing that the holders of wrong views — teachers who are the seeds of misfortune — are many who would not feel compassion for those people who long for the doctrine leading to liberation? [19] The doctrines of the three traditions — the buddhas, the naked ascetics (Jainas), and the Brahmin priests — are perceived respectively by the mind, the eyes, and the ears. Thus, the buddhas' doctrine is the subtlest. [20] Brahmin teachings are said to be mostly an outward show (to gain fame and money). So too, the naked Jaina ascetics' teachings are said to be mostly ridiculous. [21] Brahmins are revered because they acquire knowledge (of the Vedas). The ascetics are pitied because they have adopted deluded practices based on the passions. [22] The suffering the ascetics experience is the ripening of past karmic actions, and so theirs is not the valid teaching. So too, birth as a Brahmin is not the valid teaching because it too is only the ripening of past karmic action.

If rebirth and suffering are not wholesome, what is?

Reply: [23] The buddhas have explained that the teaching in brief is this: nonviolence in action, and that emptiness is nirvana. Here in our tradition there are only these two. [24] But for the worldly, their own position (i.e., their own practices and doctrines), like their own birthplace, is attractive. Why would that which defeats your own position be attractive to you? [25] But the intelligent, who seek excellence, will accept what is correct, even from others. Isn't the sun common to everyone on earth who has eyes?

13. Refuting the Self-Existence of Sense-Faculties and their Objects

[1] Not everything about a pot is perceived by perceiving its form. Indeed, what person who knows reality as it really is would also say that the pot is perceptible (in all respects)? [2] With the very same reasoning, those with supreme intelligence should refute all that is subject to smell, taste, and touch. [3] Suppose all aspects of a pot were perceived by perceiving only its form. Then, shouldn't it follow from the fact that we do not perceive the other aspects when we perceive form that we do not perceive the form either? (That is, if perceiving one aspect of an object means we are in a position to perceive all aspects of it, then from not perceiving one aspect we should not be able to see any.)

The pot's form is established by direct perception, and by this the pot's self-existence is established and perceived indirectly.

Reply: [4] There is no perception even of the entire form since it has far, near, and in-between parts. [5] This also applies when one examines whether particles have parts or not. Thus, it is not possible to establish something by means of something that itself needs establishing. (That is, the parts' existence must be established first.) [6] Indeed, in every case, whatever is a part of a greater whole is also itself a whole composed of parts. Thus, even a syllable of a sentence does not have its own existence here (because it too has parts, and so self-existence is not indirectly established).

The pot is directly perceivable because its form is directly perceivable.

Reply: [7] If its shape is distinct from its color, how is the shape apprehended? (That is, if shape and color are different, then the eye, which apprehends color, is incapable of apprehending shape, which is apprehended by touch.) However, if they are not distinct, wouldn't the body's tactile consciousness (i.e., touch) also apprehended color?

The form is visible, but we do not see the four elements that cause it.

Reply: [8] The causes of form (the four elements) are not visible apart from form. If form and its causes were not distinct but one, why wouldn't visual consciousness (i.e., consciousness arising by means of the eye) appre-hend them both? (That is, why doesn't the eye apprehend everything caused by the four elements — smells, sounds, and so forth?) [9] The earth is apprehended as solid by the body's touch. Thus, (if tactility establishes the element "earth" as self-existent), one must say that it is merely touchable (and is not the cause of visible forms, nor is perceivable by the other senses).

Vaisheshikas: A pot is not visible by its own nature. Rather, it is visible by virtue of possessing a universal — "visibility."

Reply: [10] In that case, the pot itself would have no quality of being visible and only arose as something visible (due to the independent quality). But just as the production of visibility (in what is invisible does not occur), so the pot too would have no existence. [11] The eye, like the ear, arises from the four elements. The eye sees, but the other sense-faculties do not. Thus, the Sage said that fruition of karmic deeds is inconceivable. (That is, it is hard to comprehend even why the senses work the way they do, and so how karma works is even more difficult to comprehend.)

Sense-faculties are self-existent because we experience their effect — visual consciousness, and so forth.

Reply: [12] Because the conditions are incomplete, a visual conscious-ness cannot occur before looking. Afterwards, visual consciousness has no object. If looking and a visual cognition occurs simultaneously, then the sense-faculty is useless. (That is, the sense-faculty would play no role in bringing the act of sensing and the sense-consciousness together.)

There is contact between visual consciousness and a perceived object.

Reply: [13] If visual consciousness travels to its object when form is perceived, what is distant would take longer to see (than what is close up). (But we see everything that we see all at the same time.) But (if no time is needed and the eye works through direct contact), then why are forms that are near clear and forms that are not near not clear? [14] If it is said that the visual consciousness moves after the eye has perceived a form, then this movement would have no purpose (since the eye has already seen the object). But (if visual consciousness moves to see an object that it has not yet had awareness of), it is false to maintain that the form it intends to see has been definitely ascertained. [15] If the eye could apprehend without visual consciousness moving toward an object, it would perceive everything in the entire universe (since nothing would be out of range). There is nothing distant or obscured for a visual consciousness that is without movement.

[16] If the nature of all entities is first to be seen in the entities themselves, then why doesn't the eye take the eye itself as its object?

Form is seen only in dependence on three factors: the form, the sense-faculty (the eye), and the act of visual consciousness.

Reply: [17] The eye does not have visual consciousness; visual consciousness does not have the organ of sight; form does not have either. So, how can these three collectively see form? [18] If a sound is making a noise as it travels to the ear, why isn't it considered a speaker (since it emits sound)? However, if a sound travels without making a noise, how could an aural consciousness arise in relation to it? [19] If a sound is perceived through contact with the ear, what perceives the beginning of the sound before contact? (If nothing, then it is not a sound, as discussed in the next verse.) Since sound does not come alone (but comes bundled with smells and other sense-objects), how could it be perceived by itself? (And why then doesn't the ear also sense smells and other qualities?)

What is wrong if the beginning of a sound is not perceived?

Reply: [20] Insofar as a sound is not heard, it is not a sound. And it is impossible for what is not a sound to end up becoming a sound later.

The mind perceives sense-objects after traveling to them.

Reply: [21] Without the sense-faculties, what could the mind accomplish after it has gone out to the sense-object? Because of this, why wouldn't the conventional self always be left without a mind?

[22] An object already perceived is seen by the mind to be like a mirage. (That is, just as a mirage has no water, so the memory has no essential characteristic or self-existence.) In determining phenomena, this is called "the bodily aggregate of perception." [23] The mind arises dependent upon the eye and form, like a magical illusion. It is not proper to call an entity with real existence (i.e., that is independent and self-existent) an illusion.

It is amazing to claim that the sense-faculties cannot perceive anything.

Reply: [24] Nothing on earth is amazing to the wise (after analyzing it). So, how can there be anything amazing about something like sense-perception?

[25] An apparent (solid) ring of fire created by whirling a firebrand, a magical creature, a dream, an illusion, the reflection of the moon in a pool of water, mist, an echo in a cave or ravine, a mirage, and a cloud — what conventionally exists is similar to all of these.

14. Refuting Extreme Views

[1] If an entity did not arise dependent upon anything else in any way, its self-existence would be established. But such an entity does not exist anywhere. (Thus, all entities are empty of anything giving self-existence.)

[2] The claim "The pot is its form" is wrong. The pot and the form cannot be one (because then anything with that general form would have to be that specific pot). Nor is the pot that possesses form separate from that form (since a pot without form does not exist). The form does not exist in the pot, nor does the pot exist in the form. (That is, the pot's form is not distinct from the pot but dependent upon the pot or vice versa.)

Vaisheshikas: The specific pot exists through its connection to the universal quality "existence."

Reply: [3] You claim the entity and the attribute have dissimilar characteristics (i.e., being a general quality and being a specific material entity). But if the pot is different from existence, how will it not follow that existence then must also be different from the pot? (That is, if the pot is distinct from existence, it must be nonexistent.)

The pot is a particular entity that has attributes such as "being one in number." The attributes cannot exist without there being a substance.

Reply: [4a] But if you accept that "being one in number" cannot qualify a pot, then neither can the pot come to be qualified "being one in number" (which it obviously is).

The pot possesses "being one in number" — it is not one itself.

[4b] Connection can only occur between similar things. (But a material pot and a universal quality are not similar, and so they cannot be connected, and thus the pot cannot possess the quality.) Thus, the pot is not one.

[5a] When the form is as large as the substantial entity (i.e., the pot), why is the form not qualified as "large"?

Vaisheshikas: we say that one attribute cannot qualify another.

[5b] If your opponent does not belong to your school, your scriptural authority cannot be cited.

Even if you reject the idea of separate defining characteristics, at least the pot that they characterize exists.

[6] Establishing the existence of an object having a given defining characteristic by means of that characteristic is not found. The existence of the object apart from its characteristics — "being one" and so forth — is not

found. (That is, the characteristics cannot be a separate basis to establish the pot's existence.)

Sautrantika's objection: the pot and its eight components (the four elements [earth, water, fire, air], form, smell, taste, and touch) are one.

Reply: [7] "Being one" cannot characterize the pot because the pot cannot be separated from its characteristics. Nor can the pot be characterized as "being plural" (since its parts cannot individually be characterized as "the pot.")

The eight components come together to form a single unit.

[8] Indeed, the tangible (i.e., the four elements) and the intangible (i.e., form, smell, taste, and touch) cannot be connected. (The four elements have the ability to make contact, but the last four do not.) Thus, it is not possible in any way that the components could coalesce to form a union.

The pot still exists: it is a compound entity that relies on its components.

[9] Form is a component of the pot, and thus it is not the pot itself. (The same for each component; thus, there is no pot itself to possess the components.) Since the pot itself does not exist, the components — form and so forth — do not exist. [10] Smell, taste, and touch have the same indistinguishable defining characteristic as form. For what reason then is the true existence of a pot only one (form) and not the other characteristics?

Objection: [11a] Form is different from taste and the other components but not from the pot,

Reply: [11b] The pot cannot exist by itself without smell and the others. (If smell, taste, and touch are different from form,) mustn't the pot be different from form?

[12] There is no (real, self-existent) cause of the pot, and it does not arise on its own as an effect (of itself or anything else). But no pot is found distinct from form and other components. (In sum, a pot is not self-existent.)

The pot is the effect of clay and its other causes.

Reply: [13] If the pot is established by its cause, then that cause must be established by another cause (unless that cause is self-existent). How can a cause that does not exist by virtue of itself produce something else? (Only something that is self-caused is real and thus able to cause something else.)

The pot may have many parts, but it is still a single unit.

Reply: [14] Even in a union, it is unreasonable to suppose that form could be smell. Thus, a composite object, such as a pot, is not unified into a unity.

[15] Just as the pot is not seen apart from form, smell, taste, and touch (i.e., the pot does not exist apart from them), so form and the others are not seen apart the elements of earth, water, fire, and air. (That is, the pot is dependent on form, smell, taste, and touch, and these in turn are dependent on the four material elements.)

[16] Fire is a thing that is in fact hot. (Being hot and burning are fire's defining characteristics.) How can what is not hot (i.e., fuel) burn? Thus, what is called "fuel" does not exist, and without fuel fire is not found. [17] Even if fuel becomes hot only when overpowered by fire, why doesn't it arise as fire? (That is, if it can burn, why is fuel not by nature fire and already burning?) Even if fuel is not hot, it is still impossible to claim there is something inside fire (that is not hot).

Fire does not have anything from the other three elements, and thus fire has nothing that is fuel (i.e., no non-fire elements in it and thus no material).

Reply: [18] If a particle of fire has no fuel, then there is fire without fuel. But if a particle of fire does have fuel, the particle is not unified in nature.

[19] Every entity that is fully examined is found to lack oneness (i.e., unity). And because there is no oneness, non-oneness (i.e., plurality) is not found. [20] If you assert that there is oneness where there are no other entities, then oneness is found nowhere since everything is threefold (i.e., being one in number, being made of one or more elements, and being real).

[21] Being real, unreal, both real and unreal, and neither real nor unreal — to refute these, the wise should always apply this analysis of oneness, non-oneness, both oneness and non-oneness, and neither oneness nor non-oneness.

If things are not self-existent, why do people hold that things truly exist?

Reply: [22] Just as misperceiving the continuum of events leads to claiming that entities are permanent, so misperceiving the combination of causes and conditions leads to claiming that entities truly exist (i.e., are self-existent). [23] All things that arise dependently are not independent. All this (i.e, the bodily aggregates and so forth) lacks independent self-existence. Thus, there is no "self." [24] An entity cannot in any way become a union without being an effect. That union that is unified as an effect is not a (real) union according to the noble ones. (That is, the union is not self-existent but a compound of parts and thus is an effect and not real.)

[25] The consciousness that is the seed of the cycle of rebirth has sense-objects as its sphere of activity. When objects are seen to be without self, the seed of a new birth is destroyed.

15. *Refuting Conditioned Things as Truly Real*

Assertion: [1a] What does not exist arises (as real) at the last moment of production.

Reply: How can something that is nonexistent arise at all? (If the nonexistent could arise, then the rabbit's horns could be produced.)

Assertion: [1b] What truly exists exists at the time of its causation.

Reply: How can something that is truly existent arise at all? (It would be permanent and exist prior to any arising and thus could not arise or be caused.)

[2] The nonexistent cannot arise, since an effect destroys its cause (and what does not exist does not have the power to destroy). And what already is existent cannot arise, since there is no establishing something that is already established.

[3] There is no production at the time something already has been produced, nor at any other time. If there is no production at that time or another, when can production occur?

[4] Just as something does not arise in the form it already has, so that thing does not arise in another form. (Thus, milk cannot change its defining characteristic and become something else, e.g., butter, with its own new defining characteristic.)

[5] A beginning, middle, and end are not possible prior to something arising. (When any one of these three is occurring, the other two are not.) When any two are not occurring, how will the third occur? (An "end" cannot exist without a prior "beginning"; nothing is a "middle" without both a "beginning" and an "end"; nothing is a "beginning" without something following it. Thus, none can occur without the other two.)

[6] Without other things, a thing itself does not occur. (That is, any entity is dependent for its existence on other things. In addition, these other things in turn themselves depend upon yet more things.) Thus, there is no coming into existence from either a thing itself or from another thing (since both depend on other things and thus lack the reality through self-existence to produce anything).

[7] Arising cannot be said to be before, after, or simultaneous (since no entity arises before, after, or during its own arising). Thus, the pot and its arising do not arise simultaneously. [8] What has arisen was not old when it first arose. What is still in the process of arising is not growing old. What is completely arisen does not grow old (since it cannot change its nature).

[9] An entity existing now is not produced from itself (since it is already existing). Nor does it arise from what is not yet come (since the future thing does not exist now). Nor does it arise from what has already passed (since what has passed away no longer exists).

[10] What has already arisen has no coming-into-existence. So too, what has already ceased has no going-out-of-existence. This being so, then why isn't the cycle of existence like a magician's illusion? [11] Arising, enduring, and ceasing do not occur simultaneously, nor do they occur in discrete stages — when then can they occur? [12] For each stage beginning with arising, each of the three stages occur. (That is, each stage has its own arising, enduring, and ceasing, and each of these three substages have their own arising, enduring, and ceasing, and so on and so on.) Thus, ceasing seems like arising, and enduring seems like ceasing.

[13] If the thing with these three characteristics is said to be different from these characteristics, how could it be impermanent? (That is, the thing in itself would not have the characteristics of impermanent things — arising, enduring, and ceasing — and thus be permanent, which experience shows it is not.) Alternatively, if the thing and the three characteristics are identical, there should not exist any clear distinctions between them (i.e., between the thing and the characteristics).

Arising, enduring, and ceasing all exist by self-existence since the entity with these characteristics exist by self-existence.

Reply: [14] A real entity cannot arise from another entity (since what is self-existent cannot arise from something else). An entity does not arise from a non-entity (since a non-entity does not have the reality to produce anything). A non-entity does not arise from a non-entity (since neither is real). And a non-entity does not arise from a (real) entity (since a reality cannot produce a non-reality). [15] A (real) entity does not become a (real) entity (since what is real does not change). A non-entity does not become an entity (since what is unreal cannot become real). A non-entity does not become a non-entity (since what is not real cannot change). And an entity does not become a non-entity (since what is real cannot go out of existence).

An entity in the process of arising is produced.

Reply: [16] Anything in the process of arising is not arisen since anything in the process of arising is only half-arisen. Alternatively, it would follow that everything (in the past, present, or future) would in fact be in the process of arising. [17] Anything that has the nature of "currently arising" is not in the process of arising. (That is, it is already in the state that its nature dictates and thus is not in the process of arising to that state.) Nor does anything currently in the state of arising not have the nature of "currently arising." (It could not arise without having the nature of "currently arising.")

[18] There can be no process of arising for anyone who accepts that the past and future cannot exist without an intermediate state in between, since that state too would have an intermediate state. (That is, for any segment of time, there would have also been past and future periods, with no period in between for the arising to occur.)

Objection: [19] Since what has arisen comes forth from the ceasing of the process of arising, the true existence of something other (than what was half-produced and half-unproduced) is seen in the process of arising.

Reply: [20] When what has arisen exists, then there is no longer anything in the process of arising. Why would what has already arisen be in the process of arising again?

The "process of arising" is merely called that when what has not yet arisen is progressing to the state when it will be said to "have arisen."

Reply: [21] Anything in the process of arising is said to be unarisen. Since there is no difference (for you between the not-yet-arisen and the already-arisen), why not conceive that a nonexistent pot is an arisen pot?

Objection: [22a] What is currently in the process of arising, although the process is incomplete, is different from what has not arisen.

Reply: [22b] You must claim that it is the unarisen that arises since the processing of arising is excluded from what has arisen.

Objection: [23a] What is currently arising, although not yet existent, is said to exist later. Thus, the unarisen is arising.

Reply: [23b] What is nonexistent cannot arise. [24] About what has completed the process of arising, it is said "It exists." About what has not completely arisen, it is said "It does not exist." When there is no real thing in the process of arising, what is being called "existent"? (That is, anything that is still in the process of arising has not completely arisen and so is not "real" — thus, there is nothing real that is arising to refer to.)

[25] There is no effect without a cause. Thus, it is not possible that there is a truly existing entity that could enter or exit the process of arising. (What is real is not caused and is unchanging.)

16. Miscellaneous Points Related to Argumentation

[1] For various reasons, what is empty is nevertheless seen as not empty. All the proceeding chapters have been to refute those reasons one by one.

Objection: [2a] When an objector, his subject-matter, and his assertions exist, it is incorrect to call them "empty."

Reply: [2b] Whatever arises dependent upon other things does not exist (since they are empty of self-existence), including those three things.

Objection: What is empty is nonexistent (like a rabbit's horns); since the objector and so on exist, they must be self-existent.

Reply: [3] If things can be established as non-empty by pointing out flaws concerning emptiness, then why can't things be established as empty by pointing out flaws concerning the claim that they are not empty?

Objection: [4] In refuting your opponent's proposition, you establish your own proposition. If you approve of refuting a proposition, why don't you approve of positively proving a proposition?

Reply: [5] If what does not exist when thoroughly examined cannot be a proposition, then the three claims (proposition, counter-proposition, and non-proposition) are not tenable propositions at all.

Objection: [6a] Since a pot is directly perceivable, the argument of emptiness is rendered groundless.

Reply: [6b] An argument that comes from our opponents is not valid here in our system. It is valid only within the opponent's school.

Objection: [7] Since there is nothing that is not empty (but self-existent), how can emptiness occur? How can there be a counter-proposition without something else to oppose to it? (If you deny all self-existence, then you deny there is anything to contrast with emptiness.)

Reply: [8] If there could be a proposition, then the absence of a proposition would have the form of a proposition. Since there is no proposition, what could be a counter-proposition? (That is, only if a proposition is *real* [self-existent] could there be an equally genuine counter-position.)

Objection: [9a] How can fire be hot when nothing truly exists?

Reply: [9b] This was refuted above (verses 14.16-17) — even a hot fire does not truly exist. [10] Moreover, by seeing an allegedly existent entity, that entity is shown not to be a nonexistent entity; so, what proposition is seen after the errors of the four positions (real, unreal, both real and unreal, and neither real nor unreal) are abandoned? [11] Where no truly existing entity is found even in a particle, how can there be (self-existence)? For the buddhas, even nonexistence thus cannot be implied (when the idea of nonexistence depends on the idea of real existence). [12] There is an absence of duality here (i.e., since nothing is self-existent, there is no division of things into groups of self-existent things versus non-self-existent things). If so, how could anything be a truly existent entity (since nothing is self-existent)? If this is reasonable even to you, how could you criticize it? [13] When all entities are not truly existent, it is not possible to make distinctions among them. The absence of true existence that is seen in all substances cannot distinguish them. (That is, all things are of the same ontological nature — being free of self-existence — and so cannot be divided up into different ontological categories.)

[14] You may claim that no reply is made to your proposition since we claim there is no proposition (to refute). But why is it that your own proposition can be refuted by reasons and not be established by you? [15] Even though the world says it is easy to find reasons that refute, why can't errors in your opponent's proposition (i.e., ours) be stated by you?

[16] If simply by saying "They exist" things did truly exist, why shouldn't they also be nonexistent simply by saying "They do not exist"? [17] And if things are not nonexistent because they are labeled with the name "existent," they are not truly existent simply because the label "existent" is applied. [18] If everything exists in the world simply because things can be referred to by words, how could any truly existent entity be referred to? (That is, words are not self-existent but dependent, and how could what is dependent refer to what is self-existent since they are different in nature?)

Objection: [19] If all entities are in fact nonexistent because they do not really exist (i.e., have self-existence), then in that case it is not reasonable to claim that all propositions are nonexistent. (That is, if you are claiming "All entities are in fact nonexistent because they have no self-existence," then you must accept that there is in fact at least one real thing — this claim.)

Reply: [20] Because there is no existent entity, there is no absence of an existent entity. How could the absence of an entity be established if there is no entity to begin with?

Objection: [21a] If emptiness is established by means of your arguments, then your arguments are not empty. (For only the real can be established.)

Reply: [21b] The proposition is not different (in nature) from the argument. (Both are empty of self-existence: if the argument were different in nature from the proposition, they could not be related and so the argument could not refute the proposition.) Thus, the argument is not really existent.

Objection: [22] Since you use examples of empty things, the examples are not empty. Can one say "Just as a crow is black, so is the self"? (The proposition and example must be of the same ontological nature for the example to be applicable — if they differ like a crow and the self, the example will not work.)

Reply: [23] If things did exist by self-existence, what benefit would there be in perceiving emptiness? (That is, if everything is self-existent, then it would be the perception of emptiness that is the misperception.) Perceiving things through conceptual constructs binds us to the cycle of rebirths. This discursive thought is refuted here (thereby ending the bonds fueling the cycle of rebirths). [24] To say "One thing truly exists, and another does not" — this does not comport with reality on either the ultimate level of truth or the conventional worldly level. Thus, surely one cannot say "This truly exists, but that does not exist." (That is, either conventionally or in terms of what is ultimately real, the mind and external objects always have the same nature: both exist conventionally but neither is self-existent and thus not ultimately real.)

[25] It is not possible even after a long time to level a charge against someone who has no proposition positing an entity as real, unreal, or both real and unreal.

This concludes the *Four Hundred Verses on Yogic Deeds* composed by the learned master Aryadeva, the spiritual son who sat at the feet of the noble Nagarjuna.

* * *

Notes

The text divides neatly in two: the first eight chapters on the religious life and accumulating good *karmic merit* for better rebirths, and the second half on philosophical issues about acquiring the *knowledge* necessary for gaining enlightenment. (One cannot gain enlightenment merely by accumulating merit.) But the work is not as impressively argued as Nagarjuna's works — Aryadeva's refutations in the second half do not cover all possibilities, as Nagarjuna's refutations of "time" and so forth do. Nagarjuna's central method of pointing out defects in others' positions without advancing positive arguments only comes to the fore here in the last chapter and a half. Aryadeva rarely or never uses such central Madhyamaka concepts as "empty (*shunya*)," "self-existence (*svabhava*)," "the absence of self-existence (*nihsvabhava*), and "view (*drishti*)," nor is he as rigorous in this use of terms in general. Two other works purported to be by Aryadeva that seem related to the *Four Hundred Verses* — the *One Hundred Verses* and the *Aksharashataka* — that are only partially existent today in Chinese look more impressive. (See Tucci 1929, Lang 1999b, and Lang 1999c.) But this may only be an effect of the translations.

The first half is included here to remind the reader of the religious context of Madhyamaka philosophy: it is not a disinterested attempt to know reality, but a way to end the suffering inherent in being reborn again and again. Nevertheless, it is philosophy: all that is involved are only ordinary, everyday experiences and the analysis of his opponents' alleged concepts and claims — there is no appeal to mystical or paranormal experiences or to religious doctrines as special authorities. This is not say that one can gain the peace of nirvana through ordinary experiences — rather, the insight into the way things really are is needed that is developed through *vipashyana* meditation. Philosophy will get you only so far.

The first four chapters are in effect a commentary on "wrong views" and "right views" of early Buddhism: seeing permanence in what is really impermanent; seeing as pleasurable what can only bring suffering; seeing purity in what is really impure; and seeing a self in what is without a self (*Anguttara Nikaya* II.52). This is the epistemic foundation for the rest of the Noble Eightfold Path to enlightenment. The chapters, however, are not so much a philosophical exposition as using examples to show the problems to the laity. Chapter 1 uses the death and rebirth of human beings to illustrate impermanence; Chapters 2 and 3 use the human body to show problems with pleasure and purity; and Chapter 4 presents the case against permanence through the disadvantages of being a king. Indeed, Chapter 4 should be entitled "Who Would Be Happy Being a King?" — it does not contain a philosophical argument for unreality of a "self."

Chapter 2. Pain or suffering (*dukkha*) does not mean that Buddhists see all experiences are directly painful — some experiences are directly painful and not merely the product of our conceptions (e.g., a broken leg), but obviously some experiences are quite pleasurable. Nevertheless, even the pleasurable experiences come to an end, and no experience, no matter how pleasurable, is totally satisfying. This frustration, dissatisfaction, and disappointment permeates our existence.

Verse 2.9. "Pleasure is controlled by our own conceptualizations (*kalpanas*) and our conceptualizations are governed by pain. Thus, there is nothing anywhere more powerful than pain." This verse shows that Aryadeva is not engaging in Nagarjuna's type of analysis in this portion of the work — Nagarjuna would have shown problems with the concept of conceptualizations of "pain." But it does fit with Buddhism in general — i.e., pleasure is a product of our own subjectivity and is overpowered in the end by suffering.

Chapter 5. A bodhisattva is one who has dedicated his or her lives, not to escaping the cycle of rebirths, but solely to the benefit of all sentient beings and to attaining the enlightenment of a fully-enlightened buddha. Because of this intention, even actions that would be karmically harmful if done by another do not harm bodhisattvas (v. 5). (For the ethical implications o f the bodhisattva way of life, see Jones 2004: 181-213.) They remain in the cycle of rebirths to help others (v. 16) and, since they are free of the control of karma, they are free to assume whatever rebirth is most helpful (v. 17). They acquire a huge amount of merit but use it to help others.

Verse 5.9, 15, and Chapter 6. For Nagarjuna's analysis of mental afflictions (*kleshas*), see MK 14.1, 17.25-33, 19.2-6, 19.23-24, 24.29.

Verse 5.16. The five paranormal abilities are: the divine eye (with which one can see the most subtle aspects of things), the divine ear (with which one can hear the most subtle sound), knowledge of others' minds, knowledge of past lives (one's own and others'), and the ability to perform miracles.

Verse 5.19. The word for "giving" in Sanskrit (*dana*) begins with "d," and the verse would suggest that words connected to death (*mrityur*), Buddhist doctrine (*dharma*) and rebirth ("becoming," *bhava*) should too, but they do not.

Verse 5.22. For a bodhisattva with a powerful mind, "worldly existence and nirvana are not different." Notice that Aryadeva does not say they are identical: under the Madhyamaka analysis, only what is self-existent can be *identical or different* — since worldly existence and the peace of nirvana are not self-existent, they cannot be the same or different. But having the same ontological nature (the lack of any self-existence), they are "not different."

Verse 6.11. "When dependent arising is seen, delusion does not occur. Thus, every effort will be made here to explain this very subject." However, he does not explain dependent arising in the text but merely assumes it. Perhaps he is referring to an accompanying oral commentary.

Verse 7.24. Notice that some in India at the time must have seen human beings in terms of machines for this verse to make sense. A magician making illusory beings is a more typical example, but the collection of mechanical devices also works: it is dependent and impermanent.

Verse 8.7. "One cannot attain nirvana simply by thinking that what is really empty (*shunya*) is not empty (*ashunya*). The buddhas say that nirvana is not attained through a wrong view." That is, we cannot attain nirvana simply by accepting the claim that everything is empty or by imagining the world that way — that would be simply imposing another conceptualized view onto the world. What is needed is to actually *experience* the world *as empty* — to *perceive* the way things really are.

Verse 8.9. An alternative translation for the second half of the verse is this: "But if actions were self-existent, this teaching of emptiness could not end karmic deeds." The first alternative means that accepting the doctrine of emptiness does not lead to the end of acting but to adopting the actions leading to seeing reality as empty. The second alternative means that *if actions were self-existent* then nothing could end actions or karmic effects — they would be permanent, unchanging, and unaffectable.

Verse 8.10. Aryadeva uses the word "proposition (*paksha*)" and not "thesis (*pratijna*)" or any of the other words Nagarjuna uses. (See Jones 2010: 145-47.) But it is still a matter of setting up opposing philosophical positions, and "There is no tranquility for one who lives in oppositions."

Verse 8.11. "Action (with karmic consequences) brings about rebirth again. Thus, nirvana is easy to attain when one is free of doubts; the latter is not." "The latter is not" may refer to gaining a pleasurable rebirth.

Verse 8.16. That is, all things have the same ontological nature that can be seen in anything. It is not the claim that emptiness is some *metaphysical entity* that is common to everything.

Verse 8.20. "The buddhas have mentioned what is real (*sat*), and what is unreal, and what is both real and unreal, and what is neither real nor unreal." (See MK 18.8.) This verse contains the four options that are so prominent in Nagarjuna's analysis (see Jones 2010: 155-57). (See also verses 14.21., 16.9b) This may be a "graduated teaching," since it suggests different medicines for different students. A few verses earlier (8.14-15), Aryadeva also mentioned different practices for people of different abilities. Buddhists explain MK 18.6 by claiming that the Buddha had a graduated teaching —

i.e., he taught beginners that there is a self, to more advanced students that there is no self, but to still more advanced adepts he taught that there is neither a self nor a non-self. (See R 394-96; YS 30.)

Also notice the *medical motif.* (See also verses 3.1, 5.9, 5.13, and 8.17.) This carries on the Buddha's practice: even the form of the basic four "Noble Truths" is based on ancient Indian medical practice — first the illness is diagnosed (here, the suffering and frustration that permeates life in the cycle of rebirths), then the cause of the illness is identified (craving based on our erroneous perception of reality), a cure is identified (stopping the craving by stopping the fundamental misperception of reality), and a prescription is set forth (the "Eightfold Path" of right knowledge, actions, and meditation).

Verse 8.22. Early Buddhism also had the doctrine that advanced practitioners may attain nirvana at the moment of death ("non-returners") or in the next life ("once-returners") based on what occurred in this life.

Verse 9.1. "Everything arises as an effect. Thus, nothing is permanent." This is a core Buddhist metaphysical doctrine on entities "as they really are (*yatha-bhavas*)."

Verses 9.2-4. "Nothing is *found* anywhere at any time that is not dependent." That is, nothing is *experienced* or *seen* that is not dependently arisen. It is not the claim about what is real "There *are* no independent entities," but an experiential one "We *experience* no independent entities." But this is expanded into a claim about reality in the next verse: "There is no entity without a cause. And nothing permanent has a cause. Thus, the ones who know the that-ness of reality (*tat-tva*) say that establishment (*siddhi*, i.e., "proof") without a cause is certainly not established." But in the next verse Aryadeva gives the experiential basis for the claim: "Seeing that the produced is impermanent, one may think the unproduced is permanent. If so, since we see only produced things, then there are no permanent things."

Verses 9.8-11. The first verse is like Nagarjuna on causes. It deals with the interconnection of concepts. But the next verse introduces a new idea — that causes undergo change: "When a cause becomes the cause of something else, it undergoes change. Anything that undergoes change cannot be called 'permanent.'" Verses 10 and 11 introduce new ideas: an entity whose cause is permanent is produced by something that has not come into being, and whatever arises by itself has no cause, and a cause and effect have dissimilar characteristics.

Verse 9.12-16. Aryadeva presents a philosophical argument against there being indivisible "atoms" of matter, not a scientific argument based on an empirical examination of smaller and smaller bits of matter: any bit of matter would have sides and regions and therefore could not be partless. (Also see the *Hand Treatise 3*.)

Verses 9.18-19. Part of this is not like Nagarjuna's analysis of causation. "An effect destroys its cause, and thus the cause is not permanent." But the second part is: "Or where the cause exists, the effect does not (and thus the cause is not really a cause)." So too, verse 19: "A permanent entity that shows resistance to being affected (*pratigha*) is not seen anywhere."

Verse 9.21. Aryadeva uses many different terms related to "self" — *atman* (the psycho-physical "self"), inner self (*antara-atman*), *purusha* ("eternal self," also the Samkhya's term for the pure consciousness of each individual self), *jiva* ("conventional self"), *pums* ("human being"), *pudgala* (an entity posited by some Buddhist schools that is reborn), and *ahamkara* (the "I-maker" — a sense of self). He does not make technical distinctions between the terms. For example, in verse 10.8 he uses "*purusha*" while in the following verse he uses "*jiva*" while discussing the same subject. In the state of nirvana without any residue, the bodily aggregates do not exist and thus the conventional person (*pudgala* or *jiva*) could not exist. So too, he uses "*caitanya*" for consciousness when discusses the Samkhya idea of a pure consciousness distinct from the body and "*jnana*" when discussing the Vaisheshkia idea of a consciousness connected to the embodied self.

Verse 10.6. "If the self is permanent (and thus cannot be harmed), why advocate nonviolence (*ahimsa*)?" This is important for ethics: if there is nothing to harm, we could *not* harm a sentient being even if tried. We could not but practice *ahimsa* (nonviolence in any form to any sentient being) no matter what we did. (See Jones 2004: 90-91, 331-32.)

Verse 10.12. In early Buddhism, the term "*cetana*" — translated here as "purpose" — refers to the *intention* behind an act. It is what gives the act its karmic effect. See also *One Hundred Verses* 1.22. (See Jones 2004: 152-53.)

Verses 10.18 and 20. Verse 18 brings up *prajna* (insight or wisdom) and verse 20 a knower of reality (*tattva-vid*) in connection to attaining nirvana.

Verse 11.5. This reflects one of Nagarjuna's form of argument. (See Jones 2010: 155.)

Verse 11.9. The Niyativadins hold a belief in a fixed and uncaused reality that cannot be affected by human effort. That there were materialists, fatalists, and determinists even in ancient India should be noted.

Verse 11.12. The term for "yogic discipline" is "*niyama*." In the *Yoga Sutras* II.30, "*yama*" is used for "restraints on behavior" such as nonviolence.

Verse 11.13. A claim standard to all Buddhist schools on the perishing of the impermanent: "belief in permanence is incompatible with our common experience of things having a beginning and end."

Verse 11.15. This disputes both those who think an effect is in the cause (the *Satkaryavadins*, such as the Samkhyas) and those who think the effect is distinct from the cause (the *Asatkaryavadins*): for the former, Aryadeva is claiming the effects (the pillars for supporting a house) already exist in the cause (*satkarya*, i.e., the house), and so there is no need for them to arise later; for the latter, if the pillars do not exist in the cause (*asatkarya*), they do not support the house because they are not present when the house first arises.

Verse 11.19. Another basic Madhyamaka claim: an entity and its characteristic cannot be either the same nor distinct.

Verse 12.11. Notice that there are two type of "right views" (see R 43-45). The lesser right view is belief that actions did not produce predictable effects in causation, karma, and merit; this leads to heaven. The better right view is cultivating the Eightfold Path and the insight that leads to nirvana.

Verse 12.12. The translation here amends the text to say that the Buddha spoke of the suffering inherent in the cycle of rebirths, and not the cycle or "existence" in the abstract and its causes.

Verse 12.13. Note the connection again of philosophical views with the experiential: the heterodox are those with bad eyes or weak eyesight (*kudrishti*), not merely those holding the wrong doctrines or making bad arguments.

Verse 12.19: The ears hear the Brahmin's recitation of the Vedas; the eyes see the tortured bodies of the ascetics, but the mind apprehends the Buddha's doctrine of emptiness. The Brahmin's recitation and sacrifices are for pay, and so his religiosity is only for show. The ascetic's torments do not aid in pacifying the mind, which is what is needed for liberation.

Verse 12.23. Nonviolence is for the ordinary person, but this does not mean that the "noble one" (*arya*) who seeks liberation does not also practice it. Rather, the doctrine of emptiness is simply added to this practice for those seeking liberation rather than a better rebirth.

Verses 12.24-25. For criticism of partiality, also see verse 8.10.

Verse 13.8. From Nagarjuna (SS 50): "Since color and shape never exist apart from each other, one cannot be conceived without the other, and so they are considered one."

Verse 13.21. Mind (*manas*) in classical Indian psychology is considered a sixth sense, and in its theory of perception the mind goes out to contact the sense-object; perception is not a matter of light-waves bouncing off an object and entering the brain through the eyes.

Verse 13.22. The five bodily aggregates (*skandhas*) are material form (*rupa*), feelings or sensation (*vedanas*), mental dispositions (*samkharas*), perception (*samjna*), and cognition (*vijnana*). *Rupa* covers the material aspects of a human being, but the focus is on what we *experience* — the "form" of something. *Samjna* is a discrimination based on a sensory-sensation, e.g., perceiving a *pot* rather than merely receiving a *brown visual sensation*. It is a matter of identifying the defining characteristic (*lakshana*) of something. The dispositions predispose us to see things in a certain way — i.e., conceptualized into discrete objects by our conventions — rather than to see reality as it truly is. Consciousness is not a permanent beam of awareness but a series of momentary conscious events.

Verses 13.23-25. "It is not proper to call an entity with real existence (*sat-bhava*, i.e., that is independent with self-existence) an illusion." Rather, only what arises dependent upon other things is like a magical illusion. This is common in Nagarjuna's work too (see Jones 2010: 140). But note that an illusion is not *totally nonexistent* — it is seen, but is *dependent* on something else. Thus, an illusion does not represent total nonexistence. Aryadeva was no more an ontological nihilist than was Nagarjuna. Verse 25 introduces conventional Madhyamaka examples of insubstantiality and dependent existence: the apparent solid ring of fire created by whirling a firebrand, a magical creation, a dream, an illusion, the reflection of the moon in a pool of water, mist, an echo, a mirage, and a cloud. Also verse 15.10.

Verse 14.2. This is the Madhyamaka analysis: only two real (self-existent) entities can be related to each other as either the same or different; nothing that is dependently arisen can be so related.

Verse 14.3. There is a danger here in using the word "universal" in regard to a general quality: we may start thinking in terms of the medieval Western Scholastics' use of the term. To the Scholastics, only the universals existed; the experienced world is simply the instantiation of the categories of divine reason and not actually real. We should not think the denial of self-existence in Buddhism was a response to a Scholastic-type metaphysics.

Verse 14.7. If the pot and its characteristics are in fact *united* in one entity, they cannot be identical since we cannot unite what is already *identical* but only two different things. Thus, there must be some distinction between the pot and the characteristics if they are to be united.

Verses 14.16-18. The material that would become "fuel" still exists, but it no longer has the characterization as "fuel." (See MK 10 and R 83-90.)

Verse 14.19. On the analysis of oneness, see SS 7 and R 71.

Verse 14.21. What is real (*sat*) exists by self-existence. What is unreal (*asat*) is not what exists by something other than self-existence but what is the *total absence of reality*. Thus, in this ontology there is room for what is neither *sat* nor *asat* — the dependently arisen.

Verse 14.22. On the idea of a continuum (*santana*) of changing parts, see MK 27.22: "Since the continuity of the bodily aggregates is like the flame of a lamp, neither a limit nor the absence of a limit is admissible."

Verse 15.5. See MK 7.2 and R 65, 69-70 on interdependence of characteristics. See verse 2.11 and MK 1.1, 1.3, 15.1-4 on the interdependence of self-existence and other-existence.

Verse 15.10. See R 109-115.

Verses 15.14-15. See MK 21.21. The first lines of these verses can also be read without the idea of "self-existence": "[14] An entity cannot arise from another entity (since it already exists it cannot arise from something else)." "[15] An entity does not become a entity (since it already exists)."

Verse 16.2. See VV 22.

Verse 16.3-5. This is the core of Nagarjuna's method: only pointing out errors in others' positions, not making positive arguments for emptiness. Bhavaviveka changes this, as will be seen.

Verse 16.4-8. See verse 8.10 on a proposition (*paksha*). On relating one's own proposition (*sva-paksha*), an opponent's proposition (*para-paksha*), and a counter-proposition (*pratipaksha*), see MK 13.7, R 72, and R 104.

Verse 16.10. "By seeing an allegedly existent entity (*bhava*), that entity is shown not to be a nonexistent entity (*abhava*)." Also see verse 16.20. For Nagarjuna, an *abhava* is the *denial* of an existing *bhava* —the *absence* of a *bhava*. Under the self-existence metaphysics Nagarjuna ascribes to his opponent, an *abhava* is a type of thing — an absent *bhava*. If there are no *bhavas* to begin with, no *abhavas* can be found (e.g., MK 25.7).

Verse 16.12. The Madhyamaka's ontology involves a nondualism between things in the phenomenal world — if there is nothing self-existent, then there is nothing to contrast with it and so no ontological dualism. This is not Advaita Vedanta's nondualism between the reality of the world (Brahman) and the reality of the inner self (*atman*). Advaita's is a nondualism of the phenomenal realm and a transcendental realm, while the Madhyamaka's remains in the phenomenal realm.

Verses 16.16-18. See VV 9-10, 58-59; SS 1-2. Words are conventional in nature, and the self-existent is not; thus, words could not refer to the self-existent. It is again a matter of the difference in nature: the self-existent and the dependent cannot mix.

Verse 16.20. Again, because there is no existent entity (*bhava*), there is no absence of an entity (*abhava*). See MK 15.5.

Verses 16.21-22. On the relation of the thesis (*pratijna*), the reason (*hetu*), and the example (*drishtanta*) in a classical Hindu syllogism, see VV 1, 3, 21, and 24-28. Also see Bhavaviveka's works.

Verse 16.24. The opponents here are probably the Buddhist Yogacharins (or Cittamatrins, i.e., advocates of the "mind-only" doctrine). They claim that consciousness has true existence but external objects do not.

Here also is a reference to the two types of truth — truths from a conventional point of view and truths from the point of view of things' ultimate ontological status. This is central to all Madhyamaka thought. (See Jones 2010: 147-52.)

Verse 16.25. See VV 29. In effect, this verse says that there can be no refutation of the Madhyamikas since they refuse to hold any positions that entail something is real (*sat*) or totally unreal (*asat*) to begin with. (But see Jones 2010: 145-47.) Note that this verse lists the first three traditional options (real, not real, both real and not real) but omits the fourth option — "neither real nor unreal." This also occurred often in Nagarjuna's works (MK 1.7, 2.24-25, 5.6, 8.9-11, 21.13, 23.20; R 37; SS 4, 44; VP 4, 51, 56, 73; also see Buddhapalita's commentary on MK 18.8cd). Perhaps this is because in the Madhyamaka ontology what is dependently arisen and thus free of self-existence can be accurately described as "neither real nor unreal." Only what has self-existence can be real and hence also unreal — what is free of self-existence can be neither. That is, the fourth option only must be denied with respect to allegedly self-existent entities, not what is empty. But since the unenlightened may still think in terms of "*entities* that are neither real nor unreal," the Madhyamaka found it safer in certain contexts to deny the fourth option too.

* * *

Summary of
One Hundred Verses
(Shataka-shastra)
and its Commentary

1. *Renunciation of Demerit and Merit*

I bow at the feet of the Buddha, the compassionate one, the blessed one, who through incalculable ages suffered many sorrows, who exhausted the mental afflictions and expelled the unconscious mental impressions, and who is honored by Brahma, Shakra, the Nagas (snake keepers of the Prajna-paramita texts), and the gods. I also pay homage to the doctrine that illuminates the worlds, to which there is no superior, which can cleanse every impurity and weed, and which has been preached by the buddhas, the blessed ones. And I also pay homage to the order of enlightened followers.

(1) *Opponent*: Why do you call the Buddha "blessed"?

Reply: How can you raise this doubt?

(2) *Opponent*: Because different traditions say different men are "blessed."

Reply: The Buddha is the "blessed one" because he knows the true defining characteristics of all phenomena. He has no doubts in discernment, and he has explained the profound and pure doctrine.

(3) *Opponent*: Masters in other schools also claim to know the true nature of all phenomena.

Reply: The teachings of non-Buddhist schools are all false views because they obscure the right view. Thus, they cannot explain the profound and pure doctrine that will be explained here.

(4) *Opponent*: What are the characteristics of the true doctrine as explained by the Buddha?

Reply: The doctrine is "stopping the demeritorious" and "practicing the meritorious." [In brief, the Buddha taught the true doctrine as the stopping of all demerit and practicing what is wholesome (i.e., what gains merit). The "demeritorious" are unwholesome acts by the body, mouth, and mind: the body kills, steals and engages in illicit sex; the mouth utters lies, malicious words, harsh words, and futile words; the mind covets, is destructive, and follows false views. There are also other acts (e.g., flogging). "Stopping" is putting an end to these acts and not committing more. "Wholesome acts" are the right acts of the body, mouth, and mind: the body approaching the Buddha with hands folded and paying homage, and so forth; the mouth saying true and coherent words, soft words, and useful words; the mind being friendly, compassionate, and following the right view, and so forth. Various pure phenomena like these are called the "good doctrine." "Practice" is faith in and the exercise of these good phenomena.]

(5) *Opponent*: Your texts are faulty because in the beginning they do not speak of happiness but evil (i.e, what produces sorrow).

Reply: No. In order to put an end to evil doctrines, the Buddha has expounded these texts.   [To say "This is happy and this is not happy" is to bring in wrong views. Thus, our texts have no fault.]

In addition, there is no true happiness. [The same object for some is happiness, for other unhappiness, and for others it is neither happiness nor unhappiness — because it is indeterminate, happiness does not exist. (That is, there is no objective quality "happiness.") The foolish, who do not have the means of reaching their goal, strongly desiring and searching for joy, give birth to false notions and say "This is happiness, and that is unhappiness."]

In addition, happiness cannot be established either by itself, by another, or by itself and another together. [Happiness does not arise by itself because no phenomenon whatsoever can arise by itself. Also, anything arising from itself would produce the error of having two characteristics — "being a producer" and "being something produced." Nor can happiness arise from something else: since the own characteristic of happiness does not exist, anything it arose from would also have no real characteristic; there would also then be an infinite regress of causes. Nor can happiness arise from both together since the two individually are incapable of producing it. In general, birth is only of three kinds: by itself, by another, or by the two together. If we search for happiness in these three, we cannot find it. Thus, there is no phenomenon named "happiness."]

(6) *Opponent*: Happiness arises from itself like salt does. [What is salt by nature can make other things salty. So too, happiness by its own nature can impart happiness to other things.]

Reply: No — because of the refutation already made and because in the case of salt, the characteristic is inherent in the salt. [We have already refuted the self-arising of phenomena that had no prior existence. Also salt is derived from a cause and thus that salt is not salt by its own nature. We reject your thesis and shall refute what you teach by your own thesis: if salt is combined with other things, then these things are not salty themselves since the characteristic of salt is inherent only in salt itself, as for example the characteristics of a bull are not the characteristics of a horse.]

(7) *Opponent*: Happiness can impart happiness to other things that are not happiness like a light can illuminate other things.

Reply: In the light itself and in other things, there is no darkness. [A light in itself has no darkness because light and darkness cannot be together in one entity. The light itself does not have the power to illuminate itself or another thing. There would also be the error of having two different characteristics in one thing — "being illuminating" and "being illuminated." Thus, light cannot illuminate itself. The place being illuminated also has no darkness (because it is already illuminated). Thus, light cannot illuminate other things. Because light destroys darkness, it is called "illuminating," but if there is no darkness that can be destroyed, there is no illumination.]

(8) *Opponent*: At the time when the light begins to arise, both it and the other things are illuminated together. [The light does not first arise and then illuminate.]

Reply: The characteristics of "existence" and "nonexistence" cannot be seen in one phenomenon. [When something begins to arise, it is said to be "half-arisen." What is half-arisen is not yet arisen. When it is arisen, it cannot illuminate, as already discussed. How much less can the not-yet-born illuminate? How can one phenomenon have the characteristic of existence and also the characteristic of "nonexistence"?]

In addition, light cannot reach darkness (i.e., have contact with it). [Whether the light has arisen or is only half-arisen, it cannot reach darkness because darkness is contrary in nature. If the light cannot reach darkness, how can it destroy it?]

(9) *Opponent*: Because it is like a magical formula or the (astrological effect of) stars.

Reply: If so, then the greatest errors would be true. [If light has the power to destroy darkness without reaching it, then why does not a light in India destroy darkness in China? Even if a magical formula or stars' influence can reach a distant place, still the case of light is not the same, and thus your example is not apropos.]

In addition, if in the beginning there is happiness, nevertheless what remains is not happiness. [Your texts begin by speaking of happiness, but the rest must be non-happiness. Otherwise, if what remains is also happiness, then your statement "In the beginning, there is happiness" is wrong.]

(10) *Opponent*: The beginning and the remainder are both happiness. [From the force of happiness, happiness remains.]

Reply: Because non-happiness is stronger, happiness becomes non-happiness.

(11) *Opponent*: (Because of the force of even a little happiness, a greater non-happiness becomes happiness) as with the trunk of on elephant. [Because an elephant has a trunk, it is named "having a trunk." The same does not hold for having eyes, ears, and so forth. The same with a little happiness (being the characteristic) of what has greater non-happiness.]

Reply: This would involve an error: the elephant (as a distinct entity) does not in fact exist. [If an elephant is different from the trunk, the elephant must also be different from the head, feet, and so forth. But there cannot be an elephant that is a separate entity (distinct from all its parts). However, if the whole is inherent in each part, then why aren't the feet in the head? If the elephant is not different from the trunk, there would also be no elephant as a separate entity: if what has parts and the parts themselves are not different, then the head must be the foot since both would not be different from the elephant. This is explained further in the refutation of identity below. In the same way, happiness cannot be found in its various causes. How can you claim that because there is happiness in the beginning, there is also happiness in the middle and end?]

(12) *Opponent*: The demeritorious stops, and the stopping of the demeritorious is good. Why do you not say that in the beginning?

Reply: One who acts must first know the demeritorious so that he can then stop it. Thus, we state demeritorious first and then its stopping.

(13) *Opponent*: The practice of the wholesome must come first because it produces good fruit (for auspicious rebirths). [Wholesome phenomena produce good fruits. Because one who acts desires to obtain wholesome fruits, he stops doing the demeritorious. Thus, one must first speak of the practice of the good and then speak of stopping the demeritorious.]

Reply: Because phenomena are in a series, we must first get rid of the coarse dirt and then the fine dust. [If one does not first stop doing the demeritorious, he cannot practice the good. Thus, first the coarse dirt must be gotten rid of, and then one can be imbued with the wholesome phenomena — one who washes clothes first removes the dust and then dyes them.]

(14) *Opponent*: When the stopping of evil has been taught, there is no need to speak of the practice of the good.

Reply: We must speak of the practice of good because giving gifts and so forth are the good practices. [Giving gifts is a practice of the good but not of stopping evil. When great bodhisattvas have stopped evil, then they engage in the wholesome practices — the four unlimited states (friendliness, compassion, sympathetic joy, and even-mindedness), compassion for all sentient beings, and the protection of the life of others. These are wholesome practices, not merely the stopping of the demeritorious.]

(15) *Opponent*: Gift-giving stops greed. Thus, it is stopping the demeritorious.

Reply: If non-giving were itself demeritorious, then all who do not give would gain demerit. And when the impulses are destroyed, our greed and covetousness are also destroyed — thus, what demeritorious phenomena are stopped at the time a gift is made? So too, there are people who give gifts but have not yet stopped their avaricious minds. Afterwards, they can stop their avaricious mind, and then the practice of the wholesome is considered the basis of their actions. Thus, gift-giving is the practice of the wholesome (and not merely the stopping of the demeritorious).

(16) *Opponent*: Having spoken of the practice of the wholesome, it is not necessary next to speak of stopping the demeritorious because stopping the demeritorious is the practice of the wholesome.

Reply: The characteristic of stopping is "inaction." The characteristic of practice is "action." Because their natures conflict, we say the practice of the wholesome does not include the stopping of the demeritorious.

(17) *Opponent*: I do not claim that stopping the demeritorious and the practice of the wholesome have identical characteristics but only that stopping the demeritorious is a good phenomenon. Thus, when one says "Practice the wholesome," one does not need to say again "Stop the demeritorious."

Reply: It is necessary to say both. ["Stopping the demeritorious" means stopping demerit when one takes the vow. And "Practicing the wholesome" means the exercise of good phenomena. If we only said "Practicing the wholesome produces merit" and not "Stopping the demeritorious," then there is this problem: if someone who has taken the vow but whose mind is unwholesome or undetermined, he does not gain merit at that time because he does not practice the good — but since he has stopped doing the demeritorious, he would have merit at that time. Thus, we must say both "Stopping the demeritorious" and "Practicing the wholesome."]

[The phenomena that are "stopping the demeritorious" and "practicing the good" are of three types:] They are lower, middle, and superior, according to their gifts, vows, and knowledge. [To those of lower knowledge, the Buddha taught giving gifts; to those of middling knowledge, he taught keeping the vows; to those of superior knowledge, he taught insight. Giving is the thought concerned with benefitting others, the sacrificing of wealth, and conforming the actions of body and mouth to that thought. "Keeping the rules of conduct" involves one's will to keep them and one's the mouth speaking this vow: "From this day forth, I shall never again engage in the three unwholesome actions of the body and the four unwholesome actions of the mouth." "Insight" involves a fixed and steady mind concerning the nature of all phenomena.]

[Giving produces only a small benefit for others and so is called "lower knowledge." Following the rule of conduct produces a middling benefit for others and so is called "middling knowledge." Insight produces the highest benefit for others and so is called "superior knowledge." The reward of giving is likewise is lowest, of proper conduct middling, and of insight highest.]

(18) *Opponent*: Is all giving "lower knowledge"?

Reply: There are two types of giving: the impure and the pure. Those who practice the impure type are people of "lower knowledge."

(19) *Opponent*: What is "impure giving"?

Reply: Giving in order to receive the benefits is impure. It is no more than an exchange in the market. [There are two types of benefit: phenomena that can be seen immediately and phenomena that occur later. The former are fame, honor, love, and so forth. The latter are wealth, nobility, and so forth in the next life. Giving out of a desire for these rewards is considered impure. For example, consider a merchant who comes from afar with various objects that he distributes liberally but who has no compassion for the sentient beings benefitted: many may be benefitted, but he is seeking only his own interests. This action is impure, as is any giving for which the giver seeks the benefit.]

(20) *Opponent*: What is "pure giving"?

Reply: Giving is pure if the giver loves, honors, and does good to others without seeking any benefit for himself in this life or the next, like bodhisatt-vas and all noble ones practicing pure giving.

(21) *Opponent*: Are all those who observe the rules of proper conduct people of "middling knowledge"?

Reply: The observance of the rules of proper conduct are two types: the pure and the impure. Only those who impurely observe the rules of proper conduct are people of "mediocre knowledge."

(22) *Opponent*: What is the "impure observance of the rules"?

Reply: It is when one observes the rules to gain the reward of happiness, as, for example, the "lust" is the characteristic of the gods when they descend from the heavens to earth (in rebirths after their merit is exhausted). [The reward of happiness is two types: being born a god, and wealth and nobility among men. Thus, it is impure to observe the rules in order to ascend to heaven and enjoy pleasures with the celestial nymphs, or to remain among human beings and enjoy the pleasures of the five senses. So too, an inner desire for the beauty of others and a false outer show of virtue are impure observances of the rules. When you desire but observe the rules, your action is like male goats goring each other with their horns and then retreating: although you observe the rules outwardly with the body, your mind is drawn by desire. When the action itself is impure, what is the use of the rules of proper conduct?]

(23) *Opponent*: What is the "pure observance of the rules"?

Reply: When someone acts with the thought "The rules of proper conduct are the root and the basis of all good phenomena," he has nothing in his mind to repent; when someone has nothing to repent, he is glad; when he is glad, his mind is happy; when his mind is happy, he attains a concentrated mind; with concentration of mind, true knowledge arises in him; when true knowledge arises in him, he is satisfied; when he is satisfied, he gets rid of all desires; when he gets rid of desires, he is released; when he is released, he attains nirvana.

(24) *Opponent*: If one practices knowledge, he is called a person of "highest knowledge." So Uddalaka Aruni (a famous master in the *Chandogya Upanishad*) and other non-Buddhists must be men of "highest knowledge."

Reply: Knowledge too is of two kinds: impure and pure.

(25) *Opponent*: What is "impure knowledge"?

Reply: Worldly knowledge is impure. Thus, the knowledge of non-Buddhists is impure, like that of one who hates and begins to love. [Worldly knowledge leads to births and deaths because it is bound to a desire to return. For example, when someone hates his family but begins to show love for it and becomes attached to it and after a long period commits an offence (producing demerit). The same happens with worldly knowledge.]

(26) *Opponent*: Does only such knowledge fuel the cycle of rebirths, or can giving and proper conduct do so too?

Reply: To strive for merit and to reject whatever is demeritorious is the nature of movement toward rebirth. ["Merit" means the "reward of merit."]

(27) *Opponent*: If "merit" in the text means the "reward of merit," then why does it say only "merit"?

Reply: Sometimes the effect is taught for the cause, and sometimes the cause is taught for the effect. Here, the cause is taught for the effect. [For example, when one says he has "eaten a thousand pounds of gold," this does not mean that he has eaten gold but the food obtained by the gold.]

(28) *Opponent*: What is the doctrine of the "non-movement toward rebirth"?

Reply: The renunciation of both demerit and merit. [Renunciation means the mind does not attach itself to anything. When the mind does not attach itself even to merit, one does not get reborn in any form. (That is, even the positive merit that leads to better rebirths must be renounced, not only actions that leads to demerit and worse rebirths.)]

(29) *Opponent*: Merit must not be renounced because the benefit and fruit are beautiful. And also, the reason for renouncing it has not been shown. [The benefit and fruit of all merit is good and all sentient beings desire beautiful fruits. Also the Buddha taught "Monks, do not be afraid of merit." And you do not explain the reason for renouncing it.]

Reply: When the merit ceases, there is sorrow. [When the benefit of merit is exhausted, then there is the separation from joyful things and a great sadness and suffering arise. As the Buddha taught, "When happiness arises, there is happiness. When it endures, there is happiness. When it ceases, there is suffering." Thus, we must renounce merit. The Buddha said not to be afraid of merit because wholesome practices help on the way to enlightenment. But the Buddha taught that merit must (ultimately) be renounced — how much more then should demerit be renounced!]

(30) *Opponent*: Since merit and demerit conflict in nature, if you claim "There is sorrow at the exhaustion of merit," then when demerit arises or endures there must be happiness.

Reply: When demerit is present, there is suffering. [When the reward of demerit arises, there is suffering. How much more so when it is present! As the Buddha taught, "When suffering arises, it is suffering; when it is endures, it is suffering; when it is exhausted, there is happiness." As for their conflicting nature: why don't you say "Since merit and demerit are conflicting, when demerit is exhausted there is happiness, but when happiness arises or endures there is suffering"?]

(31) *Opponent*: Merit is permanent. Since its cause is not renounced, it must not be renounced. [You teach "There is sorrow when the causes of merit are exhausted." Because merit is permanent, its reward is also permanent. Thus, there is no suffering in the exhaustion of the cause and thus it must not be renounced. As the Vedas say, "The man who can perform the horse sacrifice surpasses suffering, old age, and death." The reward from merit exists permanently. Thus, performing meritorious acts is not to be renounced.]

Reply: Merit must be renounced because of its twofold nature. [Merit can lead to both joy and suffering. It is like food mixed with poison — it is delicious to eat but it produces pain when digested. So too, the reward of merit is a cause of joy, but when felt to excess it is a cause of suffering. It is like fire: when fire is close, it stops cold and thus brings happiness, but when it comes closer it burns the body and produces suffering. Hence, merit has two characteristics, and as such it cannot be permanent. Thus, it must be renounced. As for the alleged permanence of the merit gained from the horse sacrifice:]

It is not so because it has a cause. [The reward of the horse sacrifice is not permanent because the cause has a limit. In this world, if a cause has a limit, then its fruit is also limited, as when a clod of earth is small so is the resulting pot. (If the cause is not permanent, neither is the effect.)]

So too, your gods are subject to anger and they fight and hurt one another; thus, they are not permanent (since they are not changeless).

Your acts such as the horse sacrifice are also all impermanent since they derive from a cause.

In addition, if the merit that is pure and positive must be renounced because it is not permanent, how much more must the merit that is mixed with demerit. [For example, the act of the horse sacrifice is mixed with the demerit of killing. The Samkhya texts also say that sacrifice is impure because it is impermanent. It is the same with superior or inferior merit. Thus, merit must be renounced.]

(32) *Opponent*: But to renounce merit, one must stop acting altogether. [If merit must be renounced, then there must be no action. Why would

anyone with reason suffer (with no prospects of a better rebirth)? It is like a potter who makes pots and then breaks them.]

Reply: The arising of the right path is a progressive phenomenon, as with first washing and then dyeing a dirty cloth. [When a dirty cloth is first cleaned and then dyed, the cleaning is not useless since the dirty cloth cannot receive the dye. So too, first we remove demerit and then by meritorious actions one is purified. And after that, one can receive the dye that is the way to nirvana.]

(33) *Opponent*: On the basis of merit you renounce demerit, but on what basis do you renounce merit?

Reply: The "signless" is superior. [By merit, one is born again among the gods and men; by demerit, one is born in one of the hellish destinies. Thus, knowledge of the signless is absolutely of the highest importance. When all defining characteristics are no longer thought of, when all conceptions are gotten rid of, when the mind is not attached to any past, future, or present phenomenon since phenomena are not self-existent, and when there is nothing to depend upon (i.e., nothing external accepted as real) — this is called the "signless." By these means, it is possible to get rid of merit since without the three openings to deliverance (emptiness, the signless, and the unestablished) the supreme goal is not attained. As the Buddha said to the monks, "Someone who says 'Without utilizing what is empty, signless, and free of karmic action, I desire to attain omniscience or the vision and not to increase pride' is speaks empty, false, words."]

2. Refutation of the Self

(1) *Opponent*: Not all phenomena are empty and signless. Phenomena such as the self are real. [Various schools argue that there is a self. And because of the necessity of a basis in which desire and hatred, happiness and sorrow, and intelligence can adhere, it is known that there is a self. If the self exists and you say it does not, then you cannot be liberated. Thus, you must not say that all phenomena are empty and signless.]

Reply: If there is a self, it is wrong to say that it does not exist, but if there is no self and one says so, what fault is there? And if you carefully examine the self, we see that it does not really exist (i.e., is not self-existent).

(2) *Opponent*: There really is a self, as the Samkhya texts teach. This self has "consciousness" as its defining characteristic.

Reply: Are the self and consciousness one or different?

(3) *Opponent*: They are one.

Reply: If consciousness is the characteristic of the self, then the self is not permanent. [Consciousness is not permanent — because it has different features, because it depends on causes, because it once did not exist and now does, and because it once existed but is now nonexistent. And if consciousness is the characteristic of the self, then the self is not permanent. For example, heat is not permanent, and so if it is the characteristic of fire, then fire is not permanent.]

(4) *Opponent*: Because the self is not born, it is permanent. [Things that have the characteristic of "being born" are not permanent (eternal), but the self does not have that characteristic and thus is eternal.]

Reply: If so, then consciousness is not characteristic of the self. [Consciousness is not permanent, but you teach that the self is permanent. Thus, the self must be different from consciousness. If the self and consciousness are not different, then the self cannot be permanent since consciousness is not permanent (but changes as its content changes).]

If you claim that "consciousness" is the characteristic of the self, (we reply that) there is no such possibility because consciousness is active in only one place. [According to your doctrine, the self is all-pervasive, and so if consciousness is the characteristic of the self, it too must be all-pervasive. But consciousness is active only in one place and cannot be omnipresent. Thus, consciousness cannot be the characteristic of the self.]

If they are identical, the self must be the same as consciousness. [If "consciousness" is the characteristic of the self, the self must be the same as consciousness. Then the self cannot be all-pervasive. For example, just as fire cannot have the (conflicting) characteristics of both "hot" and "cold," so also the self cannot be both all-pervasive and not all-pervasive.]

Moreover, if the self is all-pervasive, it must have the characteristics of both "consciousness" and "non-consciousness." [Because consciousness is not all-pervasive, if the self were all-pervasive, it would have a two-fold nature: the self in the condition for consciousness has consciousness, and the self in the condition for non-consciousness has non-consciousness.]

(5) *Opponent*: There is no error because of the all-pervasive power of the self. [There are conditions in which the power of consciousness exists even if consciousness is not active. (That is, the self possesses the latent power to become conscious under certain conditions.)]

Reply: The power and what has the power are not different. [Wherever there is the power of consciousness, consciousness is there and must have a function. Saying it has no function is not acceptable. So too, saying "Where there is no activity of consciousness, the power of consciousness is still there" is mere words.]

(6) *Opponent*: Because of the combination of causes, the power of consciousness has a function. [The self has the power of consciousness, but consciousness functions only under a certain combination of causes. (Consciousness is a potentiality in the self that can become active under certain circumstances.)]

Reply: The necessary implication of this would be that the consciousness has a characteristic of "birth." [If consciousness can only function when there is a combination of causes, then it must necessarily have the characteristic of "birth" since it depends on causes. (Thus, consciousness is caused and not eternal.) And if consciousness and the self are not different, then the self also must have the characteristic of "birth."]

(7) *Opponent*: It is like a light. [A light can illuminate things, but it cannot create those things. The same occurs with causes: they can cause consciousness to function, but they cannot produce consciousness itself.]

Reply: Even if the light does not illuminate a pot, still the pot can be perceived and retrieved. If consciousness cannot arise without the necessary combination of causes, the self too cannot perceive suffering and happiness (without that combination of causes). Thus, your example is not apropos.

(8) *Opponent*: It is like form: form, although it exists, is not manifested until it is illuminated. So too, consciousness, although it already exists, is not manifested until its causes are combined.

Reply: The own characteristics of consciousness are not manifested. [Even if there is no light, the characteristics of form are self-manifested. But the characteristics of consciousness are not self-manifested and thus your example does not apply. Because we know form, form still exists even when the characteristic is not seen. Not so with the self. According to you, "knowledge" is the characteristic of the self. But you must not consider something without knowledge as having knowledge. (The characteristic itself is separate from what has the characteristic.) The claim "What is without knowledge has knowledge" is wrong. In your school, knowledge and consciousness are synonymous.]

(9) *Opponent*: The Vaisheshikas say that knowledge and the self are different, and thus that the self does not fall into the condition of imperma-

nence, but also that the self is never without knowledge. (Knowledge is not identical to the self but is a characteristic that it is never without.) Why? Because the self and knowledge are united, as with a man possessing an ox. [If a man is with an ox, he is described as "having an ox." In the same way, knowledge arises out of the union of the self with a sense-perception, the mind, and the sense-object. Because the self is united with knowledge, the self is call "having knowledge."]

Reply: The characteristics of the ox exist in the ox, not in the man who owns the ox. [Thus, even if the man and the ox are united, only the ox is the ox. In the same way, even if the self and knowledge are united, the self (does not have the characteristics of knowledge and thus is not) knowledge. Even if knowledge arises because of the union of the self with sense-perception, the mind, and the sense-object, so that knowledge knows form and so forth, nevertheless it is only knowledge that knows, not the self. For example, fire can burn, but it is not the person who possesses fire that burns.]

(10) *Opponent*: The self can know because it has the power to employ knowledge. [Although people have the characteristic of "seeing," still they must employ a light to see and without it they cannot see, even though the light does not see. So too, the self has the potentiality of knowing, but it can know only by employing knowledge. Without knowledge, it cannot know.]

Reply: Knowledge is the power to know. [Knowledge arises from the union of sense-perceptions, the mind, and the sense-objects. Such knowledge can know form and so forth. Thus, knowledge is the power to know, not the instrument that is employed to know. If knowledge is the power to know, what is the use of the self?]

The example of the light is not apropos because the light does not know the form and so forth that it illuminates. [Although the light exists prior to the illumination, it cannot know form and so forth because it does not have the property of knowledge. Only knowledge can know form. On the other hand, if knowledge cannot know, it cannot be called "knowledge." Thus, if you maintain that the light has the power to know, what is the use of knowledge?]

(11) *Opponent*: Because of the union with the body of a horse, the self becomes a horse. [Although the self is different from the body of the horse, yet in these circumstances it is called "a horse." So too, because of the union of the self with knowledge, the self is called "knowledge."]

Reply: In the horse's body, the self is not the horse. [The body of the horse is the horse. You claim that the body and the self are different, and so the self and the horse must be different. How could the self be the horse? But if you compare the self only with the self, you fall into an impasse and cannot proceed with your argument.]

(12) *Opponent*: The union is like the black and the shawl in a black shawl. [A black shawl is called a "black shawl" because the black dye is united with the cloth, although the dye and the cloth are different. In the same way, the self and knowledge are different, but as the self is united with knowledge, the self is called "knowledge."]

Reply: If this is so, then the self does not exist. [If the self is called "knowledge" because it is united with knowledge, then the self itself must be a non-self since only knowledge is the power to know. If knowledge is not called "the self," the self cannot be called a "knower." If an object is named because of its union with another thing, then, as knowledge is united with the self, why is knowledge not called "the self"? And the example of the black cloth contradicts your texts. According to your texts, black is a quality, and the cloth is the substance: substance does not make the quality, and the quality does not make the substance.]

(13) *Opponent*: The self is called "having knowledge," as a man who has a stick is called "having a stick." [The man is described as "having a stick," but the stick is not described as "having a man" and is not called "a man." Similarly, the self united with knowledge is called "the knower" and not merely "knowledge." On the other hand, knowledge united with the self is not called "the self."]

Reply: A man having a stick is not a stick. [So too, the characteristics of knowledge are in knowledge, not in the self. Thus, the self is not a knower.]

(14) *Opponent*: The Samkhyas say that consciousness is the defining characteristic of the self. The self has the characteristic of "knowledge" and thus is permanent consciousness, not non-consciousness.

Reply: This has been refuted above: if the self is characterized by consciousness, it is no longer one. [Consciousness has various perceptions — of pain, happiness, and so forth. If "consciousness" is the characteristic of the self, the self must be multiple and not one.]

(15) *Opponent*: Consciousness is one but with various characteristics, as with a crystal. [As a single crystal changes according to its form — becoming blue, yellow, red, white, and so on — so too is consciousness, although one, differentiated according to its objects: sometimes it perceives pain, sometimes happiness, and so forth. Although differentiated consciousness has various characteristics, consciousness is fundamentally one.]

Reply: If that were so, demerit and merit would have one characteristic. [The thought of benefitting others is called "merit"; the thought of offending others is called "demerit." The wise believe in this doctrine. If the thought of benefitting others and the thought of offending others are one, then merit and demerit have the same characteristic. So too, for example, giving and stealing must be one. As an existing crystal changes its form, so too does consciousness arise together with its cause. Thus, your example is not apropos. Moreover, you are not right in saying the crystal is one: crystals renew, and because the new features are born and destroyed, the characteristic of the crystal is not one.]

(16) *Opponent*: Although the products are many, the maker is one, as with a potter. [A potter makes pots and other things, but it does not follow that because the maker is one that the products are also one. In the same way, a single thought can produce the action of offending and benefitting and so forth.]

Reply: The potter does not involve a different situation. [The potter's body is one and is different from the pots and other objects, and the thought of benefitting others and the thought of offending others have the characteristic of diversity. But the actions of offending and benefitting and so forth are not different from thought.]

(17) *Opponent*: The self is known to exist through inference. [There are things that cannot be directly perceived but can be known through inference. For example, since the sun disappears in the west and appears in the east the next morning, we know it possesses motion, although its movement is not seen. So too with someone who moves and reaches a place. In the same way, seeing that a quality depends on a substance, we know through an inference that there is a self (the substance). And because the self is united with knowledge, thus the self is called "the knower."]

Reply: This has already been refuted. We now add that if there is no knowledge, there is no self. [According to your school, the self is all-pervasive, wide and great, but knowledge is limited. If the self knows, there would be places and times that it does not know — thus, there are places with no self. "Places" here refers to places outside the body, and "times" refers periods inside the body such as sleep when one does not know. Thus, if the self is characterized as "knowing," then there are places and times where there is no self. Thus, when you say "There is a self because of the defining characteristic of knowledge," your words are empty and false.]

(18) *Opponent*: Simply because of the nonexistence of the function, knowledge is not nonexistent, as with smoke and fire. ["Smoke" is a characteristic of fire, but when there is ashes there is no smoke but there is fire. In the same way, although "knowledge" is the characteristic of the self, the self must exist permanently whether there is knowledge present or not.]

Reply: The self can know. [If the self is still there when there is no knowledge, then the self is not the knower and thus must not have the characteristic of knowledge since, according to you, it exists even when it is without knowledge. Moreover, we know there is a fire when there is no smoke by seeing that there is a fire. But we cannot see the self, whether it has knowledge or not. Thus, your example is not apropos. In addition, you teach that we know there is a self by inference. But this too is wrong:]

We see one who moves on account of the movement and the reaching of a place. [Without a mover, there is no movement, and without movement there is no mover. So too with "reaching a place." Upon seeing a mover, when we say that he has reached a place, we necessarily know that he possesses movement. But to say that without a self there is no knowledge is not acceptable. Thus, we must not assume that there is a self only because there is knowledge. It is not possible to see a tortoise and to have the idea of hair, or to see a barren woman and to have the idea of a child. In the same way, we cannot have the idea of a self by seeing knowledge.]

(19) *Opponent*: It is like a hand that takes. [There are times when the hand takes and times when it does not, but it is impossible not to call it a hand because of the times it does not take — a hand is always called a hand. So too with the self: there are times it knows and times it does not, but it is not possible not to call it "the self" because of the times it does not know — the self is always called "the self."]

Reply: "Taking" is not the characteristic of the hand. [Taking is an action, not the defining characteristic of the hand. You think that "knowledge" is the defining characteristic of the self, and thus example of the hand does not apply.]

(20) *Opponent*: Surely there is a self because it feels suffering and happiness. [If there is nothing that feels, then there is no feeling of the touch of the body. It would also be impossible to feel sorrow and pain. A dead man has a body, but he cannot feel pain and happiness. Thus, we know that only the possessor of the body can feel pain and happiness, and this is the self. Thus, surely there is a self.]

Reply: If the self suffers when the body is cut, the self is cut. [When a sword cuts a body, suffering arises. If the self feels suffering, then the sword hurts the self too and the self is cut (but you say the self cannot be affected).]

(21) *Opponent*: The self has nothing to touch. [Because the self has nothing to touch, it cannot be cut. It is like when a house is burned, the empty space inside it cannot be burned but only heated up, because there is nothing to touch. So too, when the body is cut, the self, which is inside the body, cannot be cut because there is nothing to touch, but it feels suffering.]

Reply: If so, there is no movement. [If the self has nothing to touch, the body cannot reach other places since movement arises out of reflection and the motion of the body. The body is without reflection since it does not have the property of thought. And the self has no force of motion since it does not have a body. Thus, the body cannot reach other places.]

(22) *Opponent*: It like a blind person and a lame person helping each other. [When the blind and the lame help each other, they can travel (by the lame telling the blind where to move). In a similar way, the self has reflection and the body has the power of motion — out of their union, there is movement.]

Reply: The characteristics of the body and the self are different. [The blind and the lame have two bodies to touch and two mental reflections and thus they can have the power of movement. The self and the body are not two material objects and thus they cannot go. Thus, there can be no movement. If it were not so, there would be the error involving cutting mentioned before. In addition, when you say the empty space in the burning house is hot, your statement is not acceptable since the space cannot be touched. Heat in a subtle condition permeates the space, and the touch of the body perceives heat, but it is not the empty space that is hot.]

(23) *Opponent*: The suffering of the self is like the suffering of the master of a burning house. [When the house is burned, the master of the house suffers but is not burned. In the same way, when the body is cut, the self suffers but is not cut.]

Reply: The house burns but is not permanent. [When the house burns, grass, trees, and so on burn and are hot since they are not permanent. The empty space does not burn or become hot because it is permanent. In the same way, the body suffers and is cut because it is not permanent. But the self does not suffer nor is cut because it is permanent. And the master of the house is not burned because he is far from the fire. But your texts say that the self is all-pervasive, and thus it must also be cut and destroyed.]

(24) *Opponent*: The self necessarily exists because of the perception of form and so forth. [The five senses themselves cannot know their sense-objects because the senses do not have knowledge as their property. Thus, we know that the self is the knower. The self employing the eyes and so forth knows the sense-objects such as form as a man with a sickle reaps his crops.]

Reply: Then why does the self not employ the ear to see? [If the self has the power of seeing, why doesn't it employ the ear to see form? Like a fire that can burn and so burns everywhere, or like a man who cut with his hands when he has no sickle, or a man inside a house with six windows can see (through any of the six windows, i.e., the six senses), so the self should be able to see everywhere (with any sense).]

(25) *Opponent*: The sense-organ that can be employed is fixed. [Although the self has the power of sensing, the objects toward which each sense is directed are not the same for each sense — each is fixed to a particular type of object. Thus, it is not possible to see form with the ear. Just as a potter who has the power to make pots cannot make them without a clod of clay, so the self has the power of vision but cannot see without eyes.]

Reply: If that is so, then the self is blind. [If the self sees by employing eyes, then it is different from eyes. If it is different from eyes, then the self itself is without eyes. Being without eyes, how can it see? And your example of the potter does not work: without the clay there is no pot because the clay is the pot, but the eyes and form are different.]

(26) *Opponent*: There is a self because of the feeling of a different sense. [If there is no self, why does our mouth salivate when we see another person eating fruits? So too, it is not possible to know tastes with the eyes, but those with eyes can still know the taste.]

In addition, only one thing is known by the eyes and touch. [If a person with eyes previously knew a pot, he knows it in the darkness by touch even though he cannot employ his eyes. Thus, we know there must a self.]

Reply: This has already been refuted above concerning the blind. In addition, if saliva is produced in the mouth when seeing another person eating fruit, then why don't the other senses have any reaction?

(27) *Opponent*: It is like a man who burns things. [A man can burn things, yet he cannot do so without fire. So too, the self can see employing eyes but cannot see without them.]

Reply: It is the fire that burns, not the man. [Man does not have the characteristic of "burning." Fire burns by itself. It arises without an agent, as when the wind causes trees to rub together and start a fire. Thus, it is not the man who does the burning.]

(28) *Opponent*: It is like the internal organ — the mind. [When a man is dead, the self does not see even though the body has eyes because there is no mind. But if there is the mind, then the self sees. In the same way, the self sees employing the eyes, but without them it cannot see.]

Reply: You maintain that it is only the mind, which goes out through the doors of the senses, that knows. But then what is the use of the self?

(29) *Opponent*: The mind does not know by itself. If the characteristic of a mind were known by another mind, then the matter would remain unresolved: there would an infinite regress of minds. But because the self is one, when we say that the self knows the mind, the matter is settled.

Reply: Even if the self also knows the self, the problem is the same. [If the self knows the mind, what then knows the self? Or if the self knows the self, then again there is no resolution of the matter but an infinite regress of selves. According to our school, we know the past mind with the present mind. Because permanence is not a property of mind, there is no error in our doctrine.]

(30) *Opponent*: If we dispense with the self, how can the mind alone know objects?

Reply: It is like fire (which has no agent) that has the characteristic of "heat." [The nature of fire is heat, although heat has no agent. There is no fire without heat. In the same way, the mind is characterized by "knowledge" — it can know, even without a self, because its nature is knowledge. And since the self and knowledge per your assumption are different, the self cannot know.]

(31) *Opponent*: The continuity of the memories of experiences in a former life that produce joy and pain as soon as one is born show that there must be a self. [A small child as soon as he is born knows objects that bring happiness and pain, although no one has taught him. Thus, we know that there is a self and that is has the characteristic of permanence.]

Reply: If the self is all-pervasive, how can there be memories? [The self, according to you, is permanent and pervades all objects, and there is no time when it does not remember — so how can a memory arise? And if memory arises in all places, then it must also pervade all places and so all places must be remembered at the same time. If memory arises in every individual place, then the self has parts, and since it has parts it is not permanent.]

(32) *Opponent*: Memory arises out of the union of self and mind. [Memory arises from the union as a manifestation of it potentiality. Conversely, although the self and mind are united, if memory's potentiality is not manifested, then a memory cannot arise.]

Reply: If the self is characterized by knowledge, it cannot produce a memory; and if it is not characterized by knowledge, it cannot produce a memory. In addition, if there is a memory, then memory knows. [When memory arises, it knows; when it does arise, it does not know. Thus, memory is knowledge. But then, what is the use of the self?]

(33) *Opponent*: There must be a self because it sees with the left eye and recognizes with the right. [When a person sees with the left eye and knows with the right, it is not possible that one eye sees and one eye knows. Rather, there is the self, and it sees with the left eye and knows with the right.]

Reply: The two eyes are interrelated. [Partial knowledge is not knowledge. The self does not see with one part of a sense-organ and recognize with the other.]

(34) *Opponent*: Because memory is attached to the self, the self knows. [Memory is called a property of the self. It is born in the self, and thus with the help of the memory the self knows.]

Reply: Partial knowledge is not knowledge. [If knowledge arises in only one part of the self, then the self only knows partially. If the self only knows partially, the self cannot be called "knowledge."]

(35) *Opponent*: The knowledge of the self is not partial knowledge: although the self knows only partially, the self is called "knowledge."

It is like the action of the body. [What is made by the hands, which are part of the body, is called "an action of the body." In the same way, the self is called "knowledge" even though it knows only partially.]

Reply: If this is so, then there is no knowledge. [According to your school, the self is all-pervasive but the mind is small. Out of their union, knowledge arises in the self. But the knowledge is small because the mind is small. If because of this small knowledge the self is called "the knower," then why do you not say that because what is not known is great that the self does not know? Your example of the action of the body does not work because it does not establish the oneness or diversity of the part and the whole (as discussed below).]

(36) *Opponent*: When a cloth is burning in one part, we say "The cloth is burning." In the same way, although only part of the self knows, we say "The self knows."

Reply: Burning presents the same problem. [If only a part of the cloth is burning, we do not say that the whole cloth is burning — we only say that a part is burning. If you say the whole cloth is burning because only one part is burning, then we must say that it is not burning because a greater part of it is not burning and still has its function. Thus, we cannot reply on your words.]

3. *Refutation of Oneness*

(1) *Opponent*: There must be a self because there are properties proper to it, such as "existence" and "oneness," just as the substance of a pot and its properties are one. If there is no self, then there are no such properties.

Reply: It is not possible to establish the self. Nor can we establish the oneness of substance and properties as with the pot.

(2) *Opponent*: What is the mistake in considering the properties and substance one?

Reply: If properties and substance are one, then everything is either established, not established, or erroneously conceived. [If existence, oneness, and the pot are one, then where there is one of these the other two will be. Thus, wherever there is existence there will be oneness and the pot. If so, (because a cloth exists) a cloth must be the pot since existence, oneness, and the pot are one. In this way, everything must be the pot since existence, oneness, and the pot are one. Thus, all things are identical. And because existence is permanent, the pot must be permanent. Moreover, when one says "existence," then one is saying "oneness" and "the pot." And since "one" is a number, existence and the pot must also be a number. And if the pot is the product of five parts (form, sound, smell, taste, and touch), then existence and oneness must also have five parts. And since the pot has a shape and resistance, then existence and oneness also must have shape and resistance. But if the pot is not permanent, then existence and oneness are not permanent. This explains the claim "Everything is established."]

[There is existence in all places, but there is not a pot in every place. Thus, because the pot and existence are not different, in every place where there is not a pot, existence will be nonexistent. And since the existence of every object is not the pot, the pot is nonexistent because then existence is different from the pot. Yet if oneness and pot are different from existence, then when saying "oneness" and "pot," one must not include "existence," but per the assumption the "pot" and "existence" are not different — thus, if existence is not the pot, then the pot must not be the pot because the pot and existence are not different. This explains the claim that "Everything is not established."]

[If one desires to say "pot," one must say "existence" (per the assumption that they are the same). So too, if one desires to say "existence" one must say "pot." And again according to you, if the pot is established, existence and oneness are established, and vice versa, because they are identical. (But establishing existence or oneness does not establish a pot.) This explains "as one, everything is erroneously conceived."]

(3) *Opponent*: Because things are "existence" and "one," there is no error. [In each thing, there is existence and there is oneness. Thus, if there is a pot, there must also be existence and oneness. But a pot is not in all places where there is existence and oneness. When we say "pot," we know that existence and oneness have been included, but when we say "existence" or "oneness," the pot is not necessarily included.]

Reply: The pot and existence are two things — how is existence and oneness not the pot? [If existence, oneness, and the pot form a unity, how is it that where there is existence and oneness there may be no pot? Why when we say "existence" and "oneness" do we not include the pot?]

(4) *Opponent*: Because in the pot itself, the existence of the pot is absolute. [In the pot, the existence of the pot is not different from the pot, but the pot is different from a cloth and other objects. Thus, there is "existence of the pot" in the pot and there is the pot in the "existence of the pot." But it is not the case that wherever there is existence there is the pot.]

Reply: According to you, the pot and existence are not different. ["Existence" is a universal characteristic — if one says "existence," then one has the firm conviction in the existence of the pot and other objects. If one says "pot," one does not have the firm conviction in the existence of other objects. Thus, "the pot" is a particular characteristic. How can a universal characteristic and a particular characteristic be identical?]

(5) *Opponent*: As one man can be both a father and a son. [One man can have the characteristics of both "being a father" (of one person) and "being a son" (of another person). In the same way, the universal characteristic is also the particular characteristic and vice versa.]

Reply: One only becomes a father on account of having a son. [If a man has not yet produced a child, he is not called "a father." As soon as the child is born, he becomes a father. (That is, the properties of "being a father" and "being a son" are not related the way the general property of "existing" and the particular property of "being a pot" are.)]

(6) *Opponent*: The pot must exist because we all believe it does. [People of this world see with their eyes that a pot exists, and so they believe it exists. Therefore, the pot must exist.]

Reply: Because the pot is not different from existence, everything is nonexistent. [If the pot and existence are not different, then the pot must have the universal characteristic of "existence" and not the particular characteristic of "being a pot." That is, if the particular characteristic is nonexistent, the universal characteristic is also nonexistent because only owing to a particular characteristic is there a universal characteristic. If the particular characteristic (of "being a pot") does not exist, then the universal characteristic does not exist (i.e., there is no pot and thus nothing to characterize as "existing"). Since neither of these exist, everything therefore is nonexistent. (That is, if the pot and the property of "existence" are not different, and if there is no pot, then there is no existence; and if the property of existence does not exist, nothing else could have that property.)]

(7) *Opponent*: The situation is like relation of the parts of the body to the body as a whole. [The head, foot, and other parts of the body are not different from the body, yet no part is the whole body. In the same way, even though the pot and existence are not different, the pot still is not the universal characteristic.]

Reply: If the foot and the head are not different from the body, how is it that the foot is not the head? [Since both the foot and the head are not different from the body, the foot must be the head, just like the god Indra and his property of "being strong" are not different.]

(8) *Opponent*: There is no mistake since all the parts are different. [The parts and the whole are not different, but this does not mean that one part is not different from another.]

Reply: If this were so, then there would be no body. [If the parts are different, then only the parts exist and there is no whole called "the body."]

(9) *Opponent*: From many causes, one effect is produced. So form and so forth are the pot. [From many causes, such as form, one single effect is produced — the pot. Not only is the form the pot, but the pot is not different from the form and the other four parts (sound, smell, taste, and touch). Thus, the form and other parts are not identical. So too with the relation of the foot and other body parts to the body as a whole.]

Reply: Since the pot comes from five parts, it is not one. [If the pot is not different from the five parts, then one must not say "one pot." If one says "one pot," then the five parts must also be one since they are not different from the pot.]

(10) *Opponent*: It is like the many parts constituting an army or a forest. [When elephants, horses, chariots and foot soldiers are united in great numbers, they are called "an army." So too, many trees collectively are called "a forest." One tree does not constitute a forest, nor without trees is there any forest. So too with an army and its parts. In the same way, neither the form alone is called "the pot," but without the form there is no pot.]

Reply: Multiplicity is also like the pot. [If trees are not different from the forest, one must not say "one forest." If one says "one forest," the trees also must be one since they are not different from the forest. In addition, a tree must not be called "one" since its parts — the root, stem, branches, joints, flowers, leaves — are not one but are not different from the tree. So too with the army and all its objects.]

(11) *Opponent*: (The pot must exist) because you admit many pots. [You say "Since the parts are many, the pot must also be many." So, wishing to refute one pot, you admit many pots.]

Reply: It is not the case that because the parts are many that the pot is also many. [We say you are wrong, but this does not mean that we admit there are many pots. You yourself said that the parts are many and thus that the pot does not exist as a distinct phenomenon produced as the effect of the parts.]

(12) *Opponent*: The effect is there because the cause is not refuted. Because there is the cause, the effect is established. [You reject the pot as an effect, but you do not reject form and the other parts that are the causes of the pot. If there is a cause, there must be an effect, since there is no cause without an effect. In addition, the causes of the pot are the effect of particles. Since you admit the form and so forth, the cause and the effect are both established.]

Reply: Since the effect does not exist, the cause also does not exist. [Since the pot is not different from the many parts, the pot must not be one. And since the many parts are not different from the one pot, the parts must not be multiple. (Thus, there can be neither one pot nor multiple parts to make one pot.) And if you say "There is no cause without an effect," then the effect being refuted, the cause is also refuted, since according to your school, cause and effect are one.]

In addition, if we accept your doctrine, the three times (past, present, and future) would be one. [The time when the pot is a shaped clod of earth is the present; the time when it will no longer be a pot is the future; and the time when it was only earth was the past. If cause and effect are one, then in the shaped clod there must be both the pot and the earth, and thus the three times are one. The distinction between what is already made, what is now being made, and what will be made would also be nullified.]

(13) *Opponent*: Cause and effect are established since they are reciprocally interdependent, like "long" and "short." [On the basis of "long" we recognize "short" and vice versa. So too, we recognize the clod of earth as the cause and the pot as the effect.]

Reply: But then the cause would not be in itself or in another or both, just as the characteristic of "being long" is not in something that is long or in something that is short or both. [If there is a real characteristic of "being long," it will exist either in something long, in something short, or in both. But none of these can be established. The characteristic "long" is not in something long because this characteristic then would have to have something else for its cause. If something is long because of something short, then "being long" is not inherent in the long thing itself, and this is a contradiction. (That is, something is long, not in itself, but only in relation to something else. Thus, the "something else" would be the cause and "being long" would not be an inherent property of long things.) If "being long" is in something short, then that thing cannot be called "short." And there cannot be "being long" in something long and something short taken together: if "being long" exists in something long and something short, there would be both of the mistakes just mentioned. The same hold for the characteristic "being short." If "being long" and "being short" are both nonexistent, how are they interdependent?]

4. *Refutation of Difference*

(1) *Opponent*: What mistake is there in admitting that there is a difference between existence, oneness, and the pot?

Reply: If these are different from each other, then they are nonexistent. [If the pot is different from existence and oneness, it is neither existence nor oneness. If existence is different from the pot and oneness, it is neither the pot nor oneness. If oneness is different from the pot and existence, it is

neither the pot nor existence. In this way, each one is lost. (Because the pot
is different from existence, it does not exist. Because the pot does not exist,
existence and oneness are lost since the object they would be embodied in
is gone.) But because of their difference, if the pot is lost, existence and
oneness are not necessarily lost; if existence is lost, the pot and oneness are
not necessarily lost; if oneness is lost, the pot and existence are not
necessarily lost — if this man disappears, then that man does not disappear.]

(2) *Opponent*: Since existence and oneness are united to the pot,
existence, oneness, and the pot are all established. [Existence, oneness, and
the pot are different, but the pot is called "existence" because it is united
with existence. And the pot is called "one" because it is united with oneness.
If you say "When the pot is lost, existence and oneness are not necessarily
lost," then your words are not acceptable because there is a union of
different things. There are three types of differences: difference between
combined things (such as a substance and a quality), difference between
separate things (such as this person and that person), and difference through
transformation (such as a ball of cow dung changing into a ball of ashes).
Because there is a oneness of different things, when the pot is lost oneness
is also lost. When oneness is lost, the pot is also lost. Existence, because it
is permanent, cannot be lost.]

Reply: If that is so, then there is a multiplicity of pots. [Because the pot
is united with "existence," the pot is existent. Because the pot is united with
"oneness," the pot is one. Because the pot is also "a pot," there is a multiplicity of pots. (That is, the pot and the characteristic "a pot" that the pot is
united with makes a multiplicity.) Why is there a different result if the items
combined are different in nature?]

(3) *Opponent*: There is a difference between the combined things, as
between a quality such as "oneness" being combined with a substance such
as "a pot." Thus, if the quality is lost, the substance is not lost and vice versa.
Since one is a universal characteristic and the other is a quality, existence
and oneness are not the pot. ["Existence" is a universal characteristic and
thus is not the pot. "Oneness" is a quality, and so it too is not the pot. The
pot is substance.]

Reply: In that case, the pot does not exist. [If the pot is a substance and
is not one with the universal quality "existence," it does not exist.]

(4) *Opponent*: You admitted earlier a multiplicity of pots in your desire
to refute the idea of one pot.

Reply: Because the one pot is nonexistent, the multiplicity of pots is also nonexistent. [You say that because the pot is united to existence, it is existent, and because it is united to oneness, it is one, and also that the pot is the pot. If this is so, then you consider what in this world is considered one pot to be a multiplicity of pots (i.e., the one united to existence, the one united to oneness, and the pot itself.) In short, the one pot has become many pots. Thus, because the one pot has become many, there is no more "one pot." (That is, its characteristic should be "multiplicity" and not "oneness.") Because the one pot does not exist, a multiplicity of pots also cannot exist.]

In addition, because of the nonexistence of the first number, there is no multiplicity. ["One" is the first of the phenomena called "numbers." If the pot and oneness are different, then the pot is not one. Because of the nonexistence of one, multiplicity (i.e., non-oneness) also does not exist.]

(5) *Opponent*: The pot exists because it is united with "existence." [Because the pot is united with existence, the pot is said to exist, but it is not absolutely existent (i.e., existence independent of any existent entity). In the same way, the pot is called "one" because it is united with oneness, but it is not an absolute oneness (i.e., oneness independent of anything that is one).]

Reply: "Existence" by itself (i.e., independent of actual existent entities) is a mere word. Your claim has been refuted already — if existence is not the pot, then the pot does not exist.

So too, the pot must be a non-pot. [If the pot exists because it is united with existence, then this existence is not the pot. If the pot is united with what is not the pot (existence), how is the pot not considered a non-pot?]

(6) *Opponent*: Because the union with nonexistence is not itself existent, the pot is not a non-pot. ["A non-pot" means "a nonexistent pot." If there is nonexistence, then there is no union. Thus, because it exists, the pot is not a non-pot. Because it exists, it must be united with existence. In sum, the pot exists because it is united with existence.]

Reply: The pot exists now because it united with existence now. [If it is a non-pot, then it does not exist. If it does not exist, there is no union. Because the pot is now united with existence, existence must be the pot. If you say "The pot does not exist because it not now united with existence," then because the pot does not exist there is no union with existence. As discussed before, if a phenomenon is nonexistent, there is no union with existence. Thus, when it is not united with existence, the pot is not a phenomenon that exists. Because it is then a phenomenon that does not exist, it cannot be united with existence. (That is, what does not exist can never be united with anything because there is nothing there.)]

(7) *Opponent*: Existence manifests the pot like a light can illuminate things. [Existence is not the only cause of such things as the pot, but it can manifest such things. As a light can illuminate things, existence can manifest things, and thus we know that the pot exists.]

Reply: If existence can manifest things in this way, the pot must already exist. [Only when things already exist are they manifested and illuminated by the light. Things must already exist in order to be united with existence. And if they already exist, what is the point of uniting with existence? If things are nonexistent prior to be united with existence but are existent after the union with existence, then existence would the "producing cause" and not the "manifesting cause." (See 9.2 below.)]

In addition, if the thing being characterized is established through a characterizing mark, how is it that a oneness does not become a duality? [If you know the pot exists because you consider "existence" as the characteristic of the pot, then without the characteristic the thing being characterized is not established. Thus, existence must also have the characteristic of existence. If we know that existence without this characteristic is still existence, then the same is true with regard to objects such as the pot.]

The example of the light was refuted above. The light shines by itself and not because it depends on some external light. So too, the pot exists by itself and does not depend upon an external "existence" to exist.

(8) *Opponent*: It is like the characteristic of the body. [From parts such as the foot, we know the whole is a body, but the foot does not have the characteristic of the body. So too, because "existence" is the characteristic of the pot, we know that the pot exists, but existence does not have the characteristic of a pot.]

Reply: If the whole is in a part, how is that the head is not in the foot? [Does a whole phenomenon exist as a totality or as a part? If it exists as a totality, then the foot must exist in the head because of the oneness of the phenomenon. But a totality cannot exist as a part.] Why? Because the whole is like the part. [If the whole in a part is similar to that part, then the whole must be one of the parts. Thus, the whole must be nonexistent (since it is merely a part and not the whole). In the same way, the existence of the parts is refuted. Moreover, if the whole does not exist, neither do the parts (because parts can only be "parts" of a whole).]

(9) *Opponent*: There are particles. [Particles exist, and the parts are not nonexistent because there is no part in which there are no particles. The particles collectively product the part as an effect. Thus, the parts exist, and so the whole exists.]

Reply: If collectively the particles are the pot, all the particles are pots. [If the collection of particles forms the pot and if the collection is in fact the pot, then all the particles must be pots. If the entire collection is not the pot, each individually is not the pot. (That is, the particles must each be a pot for the collection to have that characteristic.)]

(10) *Opponent*: As one thread cannot restrain an elephant and one drop of water cannot fill a pot but a collection of many can produce the effect, so the particles collectively have the force to produce a pot.

Reply: If each part cannot produce the effect, then collectively they cannot either. [If one barren woman cannot have a child and one blind man cannot see form and one grain of sand cannot produce oil, then many of them collectively cannot do it either. The same with particles.]

(11) *Opponent*: Each part does have the force. [The thread and the drop do separately have the power that collectively restrains an elephant or fills a pot. But the barren woman and so forth do not individually have the power to bring about the effect. So your examples are not apropos.]

Reply: There are the mistakes of the oneness and multiplicity and of the parts and the whole. [The parts and the whole, whether they are one or many, cannot be established, and the mistake in both cases has already been refuted. Again, because the whole does not exist, the parts do not exist either. If the existence of the parts cannot be demonstrated, how can they have the power of a cause? And if the whole does exist, of what use is the power of the parts?]

(12) *Opponent*: You are a man whose doctrine is refutation.

Reply: You say that existence and the pot are different. We teach that if this is so, then there is no pot. You see the nonexistent as existent, and the existent as nonexistent. [You are like a man whose doctrine is refutation, not we. In addition, the mistake here is very important: it is evident that the union of the parts of the body is the body, but you say that it is not the body and that the body as a whole exists independently of the parts. When the wheel, axle, and so forth are all united, it is evident that they make up a chariot — but you say a chariot exists beyond these separate parts. Thus, you say false things.]

5. *Refutation of Sense-Perception*

(1) *Opponent*: There is a real self and there are phenomena that are a representation of the self because direct perception exists. [Knowledge arises from the union of sense-perception, the sense-objects, and the mind. This knowledge is a direct knowledge. Because there is this direct knowledge, the perception, the objects, and the mind exist.]

Reply: If knowledge arises after having seen a form, what is its use? [If the eye first sees form and then knowledge arises, what is the use of the knowledge? But knowledge cannot arise prior to the eye seeing the form.] If the eye does not see the form, there is no cause, and there is no birth of knowledge. [If the eye does not first see the form, there is no union with the cause. With no union, no knowledge arises. But if knowledge arises when there is no union, your claim that knowledge arises from the union of the senses, sense-objects, and the mind is not acceptable.]

(2) *Opponent*: Knowledge arises at the same time as the union.

Reply: Birth and non-birth cannot be born at the same time because of the existence of one and the nonexistence of the other at that time. [The birth at the same time is not acceptable whether the perception and knowledge are reciprocally interdependent or are both previously nonexistent or are both previously half existent and half nonexistent. If the perception and knowledge were previously existing, then they do not arise again. If they were previously nonexistent, then they are not interdependent and there also is no birth (since what is nonexistent cannot become existent). They cannot be half existent and half nonexistent because each of these two possibilities has been refuted already. In addition, how can a phenomenon be existent and also nonexistent? If the perception and knowledge arise at the same time, knowledge is not dependent on the perception, and the perception is not dependent on the knowledge.]

[In addition, does the eye (i.e., the visual faculty) see a form by contact (as the Vaisheshikas argue), or does it see by not reaching the form? If the eye sees by going out and reaching the form, a form that is far away is seen later and a form that is near is seen sooner because of the law of motion (i.e., the visual faculty would have further to travel). But a pot that is near and the moon that is far are seen at the same time. Thus, we know the eye does not go out. If it does not go out, then there is no union with the sense-objects. But if the visual faculty does not reach a form (in order to see), why is it that we see things that are near but do not see things that are out of sight?]

[So too, if the eye (i.e., visual faculty) goes out to see, does it go out after having seen a form or before without having seen it? If the former, what is the use of going out? But if the eye sees the form first and then goes out to it, it cannot have the perception of what the mind perceives since the eye itself has no knowledge. It can go out to the east and west, but any place without an eye cannot perceive. If the eye goes out and reaches the form and then perceives it, then the body would be without eyes, and since a body without eyes cannot see, there would be no perception. But if the eye perceives a form without going out, there is still no perception because the form also is without eyes. In addition, if the eye perceives a form without going out, one would see forms that are above the sky or are hidden by an obstruction. Thus, this is not an acceptable thesis.]

(3) *Opponent*: There is perception because the characteristic of the eye is "perception."

Reply: If so, then the eye must be able to see itself. [It would be like fire that has the characteristic of "heat" and heats itself in heating other things. But the eye cannot see itself.]

(4) *Opponent*: It is like the finger that cannot touch itself (but has the characteristic of "touch").

Reply: Touch is the action of the finger. [It is not the finger's characteristic, unlike with the eye and vision.]

(5) *Opponent*: By means of the eye, light, and the movement of the mind, one sees the form.

Reply: If the mind goes out and reaches the form, then the body is without intelligence. [The mind then would stay with the sense-object and the body would be without mind (and thus would be unconscious), like a dead body. But the mind does not go out since what is far and what is near are perceived at the same time. So too, although it thinks of the past and of the future, the mind is not in the past or the future but in the present.]

(6) *Opponent*: The mind stays in the body but can know distant things.

Reply: If so, then the mind does not connect to the distant object. [If the mind and form stay where they are, then there is no connection. If there is no connection, one cannot perceive the form.]

(7) *Opponent*: One sees by the union of light, the mind, and the form. [The eye and mind coexist in the body. Through the force of the mind, the eye and light are united with the form. In this way, the form is seen and thus the union cannot be dispensed with.]

Reply: If perception arises out this union, then there is no seer. [If one sees form out of this union, then your statement that only the senses see the form and only the mind perceives the form is not acceptable.]

(8) *Opponent*: You admit the union. Thereby, the perception of the form is established. [You admit there is a union, and if there is a union, there must be the perception of the form.]

Reply: The mind does not see; the eye does not know; and the form neither sees nor knows. So how is perception possible? [Because the mind is different from the eye, the mind does not have the characteristic of "perception" and so cannot see. Because the eye is composed of the four elements (earth, water, fire, and air), it does not have the characteristic of knowledge. Because it is not characterized by "knowledge," it cannot know the form. Form has neither characteristic. So, even with the union of these, how can one perceive? This refutation applies to the other senses.]

6. Refutation of Sense-Objects

(1) *Opponent*: The sense-faculties must exist because objects are perceived. [It is evident that objects are indeed perceived. If the senses do not perceive them, to whom does the function of perceiving belong? Thus, it is known that the senses exist and can perceive.]

Reply: The pot is not its form alone. Thus, the pot is not directly perceived. [The form of the pot, which is in the pot, can be directly perceived, but the smell, sound, touch, and taste cannot. Form alone is not the pot. Rather, the union of form, smell, and so forth is. If the pot itself could be directly perceived, the smell and other components could also be directly perceived (when directly perceiving the form). But because they are not, the pot itself thus is not directly perceived.]

(2) *Opponent*: Because one part is directly perceived, it is said "The pot is perceived by direct perception." [People, after having seen the pot, believe and know "I see this pot."]

Reply: If only a part is perceived, the whole is not perceived. [If only one part of the pot — the form — can be seen, the other parts such as smell cannot be seen. One part does not make the whole. If it did, then the other parts — smell and so on — could be seen as well. Thus, the pot (itself in its totality) cannot be seen at all. The earlier refutation of oneness and multiplicity also applies.]

(3) *Opponent*: Because you implicitly accept the visibility by direct perception of the form, the visibility of the pot is established. [If the form is directly perceived, the pot also must be directly perceived.]

Reply: Although one part is seen by direct perception, another part is not. [You are wrong to claim "The form is directly perceived." The form has shape and only part of the form is seen at any one time. The same holds when we see another part of the shape.]

(4) *Opponent*: This is not a complete refutation because particles have no parts. [Thus, the particle can be seen in its totality by direct perception.]

Reply: The particle is not directly perceived. [Your texts say that particles are not seen by direct perception. Thus, it is not possible to establish the existence of everyday phenomena that can been seen by direct perception (since they dependent upon the particles). Even if particles could be perceived directly, the refutation related to form still holds.]

(5) *Opponent*: The pot must be seen by direct perception because the people of the world believe so [since the pot has some use].

Reply: We say that there is no direct perception of the pot, but not that the pot does not exist.

(6) *Opponent*: Since the pot is not yet united with the eye, there is no mistake. [Although the pot is characterized by direct perception, we cannot see it when the pot is not yet joined with the eye.]

Reply: Since there is no birth of direct perception, its existence is not real. [There is no birth of a new characteristic in something; thus, the characteristic of direct perception does not arise. Since the birth of the characteristic of direct perception does not exist, there is no existence of the pot.]

(7) *Opponent*: Of the five parts of the pot (the form and so forth), form has been refuted but not the others [and so the pot must exist].

Reply: If all five parts are not perceived by touch, how are they united? [Some parts like form are tangible and some are not — how can the tangible and intangible be united? Thus, the five parts do not constitute the pot.]

(8) *Opponent*: The parts are each united to the pot, not to each other.

Reply: If the pot is different from the tangible and is itself not tangible, how is the pot united with the tangible? [How can what is intangible be united with the tangible? If this phenomenon is without form and so forth, then it does not exist. But if this phenomenon does exist and is without form, how can the tangible and the pot be united?]

(9) *Opponent*: Form must be directly perceivable because this is accepted in your texts. [Your texts say form is the four material elements

(earth, water, fire, and air) and the four qualities derived from them. The basis for form is included in the quality of form and this is directly perceivable. So how can you say that form is not seen by direct perception?

Reply: The four material elements are not seen by the eye. How can they produce direct perception. [Earth has its characteristic "solidity," fire "heat," water "fluidity," and wind "movement." These four elements are not seen by the eye, and therefore the four secondary material elements are not seen by direct perception either.]

(10) *Opponent*: Because the sense-faculties perceive them, the four material elements exist. [And therefore objects such as fire that are derived from the four material elements must also exist.]

Reply: In fire all the elements have the characteristic of "heat." [Among the four elements, only fire has the characteristic of "heat." In fire, all four elements have the characteristic of "heat," and thus fire is not a fourfold body. If the other elements are not heat, they cannot be called fire. The same holds for solidity and so forth.]

(11) *Opponent*: Form must be perceived because present time exists. [Perception occurs in the present. If perception could not occur, then the present would not exist. But the present does exist, and thus what is perceivable can be perceived.]

Reply: If the time after a phenomenon has arisen is long, then the phenomenon's beginning is ancient. [If the characteristic of "being ancient" is manifested in a phenomenon, this characteristic does not arise in ancient times. The characteristic becomes manifest only gradually from its ancient initial subtle condition. If the beginning of being manifest is not ancient, then the period afterwards is not ancient either. Thus, it must be perpetually new. If so, the characteristic of "being ancient" does not arise. When a phenomenon does not last, there is no time in which it endures. If the time of duration does not exist, then there is no place for the perception of the object to occur.]

(12) *Opponent*: Because the new and the old are admitted, the present exists. [You admit the existence of the characteristics of the "new" and "old." These characteristics cannot be perceived in the past or in the future but can be seen in the present.]

Reply: Because of the birth, it is new, but because of the difference it is old. [If the phenomena arise long ago, the characteristic of "being new" would pass. What is "other than new" is called "old." If the characteristic of "being old" produces what is old, then this characteristic is itself new. "This is new" and "This is old" are only words; from the highest point of view, neither the new or the old is real.]

(13) *Opponent*: If this is so, what is the benefit obtained?

Reply: The separation of the phenomena. [If the new does not cause the intermediate in age, the intermediate does not cause the old. For example, the flower and the fruit are not united to each other: the seed ceases before the bud, and so forth. Because phenomena are not connected with each other, they do not last. Because they do not last, they are separate and distinct. Because they are distinct, they cannot be perceived (as real).]

7. Refutation of the Effect existing in the Cause

(1) *Samkhya*: The phenomena are not nonexistent — there is no loss of existence and no birth of nonexistence. [A phenomenon has the characteristic of existence. The "before" and "after" are the cause and the effect. Different causes are not lost at the time when their effects arise. If the effect is not in the cause, then the effect cannot be born. The effect is only a modification of the cause. Thus, phenomena are real.]

Reply: If because of the arising of the fruit, existence is not lost, then because of the loss of the cause, existence is lost (since the effect is only a modification of the cause). [You claim that when the pot (the effect) is born, the clod of earth (the material cause) is not lost. If so, then the pot is only the clod of earth (and not a pot). When the effect is produced, if the cause (the clod of earth) is lost, then there is no cause (since the clod is supposed to be the cause); if the cause is not lost, then one must distinguish between the clod of earth and the pot (since the pot was not manifest before its production). Thus, we see that there is a diversity of form, activity, time, name, and so forth, and thus existence is lost (since existence requires permanence and the absence of change).]

(2) *Opponent*: The clod of earth and the pot are related like a finger that is either bent or straight. [Although the finger may be in different forms, still there is only one finger. In the same way, the form of the clod of earth and the pot may differ, yet the earth is not different from the pot.]

Reply: The action and the agent are different. [Being bent or straight is the action of the finger, but the finger is the agent. If the action were the agent, then when the finger is bent it would be lost (because the straight finger would have ceased). And being bent and being straight would have to be one because, according to your texts, the pot is just the clod of earth. Thus, your example is not apropos.]

(3) *Opponent*: Cause-and-effect is like a man who is the same person in childhood, youth, and old age.

Reply: They are not one. [The child does not cause the youth; the youth does not cause the young man; the young man does not cause the old man. Thus, your example is not apropos.]

Moreover, if existence is not lost, then nonexistence is lost. [If existence is not lost, then the clod of earth must not change and become a pot, and so the pot is nonexistent. (Causation requires changes, and so if the clod does not change, then there is no causation of the effect, and therefore the pot would not exist.) But nonexistence cannot be lost because it does not exist. Thus, if existence is not lost, nothing is lost. (What does not exist, by the very fact that it does not exist, cannot disappear and leave a place for the pot to appear in. Thus, neither existence nor nonexistence disappears.)]

(4) *Opponent*: There is no mistake if nothing is lost. [If there is no loss because of permanence, the clod of earth does not change and become a pot. If the impermanent does not exist, what is the mistake?]

Reply: If the impermanent is nonexistent, then such things as merit and demerit are nonexistent. [Someone subject to demerit would eternally be subject to it and could not acquire merit, and vice versa. Giving and stealing and the observance or nonobservance of the precepts of proper conduct must in the same way be totally nonexistent. (Only the permanent cause would exist.)]

(5) *Opponent*: The effects preexist in their cause and exist because the cause exists. [If the pot did not preexist in the earth, the earth could not become its cause.]

Reply: If the effect exists because it preexists in the cause, then the nonexistence of the effect means the cause is without an effect. [If the pot is in its cause (i.e., the clod of earth), then if the pot is destroyed (then so is the cause). (But the earth is not destroyed when the pot is.) Thus, there must be no effect in the cause.]

(6) *Opponent*: The cause and effect are one [because the effect is in the cause. So they are not different phenomena when the cause changes and becomes the effect.]

Reply: If the cause and effect are one, there is no future. [The clod of earth (already exists and so it) is the present and the pot is the future. (Thus, if they are one, there is no future but only the present.) And because there is no future, there is no present (because the future is only future presents). And because there is no present, there is no past (which is only past presents). Thus, there is a confusion of the three times.]

(7) *Opponent*: One name is lost and another is born. [Only the name according to the time is different — no new phenomena are created, and no old phenomena are lost. A clod of earth becomes a pot, and a broken pot becomes earth again. The pot is not permanent, but only the names change over time. Their nature remains the same.]

Reply: If this is so, the cause is without effect. [If one name is lost and another name is born because this name did not exist before but does exist later, the pot does not exist as an effect of a cause. Only if the name "pot" existed before would the earth be the pot. Thus, the effect does not preexist.]

(8) *Opponent*: [The pot does not absolutely come out of the clod, and thus the name does not absolutely exist in the clod.]

Reply: If the cause is not absolute, the effect is not absolute.

(9) *Opponent*: The existence of the effect is in a subtle form in the cause. [The form of the pot in the clod of earth is subtle and thus difficult to recognize. It becomes manifest through the efforts of the potter. The pot cannot be known in the earth, but there is a subtle form of it in the earth.]

[There are two types of unknowable things: what is nonexistent, and what is not known because of a cause. There are eight such causes: when the object is too distant, when the object is too near, a defect in the senses (e.g., blindness or deafness), an unsteady mind (e.g., bewilderment), the object is too small, the object is obscured (e.g., by a wall), through excess (e.g., too little salt in too much water), and through similarity to its surroundings (e.g., one grain of rice thrown into a great pile of rice). The pot that is inside a clod of earth cannot be seen, but it does not come out of a willow — thus, the subtle form must assuredly be in the earth.]

Reply: If a subtle form preexists, the cause is without effect. [If the subtle form exists in the earth first and later becomes gross and manifest, then there is no effect in the cause — the characteristic of "grossness" was originally nonexistent (and thus not in the earth) and is only born later. Thus, the effect does not exist in the cause.]

(10) *Opponent*: The effect must exist in the cause because identical effects have the same cause. [To make a pot, one takes earth and not a willow — if the effect did not exist in the cause, we could use the willow as well. But we know without a doubt that only the earth can produce the pot. Thus, the effect exists in the cause.]

Reply: When the effect exists, the cause exists. When it does not exist, the cause does not exist. (That is, if the effect is in the cause, then the cause and effect exist together or do not exist together.) [When the pot ceases, it must be that the effect no longer exists. (But we see that the clod of earth continues to exist.) Thus, there is no effect in the cause.]

(11) *Opponent*: Because birth, duration, and cessation occur in a series, there is not error. [The characteristic of "cessation" is in the pot, yet the pot still must arise first, then endure, and later cease, since what is not born cannot be destroyed.]

Reply: If the effect is born in the cause, then the situation is similar to the nonexistence of the effect. [If the pot is born in the earth, then the effect ceased when the cause is destroyed to produce the effect. And when the pot is not yet born, there is neither duration nor cessation. Since the pot was not existing before, and the duration and cessation occur later, the effect cannot preexist in the cause.]

(12) *Opponent*: By rejecting the existence of the effect in the cause, your doctrine has the fault of annihilation.

Reply: Because of continuity, there is no annihilation; because of cessation, there is no permanence. [Because of the continuity of the sprout and the bud from the seed, there is no annihilation; and because of the cessation of the seed, there is no permanence. The buddhas have taught that phenomena arise according to the twelve linked steps in the formula of "dependent arising." This doctrine does not maintain either the existence of the effect in the cause nor the total nonexistence of the effect, thereby avoiding both the doctrine of ontological nihilism and permanence (i.e., eternalism). Rather, it is the middle path leading to nirvana.]

8. Refutation of the Effect Not Existing in the Cause

(1) *Opponent*: Because there is birth, there is a unity (of cause and effect). [You admit by "dependent arising" that there is birth. Whether birth exists in the cause or not, since there is birth, there will necessarily be unity.]

Reply: Birth and non-birth are not themselves born. [If there is birth, it exists either before in the cause or after. But neither option can be established by you. How much less then non-birth. If the birth of the pot does exist, do you believe it exists at the time the pot begins to be a pot or when the pot is not yet a pot? It cannot be the former because the pot already exists and thus the beginning, middle, and later states are interdependent. That is, if there is no middle and later state, there is no beginning, and so forth. But if the pot already exists, what is the use of a birth? On the other hand, the pot cannot be born when it is not yet a pot either since it does not exist at that time. If the pot has no beginning, middle, or later states, then there is no pot. If the pot does not exist, how can there be the birth of the pot? If there is a birth of the pot, it must have occurred either after there already is a pot or when the clod of earth is transforming into a pot. After there is already a pot, there is no birth because it already exists. And there is no birth when the clod of earth is transforming because the pot does not yet exist. (If the pot exists before its birth, it already exists and so no birth is possible; if it exists after its birth, then there was a time when the pot did not exist and there cannot be the birth of what is nonexistent.)]

(2) *Opponent*: The "process of being born" is itself born. [We do not say that if the pot is already born or not yet born there is the birth of the pot. Rather, when a second phenomenon is being born, this is the birth.]

Reply: The same argument applies to the "process of being born." [If it is born, then it already exists; if it is not yet born, where is the birth? If you say "It is half-born and half-unborn," then these two mistakes are also to be refuted as before. Thus, there is no birth.]

(3) *Opponent*: "Born" and "being completed" are synonymous. [We do not say that what is already completed and born has a birth, nor that what is not yet born has a birth. Rather, we see that what is completed is completed, and thus the completion is born.]

Reply: If this is so, the birth comes after the completion. [What is "completed" is something that is already born. If it has no birth, it has neither a beginning nor middle. If it has no beginning, it has no middle and no completion. Thus, it is impossible to consider the completion as the birth because the birth would then happen afterwards.]

(4) *Opponent*: The beginning, middle, and later states are born in a series. [The clod of earth produces and accomplishes the base, belly, throat, and mouth of the pot in a series. The clod does not complete the completion of the pot in a series — there is no birth of the completion. Thus, when there is only a clod of earth, there is no birth of the completion, and at the time of the completion of the pot there is also no birth of the completion. But it is not true that there is no "birth of the completion."]

Reply: The beginning, middle, and later states are not born in a series. ["Beginning" means "what has no 'before.'" "Middle" means "what has a 'before' and an 'after.'" "Later" means "what has a 'before' but no 'after.'" In this way, "beginning," "middle," and "later" are interdependent. If they are separated (and thus distinct and thus not connected), how could any of them exist? Thus, they cannot be born (separately) in a series.]

But claiming the three states are born at the same time is also wrong. [If they are born at the same time, one cannot say "This is the beginning, this is the middle, and this is later." They would also not be interdependent.]

(5) *Opponent*: It is like compound entities. [A characteristic of the compound is "existing in a series of birth, duration, and ceasing." The same happens with regard to beginning, middle, and subsequent.]

Reply: The same problem arises as with birth, duration, and cessation. [Neither existence in a series or existence at the same time is acceptable. If there is no duration, then there is no birth. (If there is no birth, there is no duration.) If there were birth without duration, then there would also be duration without birth. The same with regard to cessation. On the other hand, if they all exist at the same time, they would impossible to distinguish and say "This is birth," or "This is duration," or "This is cessation."]

In addition, they would all be in all places. [If birth, duration, and cessation have the characteristic of "being compound," then in birth there would be a three-fold characteristic since birth is itself a compound phenomenon. (That is, birth also has states of birth, duration, and cessation.) In each of these characteristics, there would also be a three-fold characteristic and then there will be an infinite regress in your argument. The same holds for duration and cessation. If the three-fold characteristic did not exist in each of the three states, then "birth," "duration," and "cessation" are not characteristics of what is compound.]

[That the "birth of birth" is born together, as with "fatherhood" and "sonship," is also unacceptable. Such "birth of birth" is either interdependent with the preceding existing cause, or is interdependent with the nonexistence of the cause, or is interdependent with a prior partial existence and partial nonexistence of the cause. These three have already been refuted in Chapter 5. Again: the father exists first and then gives birth to the child, thereby becoming "a father." Thus, the example is not apropos.]

(6) *Opponent*: Because of the existence of phenomena that are born, there certainly is birth. [If there is birth, there is something that is born; if there is no birth, there is nothing that is born. Because we see that there are phenomena that are born — e.g., the pot — birth necessarily exists.]

Reply: If there is birth, what is born is not existent. [If the pot has a birth, then it is already exists and thus cannot be called something that is born. And if there is no pot, then there also is no birth of the pot. Thus, if there is a birth, what is born is nonexistent. (What is real has no birth.) How much less what is not born (and never can never become real).]

The same applies to birth by itself, by another, or by both. [If birth and what is born are distinct, they are born by themselves, by another, or by both. But this was refuted in the refutation of happiness in Chapter 1.]

(7) *Opponent*: Birth exists because birth and what is born are established together. [Birth does not come first and then what is born — they are established together at the same time.]

Reply: Birth and what is born cannot together cause birth. [If what is born could prove birth, then birth itself would be what is born and it could not be called something that could cause birth. If there is no birth, how can "what is born" exist? Thus, both things do not exist.]

That "existence" and "nonexistence" are mutually interdependent is not acceptable. [What is to be born is nonexistent because it is not yet existent (and so "existence" and "nonexistence" cannot exist at the same time). So how can existence and nonexistence be interdependent? But birth occurs — thus, every thing is (impermanent and hence) nonexistent.]

(8) *Opponent*: Phenomena are established because birth and what is born are mutually interdependent. [Not only are birth and what is born established to be mutually interdependent, but because they are mutually interdependent, the pot and other objects are established.]

Reply: If something is born from two things, how is it that there are not three things? [It an effect is born of two things — "birth" and "what is born" — how is it that there is not a third phenomenon, as with a father and mother giving birth to a child? But besides "birth" and "what is born" there is no third thing, and so this argument is not acceptable.]

(9) *Opponent*: Birth must exist because of the cessation of the cause. [If the effect is not born, the cause has not yet ceased. Because we see the cause of the pot has ceased, there must be birth.]

Reply: Because the cause ceases, the birth also disappears. [If the effect is born, it arises either when the cause ceases or after it ceases. If the former, then the birth disappears when the cause ceases since the cause is not different from the cessation. If the latter, then because the cause has already ceased there is no cause and thus the effect cannot be born.]

There is no birth whether the effect is in the cause or not. [Whether the effect preexists in the cause or not, there is no birth. If there is no effect in the cause, how is it that the pot arises only from a clod of earth and the cloth only from threads? But if the effect does not preexist in the cause, the clod would have the cloth as its effect or the threads the pot. If the effect preexists, the cause is only the one particular effect since you claim that the cause and the effect are not different. If the effect preexists in the cause, then curd and butter would exist in milk and curd and milk in butter. If there is curd and butter in milk, then there are many effects in one cause. Thus, there is a mistake in claiming the cause and effect are one, whether one comes before or after the other or are contemporaneous. And there is the same mistake if the effect does not preexist in the cause. Thus, whether the effect is in the cause or not, there is no birth.]

(10) *Opponent*: Because you do not say that cause and effect are not existing, birth and what is born are established.

Reply: Something real does not produce another thing that is real. What is nonexistent cannot produce anything real. [Real things do not give birth to real things; unreal things do not give birth to unreal things. No real thing gives birth to another real thing. Mothers do not really "give birth" to a child since the child was already existent. The child is not born from the mother's blood and so forth because the mother cannot be conceived without those parts. Nor is birth a matter of modification — when a youth changes and becomes an old man, the youth does not cause the old man. Nor is birth like an image in the mirror since the images in the mirror come from nothing; so too, the image is similar to what is reflected, but an effect does not need to be similar to the cause. Nor does something unreal give birth to another unreal thing. A horn of a rabbit does not give birth to another horn of a rabbit. Nor does a real thing produce an unreal thing — a barren woman does not give birth to a child. Nor does an unreal thing produce a real thing — the hair of a tortoise does not give birth to a cloth. Thus, there is no phenomenon "birth." And if something could give birth to another thing, there would be the birth of two types of phenomena (the thing and "giving birth").]

[The effect does not exist in the cause or not exist in the cause. If the effect is not preexisting in the cause, the cause cannot give birth to the effect since the cause is completely different and so no effect could occur. If the effect does preexist in the cause, how can there be a birth since this is not different from the cessation of the cause? If the pot is not different from the clod of earth, the clod must not disappear after the birth of the pot occurs. But otherwise the clod is not the cause of the pot: if the clod and the pot are different, then the pot is not born and is not the effect of the clod. Thus, either way, something does not give birth to something else.]

9. *Refutation of Permanence*

(1) *Opponent*: Uncaused, permanent phenomena exist because you have not refuted them. [You have refuted the existence of caused phenomena (i.e., produced phenomena) but not permanent phenomena that have no cause (i.e., eternal phenomena) — e.g., the ether, time, spacial directions, particles, and nirvana. These have no cause and have not been refuted by you and so they exist.]

Reply: Permanent phenomena are like impermanent phenomena. [If the phenomena have no cause, they are permanent. But if they are permanent because they have no cause, then they can be called "not permanent" (as discussed below in verse 9.3).]

(2) *Opponent*: Phenomena with only a manifesting cause are permanent. [There are two types of causes: a "producing cause" and a "manifesting cause." If the phenomena have producing causes, they are not permanent. Phenomena are called "permanent" when they have only a manifesting cause. They are not called "permanent" simply because they have no cause, but they cannot be called "impermanent" when they have only a manifesting cause.]

Reply: A manifesting cause is not acceptable. [The self has already been refuted; the other permanent phenomena will be refuted below.]

(3) *Opponent*: Permanent phenomena must exist. Produced phenomena are impermanent; thus, unproduced phenomena (must have the opposite characteristic and so) are permanent.

Reply: Then unproduced phenomena would be both nonexistent and existent. [Since they have the characteristic opposite to the produced, these phenomena are called "unproduced." But because we see the characteristic of "existence" in the produced phenomena, unproduced phenomena must not exist. According to you, the unproduced phenomena are permanent because they have the characteristic opposite to that of the produced phenomena, but unproduced phenomena must not be permanent because they have a characteristic not opposite to those of the produced phenomena

— i.e., they are equally intangible. Thus, the phenomena that are considered permanent and all-pervasive are neither permanent nor all-pervasive.]

(4) *Opponent*: Obviously there are phenomena like the ether that exist and are permanent, all-pervasive, and without parts in all places and at all times because it is believed that they exist.

Reply: The ether in one place is united to that part and is not different from that part. [Is the ether inside a pot considered to be the totality of the ether or considered to be only a part of the ether's totality? If the former, then it is not all-pervasive (since it in only in the pot). If it were all-pervasive, then the pot would also be all-pervasive. If the latter, then the part in that space would not be the totality of the ether. (There would be a distinction between the ether contained in the pot and the ether containing the pot, and so ether would have parts and not be permanent.) Thus, ether is neither all-pervasive nor permanent.]

(5) *Opponent*: Obviously ether exists and possesses the characteristic of all-pervasiveness, and it is permanent because there is motion. [If there were no ether, there would be no motion — no going up or down, leaving or coming, and so on — because there would be no place where these motions could occur. But there is motion, and so the ether must be all-pervasive and permanent.]

Reply: Ether stays in ether. [If there is a phenomenon called "ether," there must be a place where it is located. (Every phenomenon must occupy a place.) If there is no such place, there is no such phenomenon. If ether stays in the middle of a hole, then it stays within ether because that is the place that contains it. But this is not what occurs. Thus, ether does not remain in inside what is full since] what is full has no void (i.e., a place devoid of ether). [If there is no void, there is no place where the ether can stay because there is no empty place that could hold it. You say the place where motion occurs is filled with ether, but then there is no place for the ether to move and so no place for the motion to go. Thus, ether is neither all-pervasive nor permanent.]

[In addition, as ether has no characteristic, it is nonexistent. Each phenomenon has a defining characteristic of its own. It is from these characteristics that we know that the phenomena exist — e.g., the characteristic of earth is "solidity" and the characteristic of understanding is "knowledge." But ether has no characteristic and so is nonexistent.]

(6) *Opponent*: Ether has a characteristic — i.e., "formlessness."

Reply: The formless is the destruction of form. It is not an existing phenomenon. If one cuts down a tree, then it becomes a nonexistent phenomenon. This characteristic of the ether indicates it is nonexistent. But in fact ether has no characteristic: at the time form has not yet arisen, there is no characteristic of ether. Nor is form a permanent phenomenon, unlike you allege ether to be. Thus, ether would have to be existing when the form is not yet existing, and so ether would be without a characteristic. What is to be destroyed is also nonexistent. But, again, if it has no characteristic, it does not exist. Thus, "formlessness" is not the characteristic of ether. "Ether" is only a name; it has no reality. Thus, what is allegedly all-pervasive and permanent is refuted.]

(7) *Opponent*: The phenomenon time has the characteristic of "permanence." [There are some phenomena such as time that cannot be directly perceived but can be known through a simple inference that generalizes from everyday phenomena. Even though it cannot be seen, we know that time exists because flowers and fruits bloom and die through the seasons. Seeing the effect, we know the cause. (Here, we see change, and so the medium for it — time — must exist.) From phrases like "one moment" and "not one moment" and from the characteristics of "sooner" and "later," we know that time exists and is permanent.]

Reply: Whatever exists does not exist in the past or future, and thus the future is nonexistent. [The time when the clod of earth is the clod in the pot is the present; the time when it was only earth is the past; and the time when it will be a pot is the future. Because the characteristic of time is "permanence," past time can never be the cause of future time and also cannot be the cause of the present (because, as a cause, the past would then have to change). If the past were the cause of the future, then there would be the mistake of diversity in the permanent phenomenon that you say time is. So too, there is no future in the past (because then it would not be future). Thus, there is no future. The present is also refuted in the same way.]

(8) *Opponent*: Because you admit the past, time must be existent. [So the future must be existent, and the phenomenon of time is established.]

Reply: The past does not have the future's characteristic. [Again, the past earth is not the cause of the future pot. If the past acquires the future's characteristic, then it would have the characteristic of "being the future." How then could it be called "the past"? There would then be no past.]

(9) *Opponent*: Time must exist because of the distinctiveness of its own characteristic. [Either the present has the characteristic of the present, the past the past, or the future the future. Any way, time exists.]

Reply: If this is so, everything is in the present. [If the three times exist with their own characteristics, then they must all be existing now. But if there is a future, it does not exist now. (If it exists now, it is not the future.) If it exists now, then it cannot be called "the future" but "the already come."

(10) *Opponent*: The past and future have their own characteristics. [The time that is past and the time that is the future do not have the characteristic of the present. The past has the characteristic of the past, and the future the characteristic of the future. Thus, each has its own characteristic.]

Reply: The past is not past. [If the past is past, it cannot be called "the past" because it is separated from its own characteristic, like fire that has lost its heat cannot be called "fire" because it has lost its own characteristic. If you say "The past is not the past," then it is impossible to claim that the time in the past has the past's characteristic. The future is refuted in the same manner. Thus, the phenomenon "time" is not real but a mere word.]

(11) *Opponent*: Space really exists because it has the characteristic of "permanence." [The characteristic of space is, for example, "the sun united with a place." The place first united with the sun is the east, and so on.]

Reply: But the eastern region has no beginning. [The sun goes through the four quarters around Mount Meru. But what is called the "eastern region" in which the sun rises changes from country to country. (Thus, the sun is not united with one specific place.) Where the sun is not united with a place, there is no space because it has no characteristic. Some people consider this region the eastern quarter and others consider it the western quarter; thus, is no truly existent space.]

(12) *Opponent*: This characteristic of space is said with respect to only one quarter. [The words "eastern quarter" are not words belonging to all. Thus, there is not the mistake of claiming the eastern quarter has no beginning.]

Reply: If this is so, then space has limits. [If the place that is first united with the sun is called the "eastern region," then space has limits (i.e., distinctions within it). Because it has limits, it has parts; because it has parts, it is not permanent. (Whatever has parts is impermanent and thus not truly real.) Thus, in your teaching, you actually consider space nonexistent.]

(13) *Opponent*: Although the particle is not all-pervasive, it is permanent and exists. It is permanent because the characteristics of its effects

exist. [Seeing the effect, we know that there is a cause and vice versa. For example, from seeing a sprout, we know that it has a seed. It is a law of this universe. Seeing that everything that is produced is at first minute and then becomes gross, it is possible to know that particle dyads are the first effect, while the particle alone is the cause. The particle exists, round and permanent, because it has no cause.]

Reply: Two particles are not united with their complete bodies because the result is not round. [When the effect of the particles arises, their bodies are not completely united because the effects such as the particle dyad are seen by the eyes not to be round (while particles are round). If the particles were completely united, the effect would be round. Also, the particle dyad would be destroyed (i.e., it would be one in nature and not a dyad). If the particles are heavy by nature, then the effect is high. If there is the conjunction of many particles, the effect is great. Because particles are (not completely united but are) united by means of only one part, they must have parts. And because they have parts, they are not permanent.]

In addition, particles are not permanent because they are separated by the ether. [If there are particles, they must be separated by the ether. Thus, particles must have parts. Having parts they are not permanent.]

Moreover, because the particles are made of different parts — form, taste, smell, sound, and touch — they are not permanent. [If particles exist, so do their parts, and because they have parts they are not permanent. They must also have a shape because all phenomena have that characteristic. If particles have a shape, they must be long or short, round or square, and so forth. Thus, they must have parts and thus are not permanent. Since they are not permanent, there is no (real, self-existent) particle.]

(14) *Opponent*: The phenomenon nirvana exists because the permanent nonexistence of the mental afflictions is not different from nirvana. [The complete extinguishing of desire and the other mental afflictions is called "nirvana." If there are mental afflictions, then there is the cycle of rebirth. If there are no mental afflictions, then there is no more rebirth, and thus nirvana is permanent (i.e., eternal).]

Reply: If this were so, nirvana would be a produced phenomenon. [If you affirm that when the mental afflictions no longer exist because of the practices on the path that there is nirvana, then nirvana (would be the result of the practices and thus) would be a produced phenomenon. Being a produced phenomenon, it cannot be permanent. In addition, when the mental afflictions are extinguished, they are nonexistent. But if nirvana is not different than the extinction of the mental afflictions, then it too is nonexistent.]

(15) *Opponent*: Nirvana is the "producing cause" of nirvana.

Reply: What is destroyed is not destruction. [If nirvana causes liberation, then it is not liberation. And when the mental afflictions are not extinguished, there is no nirvana; and when the effect does not exist, neither does a cause.]

(16) *Opponent*: Nirvana is the effect of the nonexistence of the mental afflictions. [Nirvana is not the nonexistence of the mental afflictions nor the cause of their nonexistence. Rather, nirvana is the effect of their nonexistence. Thus, nirvana does exist.]

Reply: If so, what binds someone to the cycle of rebirth, the being that is bound, and the means of release are all different from nirvana. This means nirvana is not the result of karmic actions. [The bonds are the mental afflictions and karmic action; the bound are the sentient beings; and the means is the noble Eightfold Path. Through the path, there is the breaking of the bonds and thus the sentient beings attain liberation. If nirvana is different from these three phenomena, it is not produced. The nonexistence of the mental afflictions is without even a superficial appearance, and what is without any appearance cannot be a cause.]

(17) *Opponent*: When these three phenomena (the bonds, the bound, and the means) no longer exist, nirvana exists. [The place where these three phenomena are no longer existing is called "nirvana."]

Reply: That is a terrible place — how can it be longed for? [Because impermanence is a calamity, those who know reject it and are freed from every desire for the compound phenomena. If in nirvana there are no individuals and no objects that can be desired, then nirvana is a far more dreadful place than the compound phenomena. How can your mind desire it? Nirvana is called "being freed from all attachments, the destruction of every conceptualization." It is neither real nor unreal. It cannot be conceptualized, like the light that is extinguished.]

(18) *Opponent*: Who attains nirvana?

Reply: Nobody attains nirvana. [Again, nirvana is like the light that has been extinguished — we cannot say whether it goes east, south, west, north, up, or down. Nirvana is the extinction of all words. It cannot be explained. It is without any appearance. Who could attain it? Because the self is all-pervasive and permanent, it could not attain nirvana. The five bodily aggregates could not attain it because they are impermanent and arise and perish. Thus, to whom would nirvana belong? "The attainment of nirvana" are merely words of this world.]

10. *Refutation of Views on Emptiness*

(1) *Opponent*: Some phenomena must exist because of your refutation. If there is no refutation, then other phenomena exist. [You refuted the characteristics of all phenomena. Thus, if this refutation exists, it is impossible to say that all phenomena are empty because the refutation itself exists. Because this refutation is existent, it is impossible to say that you have refuted all phenomena. (Thus, if nothing else, at least the refutation exists.) And if the refutation is nonexistent, then all phenomena are existent (because they have not been refuted.)]

Reply: The refutation is like what is refuted. (That is, it has the same ontological nature — being empty of self-existence.) [Because you attach yourself to a refutation by means of existing and nonexisting phenomena, you desire to refute this refutation. But because the refutation is established, all phenomena are empty and without appearance. If this refutation is existent, then it itself has already been refuted and is empty and without appearance. If this refutation is nonexistent, what is there to be refuted (as being real) by you? If one says that a second head is nonexistent, it does not become existent because of its refutation. When one says that something is nonexistent, it does not exist because of the mere word "nonexistence." The same happens with a refutation and what is refuted.]

(2) *Opponent*: Phenomena must exist because we have the notions of "this" and "that." [Because you accept multiplicity, you say that oneness is a mistake. Because you accept oneness, you say that multiplicity is a mistake. As oneness and multiplicity are established, all phenomena exist.]

Reply: Oneness and multiplicity are not accepted. [Oneness and multiplicity cannot be established. They were refuted in Chapters 3 and 4. Because they have already been refuted, there is nothing that can be accepted. And if one says "You have nothing to maintain, but we maintain oneness and multiplicity," then this proposition is refuted in the same way.]

(3) *Opponent*: Because you refute the teachings of others, you are a person who refutes teachings. [You like to refute the teachings that others maintain, and you try your utmost to find a mistake in them. But you yourselves have nothing to maintain. Thus, you are refuters.]

Reply: You are the refuters. [Those who teach emptiness have nothing to maintain. Since they have nothing to maintain, they are not refuters. (That is, the Madhyamika argue that nothing is real and thus that nothing exists to be refuted.) But you accept your own teachings and refute the affirmations of others. Thus, you are the refuters.]

(4) *Opponent*: By refuting the teachings of others, your own doctrine is established. [If the teachings of others are overcome, your own teaching prevails. Thus, we are not refuters.]

Reply: "To establish" and "to refute" are not the same thing. ["Establishment" means "praising and being glad for the merit." ("Refutation" means "exposing mistakes.") Being glad for the merit and exposing mistakes cannot be the same thing.]

"Establishment" means there is a fear. [Fear means "lack of strength." If one is afraid of his own teaching, he cannot establish it. Because he is not afraid of the teachings of others, he likes to refute. Thus, establishing and refuting are not the same. If the refutation of another's teaching were the same as establishing one's own teaching, why did you say that those who teach emptiness only refute other teachings and had nothing to maintain?]

(5) *Opponent*: To state that another's thesis is wrong is to state that one's own thesis is established. [If you have no thesis of your own, how do you not establish your teaching and only refute the teaching of others? By refuting others' teachings, there is the establishment of your own teaching.]

Reply: If so, everything would be unestablished. [If one's own teaching is established by such a refutation, everything else is not established. But if nothing is established, we have nothing (to refute and thus) to establish.]

(6) *Opponent*: This conflicts with the world's belief. [People here cannot accept that phenomena are empty and without any characteristic.]

Reply: This doctrine is accepted as true by the world. [This doctrine of dependency is believed and accepted because phenomena that arise dependently have the characteristic of nonexistence. You claim that there is butter in milk, that there is a fetus in a young girl, that there is excrement in food, that besides its parts there is also a house, and that separate from the threads is also a cloth. Others claim there is no effect in the cause. Others claim phenomena are born without a cause. Others claim that there is real, transcendental void. Whatever those people may affirm, who will believe and accept it? But in our teaching, this is not so because it is in accord with the beliefs of the people of the world, and so everybody accepts it. (That is, people in fact accept the impermanence and dependency of phenomena that the doctrine of emptiness conforms with.)]

(7) *Opponent*: Your nonacceptance of any thesis is the establishment of your teaching. [When you say "There is no thesis," that is a thesis. And when you say "Our doctrine is in accord with the belief of the people of the world," that is your thesis.]

Reply: The non-thesis is not called "a thesis," just as "nonexistence" (is not a form of "existence"). [We said before "All phenomena are dependently arisen and are empty of any defining characteristic" — thus, we have no thesis. For example, when we say "nonexistence," this is real nonexistence — but it is not because we say "nonexistence" that there then is nonexistence. It is the same for the nonexistence of a thesis. (Saying "There is no thesis" does not make this claim into a thesis.]

(8) *Opponent*: Because you say "All phenomena have the characteristic of 'nonexistence,'" you are one who destroys teachings. [If "Phenomena are empty and have the characteristic of 'nonexistence,'" then this thesis must be nonexistent (since it is a phenomenon), as are all phenomena. Because all phenomena are nonexistent, you are one who destroys phenomena.]

Reply: One who refutes the destruction of phenomena is one who destroys teachings. [According to me, there is no doctrine and so there is nothing to be refuted. You claim that we destroy teachings, and you wish to refute me. Thus, you are the one who destroys teachings.]

(9) *Opponent*: Phenomena must exist because they are mutually established. [If there is what is "long," there must be what is "short"; if there is what is "high," there must be what is "low" — if there is what is "empty," there must be something that is "non-empty (i.e., self-existent)."]

Reply: How can they be mutually established when the existence of one has been refuted? [If something is nonexistent, there can be no mutual establishment (because one item does not exist). If there is non-emptiness, then there would be the mutual establishment (of emptiness). But if there is nothing that is non-empty, then how could the nonexistence of emptiness be mutually established with it?]

(10) *Opponent*: According to you, nonexistence is established. [If one says "The house is empty; there are no horses in there," then the nonexistence of horses in the house is established (but this claim assumes horses are in fact real and there simply are none in the house). In the same way, although you say "All phenomena are empty and without any characteristic," this nonexistence must exist because it produces various feelings.]

Reply: Existence as well as nonexistence is nonexistent. [With regard to their true characteristic, we claim that both the existence and nonexistence of the various classes of phenomena are all empty. If existence is nonexistent, then nonexistence also does not exist.]

(12) *Opponent*: This refutation is itself empty and so is not acceptable. [If all phenomena are empty, then this refutation is not possible because it does not exist. It is a foolish person who, wishing to refute what does not exist, undertakes tiresome work.]

Reply: Although phenomena are empty of self-existence, they still bind us because we assume they have a characteristic (indicating that they are real). [Phenomena bind only because of our false conceptualizations (that make what is actually real into discrete entities). In order to refute these false conceptualizations, we expound a refutation, but there really is nothing to be refuted. It is like a foolish person who, seeing a mirage in the summertime and letting the false idea of water arise in him, runs toward it. If one who knows says to him "There is no water," he then destroys the false idea but does not refute the "water" (that was never there). In the same way, the nature of all phenomena is emptiness, but sentient beings adhere to them because they assume some characteristic (thereby suggesting the phenomena are real). In order to refute these false ideas, we expound our refutation, but there is really nothing to be refuted.]

(13) *Opponent*: This teaching is not explained because it is not in the great texts. [You refute "existence," "nonexistence," and "existence and nonexistence." So you fall into the doctrine of "neither existence nor nonexistence." This doctrine cannot be explained because the characteristic of "existence" cannot be reconciled with "nonexistence." This is called "a teaching that cannot be explained." This teaching is not found in the great texts of the Vaisheshikas, Samkhyas, Jainas, and other teachings. Because it does not exist anywhere, it cannot be accepted.]

Reply: There is a fourth teaching. [There are phenomena that are not explained in your great texts. In the *Vaisheshika Sutras*, sound is not called either great or small. In the *Samkhya Sutras*, the clod of earth is not a pot and is not a non-pot. According to the Jainas' teachings, light has neither brightness nor darkness. As with all these texts, there is a fourth teaching that is not explained. Why do you say that it does not exist?]

(14) *Opponent*: It there indeed is emptiness, there must be no teaching. [If emptiness is considered a phenomenon that is not explained, how do you teach good and bad phenomena in order to instruct others?]

Reply: Because the doctrine is in accord with worldly speech, there is no mistake. [The Buddha taught the doctrine always based on the two truths — the conventional and the absolute. These two are both true and not false words. For example, the Buddha knew that phenomena have no characteristic, and yet he spoke to (his disciple) Ananda "Go to the town of Shravasti and ask for alms." A town cannot be conceived if we take away earth, wood, and so forth. (That is, there is no entity "town" in addition to the parts.) But being in accord with worldly speech, he did not fall into false speech. Since we also follow the Buddha's teaching, we do not commit any mistake.]

(15) *Opponent*: But a worldly truth is not really true. [If the worldly truth is in fact true, then it becomes a truth from the highest point of view. (That is, any truth if indeed it is a truth is an absolute truth.) If it is not in fact true, how can it be called a truth?]

Reply: The types depend on each other, like the concepts "large" and "small." [The conventional truth accords with what people of the world consider true but what holy men consider not true. For example, a plum is bigger than a date but smaller than a cucumber. These claims are both true, but if we say simply "The date is small" and "The cucumber is large," these statements would be false. (That is, these claims would be absolute, but false.) In the same way, there is no mistake in following worldly speech.]

(16) *Opponent*: What is the profit in knowing these mistakes? [From the refutation of merit and demerit to the refutation of emptiness, you have considered all phenomena to be false — what profit will now be obtained?]

Reply: One attained profit in the same way that the renunciation of a sense of self is called "attaining liberation." [The refutation of phenomena is of three types. First, in renouncing demerit and merit, the self was refuted. Next, all phenomena were refuted. This is called the "nonexistence of the 'I'" and the "nonexistence of 'mine.'" Lastly, there is no attachment to any phenomenon whatsoever. If there is no joy in hearing of existence, then there is no sorrow in hearing of nonexistence. This is called "liberation."]

(17) *Opponent*: Why do you say with words that there is the attainment of liberation when really there is no attainment of liberation?

Reply: Because from the highest point of view, there is in fact no attainment of liberation. Because of the refutation of a self, there is no individual (who attains liberation). Because of the refutation of nirvana, there is no (real) liberation. So how is it possible to say that man obtains liberation? We say that "There is liberation" only according to worldly convention.

Notes

Verse 1.2. "Defining marks (*lakshanas, lingas*)" are the true characteristics of a particular phenomenon. Can only real (self-existent) things can have characteristics? Or does what is empty also have the characteristic of "emptiness"? Nagarjuna's answer is that everything, self-existent or not, has a characteristic (Jones 2010: 163). But the "mark" of what is empty is "being signless (*animitta*)" — i.e., being without any defining marks (v. 1.33).

"Phenomena (*dharmas*)" here are whatever falls into the widest category of what exists in the phenomenal world. Phenomena are empty in the Madhyamaka ontology, but they are still not nonexistent.

Verses 1.5, 3.13, 8.6. Note that only the three of the four options are mentioned, not the fourth — "neither *x* nor not-*x*." In 10.13, Aryadeva discusses the fourth.

Verse 1.8. The reference here is to "a magical formula (*mantra*) or the (astrological effect of) stars."

Verse 2.18. On mover and motion, see MK 2.

Verses 3.4-7, 4.3. A "general characteristic" (*samanya-lakshana*) as opposed to a "particular characteristic" of an entity (*sva-lakshana*) is a universal quality. "Existence" is a universal quality here. Even if this is not a "universal" in the Scholastics' sense of the term, there is still the problem, as in Western philosophy, of how particulars inhere in a universal or vice versa.

Verse 3.6. There are several passages in the Commentary that we would have to deem sophistry. Consider this from 3.6:

> (1) If the pot and existence are not different, then the pot must have the universal characteristic of "existence" and not the particular characteristic of being "a pot." (2) If the particular characteristic is nonexistent, the universal characteristic is also nonexistent because only owing to a particular characteristic is there a universal characteristic. That is, if the particular characteristic (of "being a pot") does not exist, then the universal characteristic does not exist (i.e., there is no pot and thus nothing to characterize as "existing"). (3) Since these both do not exist, therefore everything is nonexistent. (That is, if there is no pot and the pot and the property of "existence" are the same, the property of "existence" does not exist and so nothing else could have that property.)

Equating the existence of the pot with all existence does lead to the conclusion that if the pot does exist then nothing exists (since then there is no existence at all), but no one would accept the initial premise.

Another example is the Commentary to verse 4.4:

(1) You say that because the pot is united to existence, it is existent, and because it is united to oneness, it is one, and also that the pot is the pot. (2) If this is so, then you consider what in this world is considered one pot to be a multiplicity of pots. (That is, the one united to existence, the one united to oneness, and the pot itself.) In short, the one pot has become many pots. (3) Thus, because the one pot has become many, there is no more "one pot." (That is, its characteristic should be multiplicity and not oneness.) (4) And because the one pot does not exist, a multiplicity of pots also cannot exist.

Even accepting (2) (that the one pot has become many), (3) does not follow and thus (4) does not follow.

Verse 3.7. The argument is that if *A* is not different from *X*, and *B* is not different from *X*, then *A* is not different from *B*. In China, the classic "a white horse is not a horse" relies on the same ambiguity. That is, (1) a black horse is a horse, (2) a white horse is not a black horse, and so (3) a white horse is not a horse. The conclusion follows only if (1) is read to mean that black horses exhaust the category of horses, which they obviously do not. If (1) is read as meaning that a black horse is one instance in the category of horses, then the conclusion does not follow. In the case of Aryadeva's arguments, *A* or *B* would have to exhaust the category *X* for the conclusion to follow.

Verses 3.12, 4.9-10, 6.4, 9.13. A "particle" (*anu, paramanu*) is literally "unbreakable," like the Greek word "*atom*," but since today we would read modern quantum physics into the word "atom," the term "particle" is better.

Verse 3.13. The Commentary changes Nagarjuna's reasoning. He would argue about the independence of the concepts of "long" and "short." Aryadeva gives a more ontologically oriented argument, as in verse 4.8.

Verse 4.3. Note that *the pot* is a "substance (*dravya*)." Thus, "substance" is not merely the tiniest part of matter but also a characteristic of observable phenomena. The pot has its own substance and is not merely the sum of the substances of the particles.

Verse 4.8. The Commentary here offers a variation on Nagarjuna's refutation of "whole" and "part" by the interconnection of the concepts. Here Aryadeva argues that there is no whole, and so there are no parts to the whole; and since there are no whole and no parts, there is nothing. But his argument is oriented to the ontological and not the conceptual. Arguing that the concepts "whole" and "part" makes better sense: if there is no "whole," then there is nothing that can be labeled "parts." Nevertheless, this still does not mean that there are no things that would be labeled "parts" if they were parts of a whole. (See Jones 2010: 160-62.)

Verse 5.2. In this theory of perception, the *physical eye* does not leave the body, but the *visual faculty* does. It exits the body and makes physical contact with the sense-object.

Verse 6.9. The four material elements (*maha-bhuta*) — "earth," "water," "fire," and "air" — are not anything we see directly by the eye. Earth has its defining characteristic "solidity" in general, fire "heat," water "fluidity," and wind "movement."

Verse 6.11. If Tucci's translation is accurate, the opponent's reasoning is sometimes faulty. For example, verse 6.11 says:

(1) Perception occurs in the present. (2) If perception could not occur, then the present would not exist. But (3) the present does exist, and thus (4) what is perceivable can be perceived.

Premise (2) is not true: if we were blind, there would still be the present. This keeps (4) from following from any combination of (1) through (3): merely because the present exists does not mere that anything is perceivable. But the form is valid ("modus tollens" reasoning), even if not all the premises are acceptable.

Chapter 7. The principal Indian problem of *causation* is not the modern science of causation — e.g., the physics of mechanics. Indian causation does have a "producing cause (*karana hetu*)" that is more like efficient causation in science, but the usual problem is the ontological issue of *material causes.* Their examples are of the seed becoming the sprout and the butter being in the milk or not. In Aristotelian terms, this is a matter of the material (and perhaps formal) causes and not efficient causation.

Verse 7.12. The opponent here accuses the Madhyamikas of "annihilation (*uccheda*)." That is, they are accused of advocating the doctrine of "is-not-ness (*na-asti-ka*)" — i.e., that nothing in fact exists. In short, *ontological nihilism.* Aryadeva responds with the idea of continuity between changing entities (e.g., the seed and sprout) and thus there is no true annihilation. (So too, because of cessation, there is no permanence.) In the Commentary, he says that the Buddha taught the twelve linked steps of the formula of "dependent arising (*pratitya-samutpada*)." He adds that this doctrine does not maintain either the existence of the effect in the cause nor the total nonexistence of the effect, thereby avoiding both the doctrine of nihilism and permanence but rather is the "middle path" leading to nirvana.

Verse 9.2. The "producing cause (*karana-hetu*)" creates a phenomenon, while the "manifesting cause (*abhivyakti-hetu*)" only makes something that already exists appear.

Verses 9.12-13. The reasoning here assumes anything with parts must be impermanent. But if parts permanent and the union permanent, then the whole would be permanent. Nor is it clear in verse 13 why if particles are separated by the ether they must have parts, unless it is the unconvincing argument that because particles would have a left side and a right side they must have parts. The opponent's reasoning here is not more convincing:

> Seeing that everything that is produced is at first minute and then becomes gross, it is possible to know that particle dyads (*dyyannuka*) are the first effect, while the particle alone is the cause. Thus, the particle exists, round and permanent, because it has no cause.

The conclusion does not follow at all: the opponent gives no reason why even if the particles are the only cause of larger entities that they must be permanent (or round) and cannot have their own causes.

Chapter 10. This chapter starts out like Nagarjuna's *Overturning the Objections*. The opponent alleges that there is a Catch-22 in the Madhyamaka position: if the Madhyamaka refutation works, then it exists and so it fails — there is at least this one existent phenomenon. But if the refutation fails, then all phenomena remain unrefuted. The Madhyamikas respond that things only work if they are selfless: if things are permanent and so cannot change, nothing functions. They in turn see their opponents trapped in a contradiction: only what is real can arise (since what is unreal does not exist and so cannot do anything), but what is real is permanent and unchanging and so it cannot arise but this conflicts with the change we see in the world.

This chapter refutes the idea that emptiness is itself a real (self-existent) phenomenon. Many Westerners take emptiness (*shunyata*) to be an analog to God or the Hindu Brahman and refer to it as "the Void" with a capital "V." Aryadeva, like Nagarjuna (see MK 13.8), make clear that is not an entity of any type or the source of the reality of anything. It is not in any way an entity that can be grasped. It is not anything that transcends the world, but is merely a description of the true state of all the phenomena of the world — being empty of anything that would make them substantive, discrete realities. The Madhyamikas make no claims about anything beyond the impermanence and conditionality of the phenomena of the world. Their doctrine of "emptiness" makes no claims, nor has any implications, one way or the other about any possible source or any transcendental realities.

Verses 10.14-17. Here Aryadeva invokes the doctrine of "two truths." The opponent is alleging that if a "worldly truth (*samvriti-satya*)" is really true, then it is a "truth from the highest point of view (*paramartha-satya*)," and so there are not actually two types of truth. Aryadeva disagrees. But also note that he affirms that conventional truths are in fact *truths* and not ultimately *false*. Only the entailed ontological implications of a conventional truth that the phenomenal entities refer to in true conventional statements are *ultimately real* is erroneous. For example, the claim "The New York Mets won the 1969 World Series" is a conventional truth. The ultimate truth connected to it is that there is not real entities "the New York Mets," "1969," or "World Series" since there are no self-existent entities in the world. Nevertheless, it conveys some information about the phenomenal world that the claim "The Philadelphia Phillies won the 1969 World Series" does not. Equally important, there is no way to translate the conventional truth into an ultimate truth since the conventional claim involves the relation of conventional entities and the ultimate truth is only about the ultimate ontological status of the alleged conventional entities.

Verse 10.17. From the ultimate ontological point of view, there is no "being" who attains nirvana and no entity "nirvana" to be attained. "There is liberation" thus is only a conventional truth.

* * *

Rahulabhadra

(?)

Rahulabhadra may have been Nagarjuna's teacher, or his contemporary, or the successor to his student Aryadeva or the teacher of another Buddhist named Nagarjuna who lived in the seventh century (Ruegg 1981: 54-55, Ruegg 1990: 62) — in other words, nothing exact is known of his life. Nevertheless, his song of praise is included here to show that Buddhists in the Madhyamaka and Prajna-paramita (the "Perfection of Wisdom") traditions did not only compose philosophical treatises. Even Nagarjuna composed in this genre (at least there are several songs attributed to him). Rahulabhadra represents "a fairly distinct current in early Madhyamaka thought that was not elaborated in the theoretical scholastic texts of the classic school based on Nagarjuna's *Fundamental Verses of the Middle Way*, but which is reflected in the hymns ascribed to Nagarjuna" (Ruegg 1981: 56). He also uses language common to the devotional (*bhakti*) movements (ibid.: 55) more commonly associated with South Indian Hindu traditions. Other works ascribed to him are claimed by other Buddhist traditions (ibid.).

Stotras such as this one were meant to be sung and not merely recited. As a nod in that direction, the four-line format will be maintained in this translation, although no attempt has been made to keep the lines uniform in meter or style. It treats wisdom (*prajna*) as a person, but the style of "holy language" — "thee," "thy," "art," and so forth — has been avoided. (See Conze et al. 1954: 147-49 for a more flowery style of translation.) The Sanskrit for the translation is from Hataka 1958: 1-2.

* * *

A Song in Praise of Perfected Wisdom
(Prajna-Paramita-Stotra)

[1] Homage to you, oh perfect Wisdom,
Who is free of all conceptualizations!
All your limbs are free of imperfections,
Faultless are those who look toward you!

[2] Stainless, transcending all our conceptual projections,
Free of words, like the vastness of space.
Who sees you in your true state
Sees the Buddha.

[3] As moonlight is like the moon,
So also do you, oh teacher of the Buddha,
Who is richly endowed with all that is excellent,
And the teacher of the world not differ.

[4] The compassionate ones who take refuge with you
Who heralds the buddhas' teaching,
Easily attain the exalted state without parallel,
Oh beloved tender one!

[5] As soon as those with a pure disposition
Behold you, thereby certainly
Their complete accomplishment is indeed attained,
Oh one with an unfailing eye!

[6] To all adepts who are devoted to
The sake of others,
You are a mother who nourishes,
Gives birth, and bestows tender love.

[7] The buddhas, those teachers of the world,
Are your compassionate sons.

Thus, you are, oh gracious lady,
The great progenitor of all sentient beings!

[8] All the perfections free of impurities
Circle you at all times,
Like the stars circle the moon,
Oh irreproachable one!

[9] Persons are reaching everywhere
For instruction by the buddhas.
Although one, you are praised
As many and multi-formed, with many names.

[10] Just as drops of dew vanish
When in contact with the rays of the sun,
So darkness and the doctrines of the wise are annihilated
Once they have attained you.

[11] When you appear as terrifying
You generate fear in the childish.
When you appear gentle,
Consolation comes to the wise.

[12] When intense affection is not found
For you who offers protection,
How could desire and hatred arise
For another, oh mother?

[13] From nowhere do you come,
And to nowhere do you go.
You are not apprehended
By those who know in any place.

[14] Because they do not see you
They have attained you!
And thereby, they gain their final release.
What a wonder this is!

[15] Indeed, from seeing you, one is bound (to the cycle of rebirths).
But by not seeing you, one is also bound.
By seeing you, one is released.
Yet by not seeing you, one is also released!

[16] Wondrous, deeply profound, and glorious!
Extremely difficult you are to discern.
Like a show of magic, you are seen and
Yet you are not seen!

[17] You are approached
By fully-enlightened buddhas, solitary buddhas, and disciples alike.
You are the sole pathway to liberation —
Certainly, there is no other!

[18] For the purpose of indicating you,
The guardians of the world resort to worldly conventions.
Out of compassion for embodied beings,
You are spoken of by them
And yet you are not spoken of at all!

[19] Who is able to praise you here in this world?
You who are signless and without embellishments.
You transcend the range of speech
And are without objective support anywhere in this world.

[20] By means of the words of our worldly conventions,
We constantly praise you.
But none of our praise approaches you.
In this way, we attain the highest state.

By all the merit that comes
From praising perfected Wisdom
May the entire world attain
The final wisdom without parallel!

* * *

Notes

Insight (*prajna*) is personified here as a woman (the noun is feminine). This is more in keeping with the Prajna-paramita tradition than the Madhyamaka. Wisdom (*sophia*) of another type is also personified as a woman in the Old Testament book of Ecclesiastes.

Verse 2. "Stainless (*nir-lepa*)" means to be free of all impurities. What is "perfect" (i.e., complete or whole) is free impurities.

Rahulabhadra here uses "*nish-prapancha*": "beyond conceptual projection." *Prapancha* is the objective projection of our conceptual distinctions onto the continuum of events that is reality as it really is — in short, seeing our concepts reified in the world. (See Jones 2010: 169.) That Rahulabhadra uses this term that appears in Madhyamaka philosophy but not other key terms such as "emptiness" or "self-existence" is worth noting.

"Space (*akasha*)" means the ether filling the universe, not empty space. But, like space, it is considered all-pervading and undifferentiated.

Verse 4. The author uses the word "*bhakti*" in a compound (*bhakti-vatsala*) here. "*Bhakti*" is common in Hindu theistic traditions.

Verse 9. Note the "one versus many" reference — a problem common in theistic traditions. The one reality still has many aspects and names to aid disciples.

Verse 10. Rahulabhadra uses the term "*vadas*" here. It can mean "theses, propositions, arguments, or doctrines." But it is not a term used by Nagarjuna and the other Madhyamikas. They use thesis "(*pratijna*)" or "proposition (*paksha*)."

Verse 14. An alternative translation of this verse without paradox is this: "Those who do not see you but devoutly (*bhavatah*) take refuge (*prapad*) in you are released as soon as they are done, so great is this marvel." But since the next two verses do clearly contain paradoxes, the reading given here seems preferable.

Verse 15. Note the paradox: by seeing wisdom perfected, one is bound to the cycle of rebirths but also by not seeing it one is bound. The same holds for being released from the cycle. (A possible reconciliation of the apparent contradictions is this: whether the unenlightened know of the perfection of wisdom or not, they remain unenlightened if they do not do more. By seeing perfect wisdom — i.e., attaining it — one is enlightened, but since there is nothing to see, it can be said that one is also enlightened when one realizes that there is nothing to see. Still, this explanation may be a case of reading in something the Buddhist author did not intend.) This use of paradox is more common in Prajna-Paramita texts than Madhyamaka ones.

Verse 16. Note that here *prefect wisdom* is compared to a magician's trick (*maya*), not the appearance of *distinct entities* in the phenomenal world, as is the usual analogy in Madhyamaka texts. Again, there is a paradox: perfect wisdom is seen and yet not seen. That is, it is attained but is not an object that can be set apart from the mind and observed.

Verse 17. Perfect wisdom is the "sole pathway" to liberation (*moksha*). This is not related specifically to the issue in the *Lotus Sutra* of whether ultimately there are three vehicles in Buddhism or only one (the vehicle of becoming a fully-enlightened buddha or a solitary buddha or a listener). The claim is that there is only one path to true selflessness.

Verses 18-20. This passage does not mention the "two truths," but it does suggest part of the doctrine: the reliance on the conventional to lead to the higher truth. But here all higher truths are inexpressible.

Verse 18. Out of compassion for those who suffer, the protectors of the world (*lokanathas*) resort to worldly convention (*vyavahara*) for the purpose of "indicating" or "designating (*prajnapty-artham*) "perfect wisdom." (See MK 24.18.) But since such wisdom is not something we can conceptualize, words only indicate that there is such a thing and do not describe its nature. Buddhapalita makes much of the idea of "designating."

Verse 19. Perfect wisdom is signless (*nir-nimitta*) — i.e., free of any defining characteristics that mark entities. Despite the praise, perfect wisdom transcends the realm of what can be spoken (*vakpatha*) — i.e., it is indescribable. This follows verse 18, which says that perfect wisdom is spoken of but, paradoxically, cannot be spoken of.

Verse 20. This verse carries on the theme of perfect Wisdom being beyond language: no praise of perfect wisdom "reaches" it, yet the praise continues. The idea of ultimate silence because of the inapplicability of words is common in the Prajna-Paramita literature and comes up near the end of Nagarjuna's *Fundamental Verses of the Middle Way* (25.24). Ultimately, the Buddha is the silent one of the Shakya clan ("Shakya-muni") since he speaks no (real) words.

* * *

Buddhapalita

(ca. 480-540)

Little is known about the life of Buddhapalita. He may have been from South India, and he probably wrote early in the sixth century C.E. Buddhapalita represents a conservative current in Madhyamaka thought that resisted the adoption of the logical and epistemological innovations that were being brought into Mahayana philosophy at the time (Ruegg 1981: 60). He stuck to Nagarjuna's "*prasanga*" method of argument, i.e., poking holes in others' theses without advocating any counter-theses or advancing independent arguments for emptiness. That is, under the *prasanga* method, one does not advance any independent metaphysical claims but merely establishes errors in others' claims to prove self-existent realities by pointing out unacceptable consequences of their opponents' premises. In other words, one says "If we start with your premises on self-existence, such and such logical contradictions or other clearly erroneous consequences follow" — in short, a *reductio ad absurdum* of their opponents' theses. By doing this, one is not committed to any other premise. (However, Madhyamikas do argue that the opposite of self-existence — emptiness — does in fact follow *by default* as the only other alternative to self-existence.)

Buddhapalita composed the first named commentary on Nagarjuna's *Fundamental Verses on the Middle Way*. He is not an innovator but followed Nagarjuna closely; his commentary is not as extensive as Bhavaviveka's or as subtle as Chandrakirti's, but this makes his thought clearer and more accessible to the modern reader (Ames 1986: 313-14). In this commentary, he quotes other works by Nagarjuna, Aryadeva's *Four Hundred Verses* and *One Hundred Verses*, Rahulabhadra's *Song in Praise of Perfected Wisdom*, and one verse from another teacher (Lindtner 1981: 188). His focus is on philosophical matters rather than religious or ethical ones (ibid.).

Buddhapalita's works survive today only in Tibetan. The first twenty-two chapters of his commentary appear to be by one author and the last five by another. The last five are from an earlier unattributed commentary called the "*Akutobhaya*" (Ames 1986: 314). Presented here are summaries of his commentaries on Nagarjuna's Dedication, Chapter 1, and Chapter 18 based on translations from the Tibetan. (Translations of the *Fundamental Verses of the Middle Way*, presented below in italics, are modified from Jones 2010 when Buddhapalita's understanding indicates a change is needed.)

* * *

Summaries from
Buddhapalita's Commentary on Nagarjuna's Fundamental Verses on the Middle Way (Mula-madhyamaka-karika-vritti)

Nagarjuna's Dedication of the Mula-madhyamaka-karikas

I bow to the fully-enlightened Buddha, the best of teachers, who taught that whatever arises dependently is neither annihilated nor born, neither ceasing nor permanent, neither coming nor going, neither different nor identical; and who also taught the peaceful stilling of all conceptual creations.

The Master (Nagarjuna) salutes the perfect Buddha, who has taught the people who are roaming in the dark world and believing in Ishvara (God), time, particles, matter, self-existence, and so forth, that "dependent arising" is the ultimate truth. He also taught the peaceful stilling of the world of conceptual differentiations and the direct way to the abode of nirvana.

The Master called the Buddha "the best of teachers" because the Buddha, regarding every non-Buddhist opponent as a cheated child, had taught them "dependent arising" as if with his hand he was aiding a blind man walk.

If you ask why it is necessary to teach dependent arising, we answer that the Master observed with a compassionate heart that sentient beings are afflicted with a wide assortment of sufferings. In order to liberate them, he wished to teach the true state of entities. So he set about instructing them in dependent arising because, it has been said, "One who observes the false is bound to the cycle of rebirths; one who observes the real is liberated."

Opponent: What is the nature of entities as they truly are?

Reply: They are unsubstantial (i.e., without self-existence). Those who are ignorant of this because their insight (which analyzes phenomena) is obscured by the darkness of the root-ignorance, imagine that entities have their own self-existence; and at that time those persons develop attraction (to entities to which they attribute pleasantness) and aversion (to entities to which they attribute unpleasantness). When the darkness of delusion is dispelled by the light of the knowledge of dependent arising, one observes with the eye of insight that the entities have no self-existence. Deprived of any support, there is no opportunity (for the rise of attraction and aversion), and in that person attraction and aversion do not arise. For example, if we judge a reflected image of a woman as a real woman, our mind will conceive it as a distinct reality and an attraction to it will arise. When we conceive it according to its true nature, we do not think it is a woman, and after having gotten rid of the attraction, we are greatly ashamed. Aryadeva said "If we see that objects are empty of self-existence, the seed of existence will be cut off."

Opponent: If the all-knowing, all-seeing Buddha has already explained and taught dependent arising, what is the use of teaching it again?

Reply: (The real state of entities is that they lack self-existence, and the supreme truth is dependent arising.) The Buddha explained and taught dependent arising by means of worldly conventions such as "arising." But some whose minds are attached to mere verbal expressions do not understand the profound meaning of "dependent arising." Instead, they think that entities do indeed exist by self-existence because they are spoken of. Thus, Nagarjuna composed this treatise to teach, by means of both reasoning and the tradition's scripture, the core of dependent arising to those who, because of the supposed reality of objects, thought of them in terms of "permanent and ceasing, identical and different," and yet thought in their heart that objects, like the horn of a rabbit, do not exist.

Those who believe in self-existence teach that entities really exist because of the expressions "annihilated or born, ceasing or permanent, coming or going, different or identical" that the Buddha used as worldly conventions. Thus, we deny that these are ultimately true. Also, those who meditate or dispute on the nature of "reality" meditate or dispute relying on these terms. For example, some say that each entity is a continuous series of momentarily appearing and disappearing (real) elements. Others say consciousness or matter or substances or the ether or time or the person or the self is permanent (and hence eternal). Thus, a lot of people dispute the identity or difference of the self and the body, fire and fuel, cause and effect, characteristics and what is characterized, and part and whole. Some people say that the substance of an entity goes together with its characterizing mark. Some say fundamental particles and the mind are immovable. Others say the self and the person are movable. Thus, we deny all eight terms.

Opponent: Why do you not mention "birth" before "annihilation"? If anything is produced, it will be annihilated — e.g., death is inherent in birth.

Reply: If death is inherent in birth, then you must think that death precedes birth — if a birth were not preceded by a death, the absurd consequence would be that the cycle of rebirth had a beginning. The cycle of rebirth has neither a beginning nor an end. Thus, one can say neither that birth precedes and annihilation follows or vice versa.

In addition, if birth came first and death followed, then birth would be devoid of death and one would be born immortal.

Opponent: There are instances where production is not preceded by annihilation. For example, a forest fire is preceded by the existence of trees; if there were no trees, there would be no fire.

Reply: But the trees were preceded by the annihilation of the seeds. So the production is preceded by an annihilation.

Opponent: No — the annihilation and production here are surely different. In this case, when the seed is annihilated, a sprout arises. If the sprout is annihilated, the sprout does not arise again.

Reply: In the case of both birth and death, what is really extinguished will not be produced again. It is an absurd eternalism if the same thing that is really extinguished will arise again. Nor is a god necessarily reborn as a god or an animal as an animal. If this were so, then rebirth would not be subject to our actions and emotions, and people would become deluded.

To assume the annihilated and the arisen are different is also incorrect. If the seed and sprout were different, then the worldly convention "cause and effect" could not exist either. But since this worldly convention exists, these two are treated as different. Also, if a sprout were different from the seed, then these worldly conventions would not exist. Since they exist, you cannot say the seed and sprout are different. What is different is different in relation to another (real) entity. What is not-different is not-different from another thing. What is dependent upon something else cannot be different from it.

Opponent: Nevertheless, if a seed exists it will be annihilated. But if it does not exist it will not be annihilated. Thus, arising comes first and annihilation follows.

Reply: In the case of the seed, the seed's annihilation comes first. But since the seed is not different from the plant making seeds, after the annihilation of the seed, the spout and a seed are also produced. As Master Arydeva said, "As in the example of the seed, there is no (real) beginning, no (real) cause, and thus no (real) arising."

Thus, in the case of birth and annihilation, there is no real substance preceding or following. The Master has listed annihilation first and birth only afterwards in order to teach that there is no real substance preceding or following.

1. *The Examination of Conditions*

[1] No entities whatsoever are found anywhere that have arisen from themselves, from another, from both themselves and another, or from no cause at all.

Opponent: Why is the expression "conditionality" merely a worldly convention?

Reply: Entities do not self-arise because that would be useless: they would already have to exist (by self-existence) for such a process to occur, and thus arising would not be necessary. In addition, the arisings would go on endlessly: if a real entity arises again after it already exists, the arisings would go on without end. Second, entities do not arise from other things because then everything would arise from everything else, which clearly does not occur. Third, entities cannot arise from both themselves and others, because the faults with each of the first two options would combine here. Finally, entities do not arise from no cause at all: if that were possible, anything would arise from anything. In addition, all actions would be pointless (because we could not control the consequences).

Thus, the arising of entities is not possible in any way, and thus the expression "arising" is a mere conventional usage.

[2] There are four conditions: the producing cause, objective support within the world, continuity with previous states, and overall influence. There is no fifth condition.

Opponent: Since entities only arise out of these four conditions, which differ from the entity that is produced, it is not correct that entities do not arise out of another entity.

Reply: If the four conditions from which you have formed the concept of "another" were really different from the entities produced, then the entities could also arise of different conditions. But that is impossible.

[3] The self-existence of entities is not found in their conditions. If there is no self-existing entity, there can be no entity that can be different either.

(Only real, self-existent entities are different from each other.) When entities are dependent upon conditions, real entities do not exist. If entities do not have existence of their own, how could their conditions be different from them? It is impossible. Since there are absolutely no real entities to be different, it is unreasonable to claim that entities arise out of real entities that are different from them. Other scriptural texts agree.

Opponent: If such conditions as "matter" exist, sensation will arise.

Reply: No. If you agree that a sensation that has not yet arisen arises out of conditions different from it, then how could that sensation have its own existence? If there is no self-existence, there also cannot be "other-existence" (i.e., the self-existence of something else, MK 15.3).

In addition, there is no self-existence of an entity in its conditions, or separate from its conditions, or in a combination of the two. If the entity is self-existent, then the conditions are without a purpose — what is the use of producing something that already exists? What is the purpose of "conditions" in the case of an already existing entity? (That is, how could conditions produce what already exists?) But what is not in the conditions can have no existence of its own because it cannot be different from those conditions (as the sprout and sensation examples showed).

Thus, if there is no entity having self-existence, there also can be no (real) entity that is different from it, and thus no other real entity out of which an entity could arise.

Opponent: The eye and the other sense-faculties are the causes of sensation since they are the creators of activity producing sensation and ending in sensation.

[4a] Activity does not have conditions, . . .

Activity is not inherent in the conditions. The sense-organs cannot be the creators of vision and so forth. Does the producing activity end in a sensation that is not yet produced or in an already-produced sensation? It cannot end in something that is not yet produced because it would have no place to stay. And if the sensation has not yet been produced, neither can the activity exist. If the activity does not exist, the produced activity cannot remain in it. Nor can the producing activity end in a sensation that is already produced, since the sensation is already produced and if it already exists it is not to be produced again. Nor is it possible to think that the producing activity exists just as the sensation is being produced.

Thus, the producing activity does not exist at all since it cannot end either in something already produced or in something not yet produced.

[4b] . . . nor does it not have conditions.

Nor can there be activity without conditions. If there were, than anything could arise out of anything and then any beginning would be meaningless.

Opponent: Then the conditions alone exist (without any power to act). Entities arise directly out of the conditions.

[4c] Moreover, conditions do not exist without the power to act, . . .

The sense-organs do not have the power to act. Thus, they are not the conditions of sensation. If they were the conditions, then anything could be the condition of anything, and anything could arise out of anything.

Opponent: Then the conditions are together with activity.

[4d] . . . nor with the power to act.

No conditions exist together with activity. As previously pointed out, activity is not inherent in the conditions and there is no activity without conditions (since the activity is not itself real). If there is no self-existent activity, the conditions cannot be together with it. To assume the conditions themselves provide the activity is useless since it is impossible for the conditions to be with or without activity.

Opponent: Since the activities arise in dependence on the conditions, they are the causes of the entities.

Reply: You are striking the air with your fists! No producing activity exists, and since it does not exist, the existence of conditions is impossible.

[5] Conditions are called "conditions" because something arises dependent upon something else. But as long as that "something" does not arise, why are the conditions not really non-conditions?

It is not reasonable that something that is a non-condition first later can become a condition. The absurd consequence of this would be that anything can become the condition of anything. Nor do the non-conditions become conditions by arising together with an entity since this could occur only if there are really existing conditions, which there are not.

The fallacy of "infinity" would also follow: if anything after it is dependent upon anything else can become a condition, then that resulting entity in the same way can become the condition of anything else, and so on and so on.

Thus, real conditions are impossible.

[6] A condition is not admitted for either what is not real or for what is real: if something is nonexistent, how could it have a condition? And if something is already existing, how could it have a condition?

Opponent: Because of the dependency connection, the conditions are the conditions of a (real) entity.

Reply: Is the dependency connection a condition of a not-yet-existing entity or of an already-existing entity? If something is not yet existing, how could it have a condition? And if something already exists, how could it have a condition? How can threads be the condition of non-existing cloth?

Opponent: From the threads the cloth is produced. Thus, they are the condition for it.

Reply: It is impossible for a nonexisting entity to have a cause. A real cause is impossible, but you claim that something becomes a cause by a future production of an entity. But there is no real production anywhere or at any time. If there are no real entities, what can be a "condition"? From where does your condition, depending on a future production, become real? And if the entity already exists, the existence of a "condition" is impossible.

Thus, the threads are not the conditions of an already-existing cloth.

Opponent: We do not say that the activities of the conditions are in the entity produced. But the producing cause of the cloth is the threads.

Rely: If an entity already exists, a producing cause is unreasonable. After something exists, it cannot be produced.

Opponent: When the essence of an entity unfolds itself, it is the cause the produces the entity.

[7] So too, when no existing, nonexisting, or existing-and-nonexisting basic phenomena are produced, how is a producing cause admitted?

If the element that is to be produced by a cause already exists, what is the use of a producing cause? If an existing entity could be produced again, there would never be an end to arisings. And if something already exists, there is no cause, and thus an alleged cause could not produce any existing thing. Nor can something real produce something not real simply because what is not real does not exist. If something that is not real might have a producing cause, then a horn of a rabbit could be produced. To suppose that an entity arises out of a cause is impossible because a real cause is not possible. And if an entity does not exist, then what would have a cause and what would the cause be?

In addition, how does what is a cause become a "cause"? If there are no real entities at all, then there is nothing to which the characterization "this is a cause, and that is not a cause" could be applied. Nor could what is not real produce anything not real. Nor could it produce something that is both real and not real because "existence" and "nonexistence" cannot exist together and because the possibility of the production of both what is existing and what is not existing has already been shown to be absurd.

Thus, nothing can produce either anything real or unreal. Thus, a producing cause is impossible.

Opponent: But the condition of "the objective support within the world" must exist because it is the basis of consciousness and other entities.

[8ab] Something real is shown to be unsupported by another real thing.

There can be no such conditions if there are no real entities. "Objective support" means there is a real entity to support. But since there in no real entity, there is no real entity to be supported. Thus, you assume with your imagination that the support has an entity to combine with when there is in fact no entity.

[8cd] When a thing exists without such a support, what purpose would an objective support serve?

And if an entity is real without having such a support, why do you assume there is an unnecessary support?

Opponent: You do not understand the tradition's texts. When an entity arises, it is produced by an objective support and that support is the entity's object. Thus, we say that the support is combined with the entity.

Reply: If so, the entity at first has no object. How then will it later acquire an object? The entity does not exist and does not become real — how will support come to be exist? If the condition is not itself real, how can the entity be produced by it? If the object is not real, then the support cannot be combined with it.

Opponent: The immediately preceding annihilation of one entity is a condition for the production of another entity. Thus, the "immediately preceding" condition must exist.

[9] When basic phenomena have not arisen first, cessation does not occur. Thus, the condition of "continuity" is not applicable. And when the reality has ceased, what condition applies?

If no real entities are produced, it is not possible for them to pass away. What could cause the unproduced to pass away? There is no annihilation (of what is real). If a seed must be annihilated before the production of a sprout, then what will be the cause of the sprout? If the seed is annihilated and thus does not exist, how can it be the cause? And what is the cause of the annihilation of the seed? And how can the annihilation of the seed be the cause of a (real and thus) unproduced sprout?

Thus, your supposition results in the absurd consequence that both annihilation and production are without a producing cause. Nothing is without conditions.

Opponent: Even if the seed is annihilated exactly at the time the sprout is produced, the continuity condition exists.

Reply: Even if the sprout is produced, how will the seed's annihilation be a condition of it? And what is the cause of the seed's annihilation if the seed is immediately annihilated when the producing cause producing the sprout has ceased? And what will be the producing cause of the sprout? Again, your supposition results in the absurd consequence that both annihilation and production are without a producing cause.

If you say that the sprout is produced just as the seed is being annihilated, then both the annihilated and the produced exist at the same time. If the seed is not annihilated until the sprout has been produced, then both entities exist at the same time, and so how can there be a continuity with the immediately proceeding condition? So too, if the annihilation and production occur at precisely the same time, still an immediately preceding condition is impossible because of the simultaneity.

Thus, there can be no immediately preceding condition. In addition, no real entity can be produced; and if no entities are produced, it is not possible for them to cease (since they are real and therefore permanent). And if they (are not real and so) do not exist, what is there that could cease? Either way, there is no immediately preceding condition. Even if they could pass away, what would be the producing cause? Even if entities were produced, how would annihilation of other entities be a producing cause?

Opponent: Still, there is the condition of "overall influence" — i.e., if this exists, that arises; if this does not exist, that will not arise.

[10] Since the existence of entities without self-existence is not found, we cannot say "This reality existing, that one comes to be."

We have demonstrated that entities lack self-existence and thus that there are no real entities. This being so, there is no entity of which we could say "This existing, that arises." If there is no "this," then it is impossible to say "that arises." Thus, what and of what will there be the condition of "overall influence"? Thus, the last condition is impossible too.

Opponent: Even though it cannot be said that entities are produced by the conditions, the conditions nevertheless do exist because the effects arise out of them — e.g., the sprout arises out of such conditions as the seed. Since we experience that the effects arise out of conditions, the conditions are known to be the conditions of the effects.

[11] *An effect does not exist in conditions that are either separate or combined. And how can what does not exist in the conditions come from those conditions?*

Opponent: The effect arises; thereby, the conditions are real.

Reply: The effect does not exist separately from the conditions nor in the totality of them. So how could the effect arise out of the conditions? And if the effect does not arise out of the conditions, how can they be real conditions?

Opponent: The effect preexists in the conditions.

Reply: If so, the conditions are rendered without a purpose since something that has already been produced does not need to be produced again.

In addition, does the complete effect or only part of it exist in each condition? If the former, then there are not several conditions and the absurd consequence follows that the effect arises out of each condition and independently of the other conditions. If the latter, then the absurd consequence follows that a part of the effect arises out of each of the conditions independently of the other (parts and) conditions. Neither of these alternatives can be accepted.

Opponent: Nevertheless, the effect arises out of those conditions.

[12] *If the effect that develops from conditions does not exist in those conditions, why does it not develop without those conditions?*

If you make the distinction between conditions and non-conditions, we say that the effect exists neither in the conditions nor in the non-conditions. If the effect arises out of the conditions without preexisting in them, then why does it not arise out of non-conditions too? To say that the effect preexists in the conditions and does not arise out of the non-conditions is the fancy of your mind. Thereby, the production of the effect is rendered impossible. And if no effect is produced, how could there be real conditions?

Opponent: Still, the effect does arise out of the conditions. We say the effect is from causes — i.e., it is composed of the conditions themselves. For example, the cloth is composed of the threads themselves.

[13] The effect is not constituted by its conditions. Conditions are not self-created. So how can an effect that arises from conditions that are themselves not self-created be created by those conditions?

Conditions themselves are not self-created. They have no true reality, do not possess themselves, are not composed of themselves, and are empty of self-existence. If you assume that the effect is composed of such (reality-less) conditions, how can you form the concept "condition-composed"? If the threads ultimately were real, they could be self-composed and the cloth could be composed of such threads. But if the threads are empty of self-existence, how could the cloth be composed of them? Aryadeva has said: "If the cloth is made of threads but the threads are made of something else, how can anything not made of itself produce anything else?" (That is, only the real can produce anything, and what is not made of itself is not real.)

Since the conditions themselves are ultimately not real, are not composed of themselves, and are empty of self-existence:

[14ab] Therefore, an effect is not made either by conditions, nor by non-conditions.

No effect is composed of conditions or non-conditions. If it is impossible for the black cloth to be composed of black threads (as part of its conditions), how would it be possible to say that it is composed of white threads (that are part of its non-conditions)?

Opponent: Conditions do exist because what are non-conditions is certain: we can see what is certainly a condition and what is not a condition. It is butter and never oil that is produced from milk and neither is produced from sand. Since the matter that is the milk is the condition of butter and not the condition of oil, therefore conditions really exist.

[14cd] But in the absence of a (real) effect, where are conditions or non-conditions found?

Both "condition" and "non-condition" exist only with regard to an effect. But if the effect does not exist (i.e., is not real), where can conditions or non-conditions be found? Thus, if the existence of the effect is impossible, neither conditions nor non-conditions can exist.

Since there is neither an effect, conditions, nor non-conditions, the expression "producing" has been shown to be a mere worldly usage.

18. *The Examination of the Self*

Objection: If views about becoming and non-becoming cannot express reality because they imply the fault of permanence and impermanence, please explain what is real and how it can be attained.

Reply: Seeing that a self and what belongs to a self do not exist externally or internally is the ultimate truth. By the meditative cultivation of this view of reality, one will comprehend reality. Those who desire to see the truth should carefully consider this: is the "self" simply the bodily aggregates or it is something other than them? Everything that exists is said to be either different or identical, but in the final analysis both alternatives are not possible.

[1] If the self were the aggregates making up a person (the material form and the mental components), it would be subject to arising and ceasing. If the self were other than these aggregates, it would not have the characteristics of the aggregates.

If the self were simply the bodily aggregates, it, like the aggregates, would be marked by birth and decay. There would also be many selves (since there are five aggregates), and it would be nonsense to advocate the doctrine of "a self" since the term would be synonymous with "the aggregates."

On the other hand, it is also impossible that the self is different from the bodily aggregates. If the self is different from the aggregates, it would lack the defining characteristics of the aggregates, such as "birth" and "decay." Without birth and decay, the self must be permanent. But if the self is permanent, all undertakings (to achieve a better rebirth or nirvana) would be of no avail since something permanent cannot change or cause anything. Thus, the notion that "a self exists" is meaningless since it could not be subject to the worldly life or ceasing from the worldly life.

[2ab] When the self does not exist, how can there be anything belonging to the self? From the stilling of the sense of "self" and "belonging to a self," one is free of the ideas of "mine" and "I."

When the concept "self" is analyzed, it proves to be totally unjustified. So how can there be anything "belonging to the self"? Anything that is supposed to belong to the self must be absent as soon as the self is absent, and thus how can it be reasonable to claim "this belongs to that"? Thus, the term "mine" is also unjustified.

[2cd] From the stilling of the sense of "self" and "belonging to a self," one is free of the ideas of "mine" and "I."

Thus, not to see an "I" or anything as "mine" either internally or externally is to see reality. The yogin meditatively cultivates this and makes it firm. By developing and explaining this truth, one's devotion to "a self" or "mine" is stilled. After that, one becomes free of a sense of "I" and free of a sense of "mine."

Objection: But it is definitely the self that becomes selfless and mineless when it sees reality correctly. Thus, a "self" and "mine" must exist.

[3] One who is free of the ideas of "mine" and "I" is not found. In addition, one who sees someone as "free of mine" or "free of I" still does not see correctly.

A "self" that is said to be "selfless" and "mineless" does not exist. The word "self" is based on the acquisition of the bodily aggregates (quoting the Buddha). There can be no "self" that becomes selfless and mineless. And if there were such a self, it could not become selfless and mineless.

Those who have a sense of "I" and "mine" would have wrong views, and thus seeing reality would be absent. (Aryadeva's CS 10.20 quoted.) One who perceives a self that has no "I" or "mine" does not perceive reality — his mental eye is impaired and he has a wrong view. (Thus, seeing a self that is without a self as real is not the same as seeing the person as selfless; one still see reality through the prism of "self-existence.")

[4] When "mine" and "I" are destroyed with respect to both outer and inner phenomena, the acquisition of a new rebirth is stopped; and from the stopping of such acquisition, future births are destroyed.

Once the false belief in an "I" or "mine," internally and externally, has ceased, then there is no acquirer nor anything to be acquired. The fourfold acquisition — desire, views, rules of proper conduct, and the doctrine of a self — is thus stopped. When acquisition has stopped, a new cycle of rebirth is stopped. By the cessation of cyclic becoming, birth ceases, and this is called "liberation." One who thus sees things as they really are attains reality. By attaining reality, one is liberated.

[5] From the destruction of the afflictions and karmic actions, there is the liberation from rebirth. The afflictions arise from thoughts that make distinctions between entities. These thoughts come from projecting distinctions onto reality. But such conceptual projections cease through emptiness.

In the cycle of rebirths, action and mental afflictions are the causes of a new birth. Such action and afflictions arise from discriminations of objects devoid of reality and so do not exist by their own self-existence. Each affliction arises from insignificant discriminations since with regard to the same object one person desires it, another hates it, and another is confused by it. Thus, the afflictions arise from discriminations. Karmic action are the acts of the body, speech, and mind of one afflicted.

These groundless discriminations arise from worldly conceptual projections. Those whose mind adheres to the notion "This is real" concerning such phenomena as worldly profit and loss form discriminations among the phenomena arising from their conceptual projections. (That is, the mental discrimination of distinct concepts arises from the process of our projecting distinctions onto what is real.)

However, this process of conceptual projection is stopped by emptiness. By understanding that the own nature of entities is in fact emptiness, conceptual projection is stopped. Thus, such projecting is stopped by understanding emptiness. Emptiness is the that-ness of reality, and only by meditatively cultivating emptiness is reality attained. The attainment of reality is called "liberation." (Aryadeva's CS 12.23 quoted.)

Objection: If there is no "self" or anything "mine," why have the buddhas occasionally taught that there is a self?

Reply: They have not even advocated a doctrine of non-self! "Thus, it (the self) is neither different from acquisition nor identical to it. There is no self apart from acquisition, nor is it true that it does not exist (MK 24.8)."

[6] The idea "There is a self" has been disclosed. That "There is no self" has been taught. But by the Buddha it has been taught "There is neither the self nor indeed what is not the self whatsoever."

There are some people who need discipline who cherish views such as "This world does not exist," "The other world does not exist," and "Self-produced beings do not exist." Their minds are disturbed by clinging to false views; they do not care about life after death and transgress principles that lead to a hellish rebirth. The Buddha indicated a "self" in order to dispel the view of "no self" of those who were heading for the great abyss of a hell. (That is, the correct view that actions have consequences, as in R 43-44, required the Buddha to teach that there is a self that continues after death to those people who did not believe in any life after death and thus were acting in a manner that would lead them to one of the hells.)

Other people who also need discipline accept the view that there is a (real) actor, who performs good and bad acts and who reaps their karmic good and bad results, and a (real) self subject to bondage and liberation. To these people, the Buddha taught "There is no self" in order to repudiate any view about a (real) self of those beings who are mired in the ocean of rebirth, who have been grasped by the monster of the belief in "I" and "mine," and who cherish the joys of life.

But there are well-disciplined people who have a large collection of merit, who are capable of crossing the ocean of rebirth, and who are attentive to the discourses on the ultimate meaning. To them, the buddhas have taught that the everyday illusion deludes fools. At this stage, he taught "There is neither self nor non-self." (Aryadeva's CS 8.20 quoted).

But there is also another group of people: to them, a "self" has also been indicated to exist by those who do not perceive the truth and who without understanding anything imagine that they understand everything. They follow their own conjectures and fear that if there is no self then all this is without a foundation.

In addition, there are others who have taught that there is no self. But their minds are muddled, and with an unreal self they cause misery in the world. To them, action and the field of rebirth is unintelligible. (That is, they deny any life after death and not merely that there is no real self.)

From a desire to benefit the world, the buddhas, who have attained the knowledge of liberation without coverings, who know everything, and who see everything, have taught the middle path without "I" or "mine." It is absolutely clear that these two do not exist. Rather: "When this exists, that arises, but when this does exist, that does not arise."

[7a] When the domain of thought has ceased,...

When it is seen that all entities are empty, what can be named disappears. Thus, conceptual projection is stopped by emptiness. When the named exists, conceptual projection arises dependently upon it. But when the named does not exist, conceptual projection is without a basis, and so how can it arise?

[7b] ... then what can be named has ceased.

The nameable disappears when the domain of thought disappears. The domain of thought is an object with form and so forth. Since the domain of thought has disappeared for a yogin, form and so forth have disappeared and thus the nameable has also disappeared. If the nameable is in fact form and so forth, how can nameable exist when these are not present?

[7cd] The nature of all things is, like nirvana, unarisen and unceased.

The domain of thought disappears because the nature of things is, like nirvana, unborn and unceased. When perceiving correctly, the yogin understands that the unborn and undestroyed nature of things is like nirvana. Thus, the domain of thought for him disappears. Thus, conceptual projection is stopped by emptiness. (Aryadeva's CS 14.25 quoted.)

The difference between the view "This world does not exist, the other world does not exist, and self-produced beings do not exist" and the view "All things are unborn and unceased" is enormous. Because you fail to discern the meaning of emptiness you consider those two to be similar. In our school, one who is unreflectingly even-minded and one who is reflectively even-minded may be similar to the extent that they are both even-minded, but there still is a very great difference between them since one who is unreflectively even-minded is fettered by the root-ignorance whereas the other one is cherished by the buddhas. In the case at hand: the one, who perceives that this world does not exist, has a mind confused by the root-ignorance; the one, who perceives that this world is unborn and unceased because it is empty of all entities, is backed by cognition.

Not seeing the unreality of the world, someone may make a mere verbal statement "This world does not exist." For example: a blind man could state that a certain place is pleasant, but since he cannot see its beauty, due to his lacking sight, he will err and stumble as he walks. Likewise, someone may state that this world does not exist but lacking the eye of knowledge he does not see the unreality of the world and so he is defiled by errors.

Take another example: during a dispute, two witnesses to an event are appointed who give the same testimony, but one has actually seen the event in question with his own eyes, whereas the other testifies because he was bribed or was partial to one side in the case. When both are required to give evidence, the second one relates the true story, but not being an eye-witness he is lying and unvirtuous and brings disgrace upon himself. When the first one gives evidence, not only does he speak the truth but he also is virtuous and honorable, for he was an eye-witness to the case. Likewise, one who has personal knowledge of the fact that all entities are empty, and, since they are empty, unborn, and undestroyed, is expert and laudable, while one who has not seen emptiness is defiled by the error of views and despised by the wise. (The *Song in Praise of the Perfected Wisdom*, verse 15 quoted.)

Thus, emptiness is the object of those who reality-knowing mental eye is clear, whereas it is not the object of those whose mental eye is enveloped in the profound darkness of the root-ignorance.

Your understanding is accompanied by a conceit about your learning that makes you equate us with those who hold views of self-existence, and you charge us accordingly without acting so toward those who advocate being and non-being. But we are at variance with this. Statements about being and non-being take place under the sway of views. We see that entities are unreal like the horns of a rabbit, but in order to avoid defects of speech, we do not say "Being does not exist" or "Nonbeing does not exist." We state that "being" and "nonbeing" are like reflections because they are dependently arisen. It is as if you would sell a glass pearl for the price of a sapphire. You would not obtain the expected profit and you would be shown to be despicable.

Objection: If all entities are like nirvana, won't all undertakings be useless since there would then be no difference between virtuous conduct and unvirtuous conduct?

Reply: If you see reality as it really is, is there any such thing as an "undertaking"? For when the domain of thought has ceased, then what can be named has ceased. One whose mind is perplexed may show active engagement, but for one who sees reality there is nothing further to be done. (Aryadeva's CS 8.9 quoted.) Thus, the statement that "Things are like nirvana" has been spoken from the point of view of ultimate truth.

[8ab] Everything is real, and everything is not real; everything is both real and not real.

The Buddha said "What is acknowledged to exist in the world, I also affirm that to exist. What is acknowledged not to exist in the world, I also deny that to exist." Thus, when it comes to worldly, conventional action, the Buddha also affirms what is acknowledged by the world to be real, and affirms to be unreal what is acknowledged by the world to be unreal, and affirms to be both real and unreal what is acknowledged by the world as both real and unreal.

For example, when a monk was asked which god was which in a picture, he said "Indeed, you know that there are no such gods for they are only pictures on the wall, but they are real by virtue of worldly convention." He did not commit the fault of lying. Likewise, the Buddha, though he has seen that things are empty of self-existence, still has said that by virtue of worldly convention "This is real, this is not real, and this is both real and not real."

[8cd] The buddhas' teaching is this: everything is neither real nor not real.

Ultimately, the teaching of the buddhas is "Nothing is real or not real." How can one claim that things that are empty of self-existence — like illusions, dreams, reflections, and echos — are real or unreal? Thus, the Buddha's doctrine is free of the faults of existence, and nonexistence and it elucidates the ultimate point of view in which none of the founders of other traditions have any share.

Some claim "Everything arises from what is real." Others claim "An effect did not exist before and arises from a cause." Others claim "An effect arises from what is real and unreal." The teaching of the buddhas is "There is nothing real or unreal, although one can indeed form mental designations of entities based on causes and conditions." It has been said "Katyayana, this world rests on duality. It most rests on 'real' and 'not real.'" Thus, though the buddhas affirm "this" or "that" according to worldly usage, those who wish to see the that-ness of reality as it really is must not cling to the words spoken according to worldly conventions, but must grasp the reality.

The Buddha, although he saw that entities are empty of self-existence, did say "This is real; this is unreal; this is both real and unreal." The Buddha's teaching is that an entity is simply designated due to causes and conditions, but it does not exist or not *not* exist. How can it said that entities that are empty of self-existence — like magical illusions, dreams, mirages, reflections, and echoes — are real or unreal? Thus, the Buddha's teaching is "not real, not unreal," free of the faults of existence and nonexistence, not in common with the founders of other traditions who elucidate the ultimate nature of reality.

Opponent: what is the defining characteristic of what is real?

[9] The characteristic of what is actually real is this: not dependent upon another, peaceful, free of being projected upon by conceptual projections, free of thoughts that make distinctions, and without multiplicity.

"Not dependent upon another" means that it cannot be known from others — i.e., it is self-evident without the teaching of a tradition and evident to oneself. "Peaceful" means it is empty of self-existence. "Free of being projected upon by conceptual projections" means that it is devoid of worldly phenomena. "Free of thoughts that make distinctions" means that it cannot be conceived as "this" or "that." "Without multiplicity" means that it does not vary whether it is this or that. Since it is free of distinctions, it cannot be projected upon by conceptual projections. Since it is free of conceptual projections by worldly phenomena, it is peaceful. Since it is peaceful, it is without multiplicity. Thus, the defining characteristic of reality is "knowing that nature directly oneself, not learning it from another."

Here is another defining characteristic of what is real:

[10] Whatever arises dependently upon another thing is not that thing, nor is it different from that thing. Therefore, it is neither annihilated nor eternal.

Whatever arises dependently upon another thing is not identical to that thing, nor is it different from it. If it were different from the other thing, it would come into being without it. Since it does not come into being without it, it is not different from it. For example, a sprout arises dependently upon a seed. The seed is not identical to the sprout, nor is the sprout different from the seed since the sprout does not have a nature different from the seed. Thus, what is dependent upon something else is neither identical to it nor different from it, nor is it either annihilated or eternal. Indeed, if the sprout were identical to the seed, the seed would be eternal, which it is not. So too, if the seed were one thing and the sprout another, then the seed would be annihilated since it would be totally destroyed, but since the sprout is not different from the seed, the seed is not destroyed. (Aryadeva's CS 10.25 quoted.)

Thus, since one cannot say that something is identical to or different form something else, it is neither eternal nor annihilated. Thus, this is a defining characteristic of what is real.

[11] Not one, not diverse, not annihilated, not eternal — this is the immortal teaching of the buddhas, the guides of the world.

Thus, the investigation of the way to the heavens and to liberation is (to determine) that what is real is not one, not multiple, not annihilated, and not eternal. It is beyond the faults of one or multiple, annihilated or eternal. It is very profound.

This exposition of what is real from the ultimate point of view is a happiness beyond the world and all things worldly. Thus, it is the ambrosial message of the buddhas who know everything, who see everything, who are armed with the ten powers (to help all sentient beings), and who are friendly without a personal motive. It must be realized directly. Thus, those who are proficient in this will immediately achieve success as they personally experience reality. Those who finished the requisites of both (merit and knowledge) will certainly achieve success in another rebirth in establishing the immediate method. (Aryadeva's CS 8.22 quoted.)

[12] When the fully-enlightened buddhas no longer appear, and when the disciples have disappeared, the knowledge of the solitary buddhas will come forth without a teacher.

Among those who have exerted only a small effort in this life, perhaps there will not arise any buddhas or listeners (disciples) may vanish. But granting that solitary buddhas, who achieve enlightenment by themselves (and do not teach others), will arise due to their prior efforts. Such persons achieve the fruit of the instruction that is like ambrosia. Thus, those who desire to leave the wilderness of the cycle of rebirths must, when desiring to obtain the state of immorality, achieve that state through effort. Certainly it is only through this that the ultimate truth about reality is achieved.

* * *

Notes

Dedication. Note that Buddhapalita brings up early in his Commentary that the Buddha utilized worldly conventions to communicate his doctrine.

Also note that the idea of a *beginning* to the cycle of rebirths and by extension the universe is considered abuse. Aristotle would agree concerning the universe, but most theists believe that it is the idea that the universe did *not have a beginning* that is absurd.

Verse 18.7cd. The example of the two witnesses in court highlights the point that the enlightened *see* the emptiness of the world experientially, not merely *subscribe to the idea* that the world is empty of self-existence.

Verse 18.8cd. This discusses the fourth alternative as the Buddha's final position: "everything is neither real nor not real" rather than "real," "unreal," or "both real and unreal." In this ontology, entities are merely designations that neither ultimately exist nor not exist; rather, they are like dreams and magical tricks that arise dependently but do not totally not exist.

A reference to the *Discourse to Katyayana* also occurs in MK 15.7. Also see Jones 2010: 107.

Verse 18.12. "Solitary buddhas (*pratyeka-buddhas*)" become enlightened without the aid of a teacher who knows the total path to enlightenment. But in this text they are deemed to be out of the cycle of rebirths.

* * *

Bhavaviveka
(ca. 500 - 580)

Bhavaviveka (also called Bhavya or Bhaviveka, among other variations) lived from the early to late sixth century C.E. and may have come from a Brahmin Hindu family in the south of India. (For the legends, see Eckel 2008: 9-12.) He was twenty years or so younger than Buddhapalita, but he apparently did not study Buddhapalita's work until after the latter's death. His major innovation was to introduce into the Madhyamaka school the idea of the independent defense of Madhyamaka theses, as discussed in the Commentary. In doing so, Bhavya was explicitly going against Nagarjuna's method exemplified in Buddhapalita's work. In fact, Bhavya was directly responding to his esteemed older contemporary — not that he thought of Buddhapalita as an opponent who belonged to another subtradition of the Madhyamaka. He influenced Madhyamaka thought in India, but he had less impact in Tibet and East Asia. He also was the first Madhyamika to discuss non-Buddhist schools extensively. Indeed, he was one of India's first systematic comparative philosophers — indeed, "no Indian Mahayana thinker played a more crucial rule in mapping the landscape of Indian philosophy and defining the relationships of its different traditions" (Eckel 2008: 3).

Bhavya's commentary on the *Fundamental Verses of the Middle Way* — the *Lamp of Insight (Prajna-pradipa)* — no longer exists in Sanskrit. For English translations of various parts, see Eckel 2008: 449-450.

The first text translated here — the *Summary of the Meaning of the Middle Way* — is a short work that places the doctrine of "two truths" as central. It may well be not be by Bhavya but by a much later author, perhaps the eighth century or even later (Ruegg 1990: 68). However, it is in keeping with his thought. It too no longer exists in Sanskrit, and the translation here is based on the reconstruction of the Sanskrit in Sastri 1931.

After that, selections from *Verses on the Heart of the Middle Way* are presented. There is also a commentary — the *Flame of Reason (Tarka-jvala)* — ascribed to Bhavya that is no longer extant in Sanskrit, as are some missing lines. Some material based on translations from the Tibetan versions is included here. It is treated here as if it were part of the work, although it was probably not written by Bhavya himself (Ruegg 1990: 65). First, a few introductory verses from Chapter 1 are translated. This is followed by parts of Chapter 3. This is the longest chapter — 356 verses out of a work of 928 verses in the Sanskrit version (Gokhale & Bahulkar 1985: 76). In comparison, the entire *Fundamental Verses of the Middle Way* is only 422 verses. This chapter is also the most central chapter of the work. It involves the knowledge of reality (*tattva-jnana*). The last third of this chapter involves the nature of the Buddha and is of less general philosophical interest. (For a translation, see Eckel 1992.)

The first three chapters of this text constitute a work in themselves — the first chapter discusses maintaining the thought of enlightenment (the *bodhi-chitta*); the second analogizes the traditional aspects of a silent Indian ascetic (*muni*) in terms of Mahayana virtues (see Gokhale 1972). The chapters after Chapter 3 provide a tour of Indian philosophy — in Chapter 9, he even refers to the magi from Persia.

The other chapter chosen for inclusion here concerns Vedanta. It is of interest because Bhavya lived two hundred years before Shankara, the most famous teacher of Advaita Vedanta, and before any specifically theistic Vedantist traditions developed. Thus, it shows a Buddhist view of an earlier Vedanta. (See Eckel 2008: 450-51 for a list of English translations of the other available chapters.)

* * *

Summary on the Meaning of the Middle Way (*Madhyamaka-artha-samgraha*)

[1] I bow to the glorious one! I continually pay homage to the buddhas, the great victorious ones who realized the truth of nonarising, but who, out of compassion for the worldly, continue to live in the world of rebirths until the end of the cycle of birth and death and yet remain without stain.

[2] I have composed this brief work to make intelligible the true meaning of the doctrine of "two truths." [3] The teaching of all the buddhas is, in brief, that truth is twofold — the ultimate and the conventional.

[4] Ultimate truth is free of all conceptual projection. It is of two types: the ultimate truth that can be expressed, and the ultimate truth that cannot be expressed. [5] The former is of two kinds: the ultimate truth expressed in terms of argument, and the ultimate truth expressed in terms of arising.

[6] The "ultimate truth expressed in terms of argument" is concerned with the reasons refuting the four options concerning arising. (That is, the argument that something arises from itself, from something else, from both itself and something, and from neither itself or something else.) The "ultimate truth expressed in terms of arising" negates the true arising of every apparent entity.

[7] What is empty of all conceptual projection, clear and subtle, is known as the "ultimate truth that cannot be expressed in words." [8] The ultimate truth is approximately this: totally empty of the two extremes of "being" and "nonbeing" (i.e., neither eternal nor totally nonexistent).

[9] "Conventional truth," as it is called, is also known to be of two types: "authentic conventional truths" and "inauthentic conventional truths." [10] Something that has the capacity to produce results is called an "authentic conventional truth," and what appears conventionally but is without such a power is called an "inauthentic conventional truth." [11] The latter is of two kinds: "with mental discriminations," and "without mental discriminations." An "inauthentic conventional truth with a mental discrimination" is, for example, taking a rope to be a snake. An "inauthentic conventional truth without a mental discrimination" is, for example, perceiving two moons (due to a physical defect in the eye rather than our imagination).

[12] Thus, it must be taught that everything comes within the domain of the "two truths." Having realized the meaning of this doctrine, complete perfection is achieved.

[13] May the virtuous act of my composing this tract procure to all sentient beings what they desire!

* * *

Notes

Verses 3-10. The distinction of "ultimate truth (*parama-artha*)" and "conventional truth (*samvrti*)" is a major point in Madhyamaka thought and is discussed below in the Commentary.

Verse 4. It is the distinction of two types of higher truth that suggests this work is not by Bhavya: higher truths that can be conceptualized or expressed (*saparyaya-paramartha*) and higher truths that cannot (*aparyaya-paramartha*). There is no other reference to this idea in any of his works (Ruegg 1990: 67). Verse 3.27 draws a different distinction between higher truths based on the idea of conceptual projection (*prapancha*). The distinction between two types of lower truth is assumed in MKV 3.7 and 3.12.

Verse 5. "Argument (*yukti* or *nyaya*)" is epistemic in nature. It concerns our reasons (*hetus*) and also our concepts. The other type of higher truth — involving "arising" — is ontological, i.e., involving the nature of reality.

Verse 6. On the four options, see Jones 2010: 155-57. N. Ayyaswami Sastri (1931: 43), following another tradition, sees the four options here in terms of four oppositions: (1) birth and death, (2) immorality and extinction, (3) existence and nonexistence, and (4) phenomena and emptiness.

Verse 11. "Mental discrimination (*vikalpa*)" is related to conceptual projection (*prapancha*): it involves seeing reality in terms of discrete entities corresponding to our conceptualizations. Seeing a rope as a snake involves imposing our conception (our idea of a snake derived from our experience and knowledge) onto what is really there. Seeing two moons due to an defect in our vision does not involve our conceptions in any way. (This image is also used in Advaita.) It is an experience free of conceptual mistakes, and no correction to our knowledge will change the experience. Thus, there are nonconceptual experiences on both the conventional and ultimate levels, although those on the conventional level involve error.

Selections from
Verses on the Heart of the Middle Way
(Madhyamaka-hrdaya-karikas)

1. Maintaining the Thought of Enlightenment

[1-3] Homage to the Master whose speech is without error who from compassion promulgated by means of words the that-ness of reality that is without words, inexpressible, not knowable, not a receptacle storing mental phenomena, without any defining characteristics, unascertainable as "this" or "that," free of mental distinctions, without beginning or end, auspicious and thus free of calamities, without mental constructs (of a perceiver, object perceived, and perception, or of a self or nonself), without any false appearance, without any material or immaterial sign, without the embellishment of birth, duration, and destruction, neither dual nor non-dual, tranquil and so is realized through tranquil knowledge, and outside of the range of intellectual cognition and so the insight into the ultimate truth comes through the inaction of intellectual activity. "That-ness" is a synonym of "such-ness," the fundamental realm, and emptiness. It can be conceived only through the method of nonconception.

[4] With whatever abilities I possess, I will strive here briefly to guide in the intelligibility of the truth that is like ambrosia. This truth was proclaimed by those who, having taken a vow to work forever for the welfare of others, dedicated all their of understanding to the attainment of the great enlightenment.

3. Quest for the Knowledge of Reality

[1] The one who has an eye consisting of knowledge and not another eye is the one who sees. Thus, an intelligent person concentrates on the quest for the knowledge of reality. [2] Even a person who is physically blind but is intelligent sees the three worlds (the realm of desire and the formed and formless realm created by meditation) without obstructions. Such a person sees the objects he wants to see, whether they are far away, subtle, or concealed. [3] But a person who is bereft of intelligence is sightless even with

a thousand eyes since he does not see the truly real path to the heavens through wholesome actions and to release through the noble Eightfold Path.

[4] One whose eye is opened by insight does not proceed with giving, ethical conduct, and so forth out of desire for their special fruits. For longing for the fruits in this life and future life is a poisonous thorn. Acting out of expectations of the fruit is poisonous because it is a hindrance to becoming released. [5] Instead, he strives, out of compassion and for omniscience, for the threefold purity of mind, word, and deed in his acts of giving and so forth. But his mind is not fixed there either. Moreover, there is a threefold purity of conforming to "emptiness" because it is free of the apprehension of a giver, gift, or recipient; conforming to the "signless" because it is free of the false view of a real entity, false views that deny causation, and the false views of eternalism and total nonexistence; and conforming to the "unfixed" because there is nothing to crave in the world of sense-desire and in the formed and formless realms created by meditation (i.e., free of any discrete realities to wish for, including enlightenment).

[6] Insight is ambrosia, giving satisfaction, the lamp of unimpeded light, the stairs to the throne of release, and the fire that burns the fuel of mental afflictions. [7ab] Insight falls into two parts because of the twofold nature of truth.

[7cd] Conventional truth is "true" if it accords with the discernment of the real object. [8] With the equipment of giving and so forth, knowledge, and merit complete, the characteristics and the connection between cause and its fruit are ascertained. [9] Healed by the continuous practice of great friendliness and pity, the insight that has as its basis the domain of the six senses and their objects is known as "conventional insight."

[10-11] Insight causes the destruction without remainder of the net of conceptualizations. When insight is still — free of all conceptual projection, being realized alone, without the mental discrimination of entities, beyond the realm of speech, seeing the appearanceless appearance of the such-ness of phenomena, with the disappearance of oneness and multiplicity, as free of impurities as the sky — then it is the insight belonging to the ultimate nature of reality.

Question: Of the two types of insight, which should be practiced?

Reply: Both. It is a matter of steps. [12] Indeed, without the stairs of true conventional truth, the ascent to the highest throne cannot be performed. [13] For this reason, understanding is first isolated by conventional truth. It is "truth" because it is the means of knowledge that leads to establishing all things in the world. Then, the self-characteristics and the general character-istics of phenomena need to be investigated thoroughly. Having finished the thorough investigation here, [14] the wise practice the concentration of the mind. In the knowledge of the texts, there is the cause of the other (higher) knowledge. [15] Just as one cannot see a face in muddy and rippling water, so the reality of phenomena cannot be seen by an unconcentrated mind that is covered by a disturbance and thus is scattered.

[16] Having been tied with the rope of mindfulness to the post of a meditative object, the mind, like an elephant that has wandered astray, should gradually be brought under control with the hook of insight. [17] Pride can be pacified by orienting the mind toward impermanence, emptiness, and selflessness. Depression can be alleviated by holding to the great doctrine or another object by repeated meditative practice. [18] The mind scattering by shifting attention can be concentrated by observing the danger caused by straying. The sluggish can be encouraged by observing the benefit of energy. [19] The mind not held together and also muddied by greed, hatred, and delusion is cleansed by the water of dependent arising, friendliness, and the unembellished (i.e., what is empty of distinctions). [20] Totally involved with a meditative object, and knowing skill and gentleness, he perceives correctly the pure, the immovable, and the pacified.

[21] After his mind is concentrated, the yogin annihilates the idea of the self-existence of phenomena, which can be grasped by conventional expression, with his insight in this manner. These phenomena are estab-lished by conventional truth, which is understood by the world's conven-tional expressions. [22] By the cognition of the analyzing mind, he asks how could entities be self-exist from the ultimate point of view? If entities are self-existent, then they are ultimately real. If not, then their cause should be searched for without prejudice. [23ab] With the torture caused by adhering to a proposition, he is never worthy of tranquility.

The Bodily Aggregates and the Four Elements

[23cd] The five bodily aggregates, the sense-fields, and the elements are conditioned and unconditioned phenomena. The conditioned phenomena are caused and associated with conditions. Unconditioned phenomena are distinct from arising, enduring, and ceasing. [24] The Buddha therefore proclaimed to the disciples the abandoning of the covering of the mental afflictions. The guiding principle is that ultimately there is no arising, no entity, no causation, no ceasing, nothing leading to formation, and no con-

cealment of the knowable. The teaching of the compassionate ones is for the removal of the defilements of the mental afflictions covering the knowable.

[25] First, the bodily aggregate of form is examined since it is most manifest to the gross intelligence. In addition, for that reason the four great elements are examined first. [26] As to that, from the point of view of ultimate truth, earth and the other elements (water, fire, and air) indeed do not have self-existence from the underlying great elements because they are produced and because they have a cause and conditions, like knowledge. "From the point of view of ultimate truth" means "in accordance with what is ultimately real." "Elements" are "things that came into existence" since they are self-generated or generated by other things. The negation of the self-existence of the elements is absolute (i.e., some other essence for these elements is not implied).

Objection: You accept the existence of the elements, and so if you negate them your proposition is hurt. There is no superior means to knowledge than seeing, and you yourself have seen the form of the elements with your own eyes and yet you still search for self-existence. Also, everyone in the world recognizes that the elements do the work of sustaining things. So too, the bodily aggregates and nature of the elements are well known even to savages. By negating what is generally known in the world, your proposition is again impossible to maintain.

Reply: There is no inconsistency between our proposition and experience. We make the qualification "from the point of view of ultimate truth." The Buddha established the self-existence and defining characteristics of phenomena from the conventional point of view; however, from the ultimate point of view, he proclaimed there is no self-existence to phenomena — no entities exist, let alone the self-existence of entities. The worldly do not understand the ultimate truth, just as the blind cannot see a precious jewel.

Objection: How can what is ultimately real transcend every intelligence when the negation of self-existence can be expressed? Shouldn't the negation be negated?

Reply: The ultimate truth is of two types. One is free of self-will and all that is worldly, without empty of mental impurities, and beyond conceptual projection. The second is with self-will, what is worldly, conceptual projection, and what leads to conceptual formation. Here, insight is qualified as the second type.

Objection: Since your objection is without its own proposition and only refutes another proposition, isn't it a mere cavil?

Reply: No — it is not a cavil because our proposition is "Everything is empty of self-existence."

Objection: You say knowledge too is produced.

Reply: Because it is the product of inquiry into what leads to the heavens and into what accomplishes release from rebirth. Whatever has a cause and worldly objectivity and is knowable and expressible does not have the great elements as their source of self-existence, as with knowledge. All means of knowledge should be understood according to this proposition. Having refuted the self-existence of the great elements, we can turn to specifics.

[27] The earth has no self-existent solidity because of its state as a great element, like the air (and hence is produced and is not self-existent). Nor is it a cause of support for things because it itself has causes, like water does (and thus cannot be an ultimate source of support for anything). There is no entity "earth" apart from water, fire, and air (i.e, they do not exist separately but only together). It is simply impossible to talk about a self-existent earth apart from them. Thus, there is no self-existence.

Abhidharmika objection: [28ab] Even though there is no self-existence, earth still has solidity as a self-existent property from the ultimate point of view.

Reply: [28cd] If so, then yogins here could not submerge downward into the earth and emerge upward as if the earth were water. Yogins also have other supernatural powers connected to the other elements — e.g., walking on water, or turning a blazing forest into the coolness of frost. [29] That the earth is made fluid by the power of yogins' meditation is not tenable because the earth's self-existent nature is not changeable; or if it is changeable, then the earth has no (self-existent, inherent) solidity. [30] Likewise, water, air, and fire have no self-existent natures. It is also untenable that the earth's proper action is holding things together, separating things, or completing things. Since all things are endowed with the qualities of each element — solidity, wetness, combustibility, and mobility — it is difficult to talk about the self-existent nature of each one. Thus, no particle has self-existence. If they did, yogins could not, for example, make a fiery forest cool.

Objection: Granted, yogins have supernatural powers, but the elements are obstacles to other sentient beings or else we too could move around like the yogins do. And even a yogin practicing meditation on space would bump against a pole in the dark.

Reply: That yogins can manipulate the elements only in their meditation is sufficient to make the point. [31] We do not deny that the elements all have qualities as seen from a conventional point of view, because they are like the earth that is an element perceivable by the tactile sense-faculty. [32] The four elements are not real substances because they cannot be grasped when the parts of a collection are not grasped. (That is, earth and so forth do not exist apart from collections of different parts.) That real entity that is mentioned by you cannot be seen, just as a forest cannot be seen apart from the trees (because apart from its parts it does not exist). "Substance," like "forest," exists only as a conventional designation.[33] We maintain that the perception that has the elements as its object is not a real substance because it has a cause and is destructible, like the perception of a "forest."

[34] We do not maintain that the designating sound that is the naming of the elements is a real substance, since something that is heard — e.g., the sound that is the indicator of an army — is not regarded as a real substance (because it is dependent on a source and the hearing sense-faculty).

Vaisheshika objection: Real substances arise from the conjunction of things. Thus, a forest is in fact a real substance. [35] Or your reason in your example is inconclusive because it is uncertain whether the power of cognition is the consciousness or instead belongs to consciousness. As that is refuted, so is what is to be concluded, due to their resemblance. Moreover, the Samkhya say that a forest is also a real substance because it is one unit.

Reply: [36] We do not maintain that the various trees are the cause of the beginning of the forest since they have a cause, e.g., roots. [37] A forest that has parts is not formed by the trees because it is not complete in each of the trees, just as a tree is not complete in the branches and its other parts. Thus, the various trees are not the cause of the beginning of the forest, and thus forests are not real substances. [38] Thus, the Vaisheshika proposition "Your example is faulty" is not established. In addition, there is no claim "The forest is also a real substance because it is one unit," contra the Samkhya. [39] The word "forest" is not a common usage for measuring an indefinite number of substances since the word is caused by a distinct cognition, as with "pot."

Abhidharmika objection: The various elements each have their own self-existent nature. Nothing whatsoever arises based on the absence of self-existence. What is called "form" has its self-existent nature of color and shape and is perceivable by the eye, but it arises from causes, i.e., the elements. Thus, the elements indeed must have self-existence.

Reply: Form arises conventionally from the imagining of something unreal. The unwise are confused, just as with seeing a magical illusion or a mirage. Even less accomplished yogins who dwell in the contemplation for attaining the abode of unlimited space, the abode of unlimited consciousness, or the abode of no existence can vanquish temporarily the idea of form and the idea of unvanquishability in all respects. How much less would those yogins of the supreme Mahayana who dwell on the edge of the contemplation of "emptiness," the "signless," and the "wishless (i.e., free of any distinct objects to be desired)," having contemplated the self-existence of substances for countless ages, seize on form?

[40] Indeed, from the ultimate point of view, form is not graspable by the sense-faculty of sight because it is resistant and produced from the elements, like such things as sound. (That is, there is no self-existent entity to see.) Our proposition is "From the ultimate point of view, form is not the object of the sense-faculty of sight." [41] The eye does not see form because form is produced from the elements, like the eye's own form. (Because the eye's form is produced from the elements, the eye cannot grasp what is also made from the elements. It would have to be different in nature from form to see form.) And because the eye has a cause for its arising, like happiness and so forth, and because it is expressible, like such things as taste. [42] So too, form is not real because it is produced (and thus dependent), like fire and so forth, and because, like both thought and learning, it has a cause. Thus those who know indicate.

[43] The mental fabrications of the characteristics of form are from different colors, shapes, and configurations, whether gross or subtle. [44] The negation of these fabrications is to be understood by the application of the reasoning already explained in verse 42. The negation of the fabrications of sound, smell, taste, and touch is also accomplished in the same manner.

[45] From the ultimate point of view, the visual sense-faculty does not see form, just as the taste-faculty does not see, because it is different from consciousness and what belongs to the mind. (The eye is only an instrument and does not actually see.) If there were the power of seeing in the material eye itself, then it would see all the time, even in times of sleep, intoxication, and death, and in a dark cave. If it does not see, then the act of seeing does not exist in the eye itself. If one claims "Cognition sees," then a blind man could see form. Also in that case, the eye alone is not the agent of sight because the act of seeing depends on a group of agents — form, light, space, and consciousness. [46] In addition, from the ultimate point of view, the eye

does not see form since seeing cannot arise where there is no self-existent cognition, as with the skin and the other senses. [47] From the ultimate point of view, the visual sense-faculty is not pure form having color as its domain because it is produced and so forth. For the example, it is like skin and so forth. [48] We maintain that the eye does not have the domain of form because it cannot grasp its own form and because it has a form, like taste and so forth. (If the eye could see form, it would see itself.) The same for the hearing-faculty and so forth.

Samkhya and Vaisheshika objection: The eye is an instrument of seeing — one who sees sees with the eye. Just as one cuts with an axe and cannot cut without it, so with the eye and seeing. It is a person who sees form.

Reply: [49] If what is by nature free of sight (the Samkhya's "person") could see by joining sight to it, then the idea of seeing by an eye-less seer is not groundless. But how is it possible for something that does not have the nature of seeing to see form? [50] Or how can the seeing of form be joined to a seer without form? Even if a seer is also a listener, how can there be the quality of listening in him? If there is the self-existence of a seer, how can other self-existent natures arise in him? (A "self-existent seer" could only see and not have other sense-qualities as part of his nature.) If they are joined, then the self-existent natures were first separated, which is untenable.

[51] In addition, the claim that a seer has the attribute of knowledge and is eternal cannot be maintained because a seer has the attribute of change and does not remain one form, just as the body is varied and not one in form but is different from another body (due to its changes). The self as a seer that could become a listener has neither knowledge as an essential attribute nor is permanent in nature because it has changeable distinctions (and knowledge does not change). Something that is changeable in nature neither has an inherent nature nor is permanent. When a self is without inherent knowledge or permanence, it is without self-existence and thus is not real.

[52] It is not claimed that the visual sense-faculty is the cause of perceiving form because it does not have the nature of the mind and is other than the seer, just as with hearing and so forth. [53] The self cannot be the seer because of its dependence on the eye and other sense-faculties, like the mind, or like a transformation, or like a reflection. What has the nature of a seer does not depend on the collection of the instruments of seeing, nor would it be impermanent or changing. It is unreasonable to say that the self is the seer because it reflects images, just like water, and cannot grasp a

sense-object that is not seen by the eye and so forth. [54] How can the self have the nature of a seer, since, like the mind, it cannot be seen by another sense-faculty? From the point of view of the that-ness of things (i.e., what is real), it is not proclaimed that the mind has the nature of seeing. The mind, like the self, is neither identical to nor different from what has the nature of seeing. [55ab] Or there is no seeing by the mind because there is no real substance to the assembly of causes and conditions of sight, like a forest.

Objection: If there is no self, who does the seeing? If the mind is momentary, it cannot be the causal agent of seeing.

Reply: [55cd] From the point of view of conventional expression, the mind can be the causal agent because of the production of other phenomena through the assembling of different causes and conditions, like how a bell produces sound. Thus, we admit the reality of seeing in the conventional sense because of the assembly of causes and conditions. However, from the ultimate point of view, the causes and conditions do not exist at all — seeing does not exist in the eye or in the form, or in both together, so where does it exist? It is neither real nor totally nonexistent.

Objection: But the eye has light — how else could a cat or owl in the dark have a lamp-like glare in their eyes?

Reply: [56] It cannot be claimed that the eye as a sense-faculty has a ray of light, as the other sense-faculties do not. The sense-faculty is visible in the eyeball of an animal moving at night, but it is not visible by the eye. The eyeballs shine, not the sense-faculty itself. The sense-faculty is invisible.

[57] The eye does not have the nature of pleasure by seeing something pleasurable because it is an object, just as the individual self is void of it. Nor does the eye-faculty reach everywhere because it has the nature of an entity, just as do the eyeball and so forth. The eye stays in its own place and does not go out. [58] Rather, the eye does not have the nature of one who can move elsewhere because it exists for the sake of another (i.e., the self), like a pot exists for the benefit of another. It also does not move elsewhere because it is a cause of apprehension of form, like a form that is also a cause of apprehension does not move.

The eye does not have the self-existent nature of fire. Nor can it move as fire does. [59] The eye is not joined with fire because it has the nature of a sense-faculty, like skin has. In addition, the eye does not have the nature of fire alone but is made a pure form by all four of the great elements.

Naiyayika objection: The visual sense-faculty moves out from its base and grasps the sense-object outside.

Reply: [60] The eye does not reach a sense-object because of its nature as a sense-faculty, like the mind. (The visual sense-faculty does not move out of the body when it sees fire any more than the physical eye does.) In addition, it has the nature of a cause and is produced from a cause, like form.

Abhidharmika objection: The sense-faculties of the mind, eye, and ear (unlike the nose, tongue, and body) can grasp distant objects.

Reply: [61] We do not maintain the claim "The nose grasps the sense-object it can reach" because it perceives the external object directly (by touching it) and also because it does not perceive the past or future, like the eye does not. [62] This does not commit the error of an uncertain reason (see verse 35) concerning touch, because it negates the immediate grasping for the other three sense-faculties. (That is, the two groups of senses are distinguished concerning contact. When we see fire, the eye does not go out and come in contact with the fire and get burned.) The criticism of the nose and taste should also be understood as untainted reasoning. [63] The three characteristics of mind, hearing, and sight do not grasp unreachable objects because they are sense-faculties and the cause of consciousness, like smell, taste, and touch.

[64] From this extensive exposition of sight, the repudiation of other sense-faculties — hearing, smelling, tasting and touch — should be attended to. (Mind is not mentioned.) Just as it is unreasonable to maintain that a seer, seeing, and its form exist in only the eye and mind of the seer, so too a hearer, hearing, and its form do not exist solely in the sense-faculty. [65] This is also the means for the negation of sound, smell, taste, and tactility. This is understood properly by the wise with correct cognitions.

Objection: The defining characteristic of feeling is experiencing the coming together of a sense-faculty, sense-object, and cognition.

Reply: [66] From the ultimate point of view, the claim "Feeling has the nature of experience" is untenable because of its association with cognition, like any other thing that belongs to consciousness. Feeling is not endowed with enjoyment since during concentration in meditative trances all pain and pleasure are in abeyance and in nirvana all feelings are completely annihilated. [67] We do not maintain the claim "Pleasure is a necessary feature of anything beneficial" because pleasure is produced by any touch, as with anything other than pleasure is (i.e., painful and neutral sensations are also produced by touch). Suffering does not have the nature of pain for a reason that is knowable since it has already been explained. [68] That feeling is either free of suffering or free of pleasure is not maintained, for its fruit is desire, as is feeling itself. There is also the refutation of the self-existence of consciousness, as will be discussed later. [69] The refutation of the self-existent nature of both perceptions and dispositions is similarly explained. This is understood properly by the wise with correct cognitions.

[70] From the point of view of what is real, consciousness is not a self-existent, real object that recognizes things because it depends on an external support, as does perception, or because of the fact that is does not exist, like a lamp light doomed to extinction.

[71] From applying the analysis of the five bodily aggregates as discussed, the nature of the sense-fields and their constituents should be known. They exist merely as designations in the conventional world.

Objection: In the ultimate sense, the bodily aggregates, sense-fields, and constituents are self-existent because they have the three defining characteristics of conditioned phenomena — arising, enduring, and ceasing.

Reply: Are the entities conditioned or unconditioned? If they are conditioned, you have to offer your example for your proposition that proves the existence of the things that give rise to these entities. These things would not have the defining characteristics of conditioned things because they give rise to them. If on the other hand, these entities are unconditioned, how could they have the defining characteristics of conditioned phenomena? If the aggregation of the entities has the defining characteristics of conditioned things, it is impossible to maintain the aggregate for any length of time (because of change and impermanence). If the defining characteristics are in the entities individually, there is no duration or cessation in what is unproduced. Since there is no production or cessation of what endures, this also is not conditioned. Hence, there is no real conditioned entity.

[72] Thus, the claim "The arising, enduring, and ceasing are the defining characteristics of the constituents because they are conditioned phenomena" is not acceptable because the constituents are conditioned and the object of understanding, like other things. (What is real is beyond understanding.) Conventionally there are entities because they have defining characteristics. Nonexistent entities like the son of a barren woman have no defining characteristic. [73] But we also do not maintain "There are essential natures to entities" because there are no real defining characteristics. (Thus, nothing real that could have defining characteristics.) Thus, your reason is not established and is contradicted.

Defining Characteristics

Next we explain the absence of any defining characteristic. [74] One cannot claim "Solidity is the defining characteristic of earth because it is the nature of earth" because solidity is the cause of the tactile cognition, just as it cannot be claimed that solidity is the defining characteristic of fire. If the defining characteristic and what is characterized are the same, then apart from the characteristic, which is only a designation, there is nothing to be characterized. Likewise, [75] we do not maintain that the defining characteristic of a cow are the lump on its back, the skin hanging from its throat, and so forth, since they are the properties of "a cow" because the properties are known by a particular cognition, as with the properties of a donkey.

Objection: The defining characteristics are different from what is characterized because what is characterized is an activity of the defining characteristics.

Reply: [76ab] If the defining characteristics and the characterized are identical, how the defining characteristics be defining characteristics since the thing could not indicate them by itself? Thus, the conventional expressions "This is the characterized" and "This is the defining characteristic" would not be possible. In addition, there would be a redundancy when the referent of two things is identical.

Objection: What is characterized and the defining characteristic are different because the defining characteristic denotes something else.

Reply: [76cd] If they are completely distinct, how could the defining characteristic be a defining characteristic? A distinct thing could not denote something completely distinct from it.

Thus, the defining characteristic and what is characterized are neither identical nor distinct. In addition, if the defining characteristic itself had a defining characteristic, there would be an infinite regress. But if it did not have a defining characteristic, then a defining characteristic would be utterly nonexistent. Thus, a defining characteristic exists conventionally.

Going

Objection: Bodily aggregates, sense-fields, and constituents must have defining characteristics because they have activity given in conventional expressions. For example, the son of a barren woman does not go but a person is described as a "goer." Thus, there must be defining characteristics.

Reply: If one maintains that there is the conventional expression "having gone" according to the well-known fact of the world, then one is committing the fallacy of proving what is already proven (i.e., that conventionally there is "going"). On the other hand, if there is "having gone" from the point of view of what is ultimately real, then it is in the process of "gone," "not gone," or "going." [77] But "There is going in what has not gone" is not acceptable from the point of view of what is ultimately real because there is no current movement in what has already gone, just as there is no current movement in what has not yet gone.

[78] Moreover, in the ultimate sense, there is no "going" in current movement because apart from "having gone" and "not yet started to go" no actual movement can be seen. "Actual movement" is either "already gone," "not yet gone," or a bit of both. The first two are already been refuted. If actual movement has the self-existent nature of both, then lifting the foot from a given place is "already gone" and putting the foot down is "not yet gone." Thus, no actual movement occurs. (There are only two motionless situations.) [79] Thus, there is no "going" in actual movement. The actual movement cannot be expressed in terms of "having already gone" or "not yet going" because it is traveling (i.e., in a process), just like "having gone" is. This is also so for any future process of "going." The actual movement is not the thing expressed by "going," nor is it in the domain of the cognition; thus, it does not exist. Even if actual movement did exist, it is still unreasonable to say going is real since it is a process. (That is, what is ultimately real is permanent and unchanging and not in a changing process as motion is.)

Objection: Going certainly exists because there is the conventional expression "goer" who possesses it. In the absence of going, there is no conventional expression for who posses it, just as with the absence of the conventional reality of a rabbit's horn.

Reply: The conventional expression "He goes" is understood whether there is or is not a goer in the ultimate sense. [80] Because "going" is not established, a "goer" does not exist. Thus, "He goes" cannot be maintained. When there is no going, there is no one who goes. If someone had the self-existent nature of a goer, he would never depart from the act of going.

It cannot be said that there is the going of someone who does not go because he is not joined to the act of going, like the former. One who has the nature of "not going" cannot go. Otherwise, inherent natures could change. In addition, how could a non-goer change natures and become a goer? Some accept that one can have the nature of a goer and still not go, according to different modes. But there is no third position apart from going and not going.

Moreover, can a goer stay or a non-goer stay? A goer cannot stay for he cannot exist separate from going. A non-goer cannot stay for there is no "staying" apart from "going" even in a conventional expression. There is no third party apart from a "goer" and a "non-goer." Thus, your reason for claiming "one who stays" is dissimilar from a "goer" is unacceptable.

Vaisheshika objection: The substance in which the act of going arises does not go, but whenever the act of going arises it goes because the going is other than the substance. It is like "He has a stick."

Reply: [81] In the Vaisheshika's opinion, it is believed that the goer is real in connection with an object other than himself because the word and the thought agree, like a person with a stick. But in reality this is not so because there is no inherent connection between the person and the stick. For "a stick" and "a person holding a stick" are both without self-existence from the point of view of what is actually real. (Being unreal, there is nothing to connect, and thus their example fails.) In addition, from the ultimate point of view, there is no such thing as "holding." We maintain that "There is motion" only as a conventional expression. Thus, your argument fails.

Buddhist objection: Going is totally nonexistent. "Going" is not a separate reality from the goer but perishes each instant like the continuation of a whirling firebrand that is seen as a spinning wheel of fire.

Reply: "Going" does not exist in the ultimate sense but is real conventionally. [82] The bases from which conditioned things go forward spread out continuously, like the firebrand. This rolling motion exists only conventionally, not in the ultimate sense.

Samkhya objection: A goer exists whenever there is a manifestation of the activities of the amalgam in which passion dominates.

Reply: [83] From the ultimate point of view, the Samkhya's imaginings of a "goer" are unreasonable because the amalgamated thing has no substance and does not have the nature of exertion. [84] Samkhyas claim that the amalgamated thing is a real substance because it is not grasped when the activity of the amalgam is not grasped. But "The amalgam is real, just as the self is" is not to be claimed because the amalgam is not a real substance. That is, it is unreasonable to maintain that the elements are real as the agent of activity because the amalgamated thing that has the activity is not a real substance. Thus, we must conclude that "going" and "not going" are established only in the conventional sense, not in the ultimate sense.

[85ab] This way of explanation is also the refutation of all remaining actions — e.g., speaking, eating, and cutting.

Rebirth and Release

Vaisheshika and Buddhist objection: Entities of a mental nature are certainly self-existent in the ultimate sense because there is bondage to the cycle of rebirths and release from it. If they were nonexistent, it would be like the bondage and release of a child of a barren woman. So too, the Buddha declared bondage and the noble Eightfold Path of release from the prison of rebirth. If there is no self-existent things, how is bondage and release possible?

Reply: [85cd] If self-existence is declared because rebirth and release are real entities, [86] then when the imagined form is not attested to (as real), where and how could there be bondage and release? [87] It is claimed that there is no self-existence in rebirth and release, as with a magical illusion or a dream. However, they acquire a distinctive (conventional) self-nature by the force of their own cause and conditions. It is acceptable to posit release by means of insight conventionally, however "release" and "bondage" do not ultimately exist. [88] From the ultimate point of view, the cycling of name-and-form (i.e., a being) is invalid, like the rebirth of earth is not accepted because it is conditioned. [89] From the ultimate point of view, name-and-form cannot be released in any way because it arises and perishes, like external things such as waves. Are beings continuous or momentary? If they are continuous, they rise and perish like waves. If they are momentary, then bondage arises and disappears each moment, and so where could release be?

[119cd] Bondage is not established. It is without the nature of self-existence and is immovable. Bondage and release only exist in the conventional sense, not from the ultimate point of view.

The Person

Buddhist Pudgala objection: The person is different from the bodily aggregates, sense-fields, and constituents. It cannot be described, but it is reborn and is released.

Reply [90]: In reality, the "person" is not reborn nor released because it is merely a designation like a "house" or because it can be expressed, like "good perfume" or "bad perfume." Since the bodily aggregates, sense-fields, and constituents do not ultimately exist, neither does the designation "person." [91] Or, the dispositions are without anything of the nature of a "person" because they have a cause, like a pot does; also because they have the nature of arising and of destruction, because they are knowable, like a lump of clay. If the person is different from the bodily aggregates, it is nonexistent. If it is identical, then when the aggregates are destroyed so is the person.

Objection: Although the person is inexpressible as either identical to or different from the bodily aggregates, it is still a real object.

Reply: [92] Your position — that "Although the person cannot be designated explicitly and is inexpressible, it is a real substance, like the best perfume" — cannot be maintained because of an uncertain reason or because it is inexpressible because it does not exist like the color of the child of a barren woman.

The Universal Self

[93] Thus, the bodily aggregates are without any self-nature, without living beings, and deprived of being. The universal self (of Vedanta) is refuted in a similar manner of refuting the person (of Samkhya). [94] According to what is real, the amalgam of the body and sense-faculties is without any self-nature (i.e., is not self-existent), either because it has a cause, like a pillar, or because it is an accumulation, like an anthill.

Objection: The amalgam of body and sense-faculties must be endowed with a universal self since it, unlike a pot or cloth, generates recollections, memories, knowledge, and so forth. Such activities must be the activity of the self. So anything with sense-organs must have a self.

Reply: [95] The thesis of the reality of the universal self cannot be established by this reason: the arising and so forth of recollections, memories, and knowledge. These things do not have any self but are particular states of the mind or what belongs to the mind based on causes and conditions. Thus, your reason falls into the fallacies of inconclusive evidence and the impossibility of its basis.

[96] If it is argued "A body with a sense-faculty has its own nature," then the reason is false because it does not agree with the proposition — the occurrence of memory and knowledge can be seen, but the self is not seen anywhere. Thus, the reason conflicts with the proposition.

Vaishesika Objection: [97abc] The word "self" has a real meaning (and hence the self is a real object) because it can be used metaphorically for something real. For example, we may can a young Brahmin a "lion" only because there are real lions with which he shares attributes. So too, if the designation "recollections, memories, knowledge" can be conceived, then there must be a real object apart from the amalgam of body and sense-faculty — the "self" — in which these attributes appear. (A word can be used metaphorically only if it has a direct meaning, and so there must be a "self.")

Reply: [97d] We say that the self cannot be established this way. For your argument to work, the entity in the example must be an amalgam, like "lion," but "I" is not. Thus, there is no valid example, and the argument establishes only what we have already established (i.e, the self from a conventional point of view). We also posit the word "I" in a cognition from the conventional point of view that takes a new rebirth in the amalgam of body and sense-faculties. Like "This is a carriage" in an amalgam of parts, so too we conventionally say of what is dependent on the bodily aggregates "This is a sentient being."

Objection: [98ab] Here the existence of the universal self is established, as with the domain of cognition. That is, if you establish cognition as a self-existent object, you establish the existence of the universal self.

Reply: [98cd] If so, then a contradiction arises because of the obstruction of permanence, omniscience, and so forth (i.e., the attributes of the universal self). That is, since cognition is without permanence and so forth, then so would be the universal self.

[99] Thus, from the point of view of ultimate truth, there is no bondage or release in the mind whatsoever. The rest of the mental life should be explained like the "gone," "not yet gone," and "currently moving."

Objection: Release exists for a person in the process of release.

Reply: What is in the process of release? If it is bound, then there would be the fallacy of the simultaneous existence of bondage and release. If it is not bound, then what is the point of release? That is, if it is bound, then there is no release; if it already released, then it not in bondage. If you say both of them are inexpressible, then this injures any (claim to) essential nature. If you say that release occurs in the mind that needs religious training, then this is an argument about conventional reality, which does not concern us here (only ultimate truth does).

Thus, in the ultimate sense, "bondage" and "release" in the mind cannot be maintained. There is neither rebirth nor nirvana, neither defilement nor purification in reality.

Nirvana

Buddhist objection: Passion is real because its abandonment is taught by the Buddha. The extinction of craving, which is born simultaneously with the passion for greed, is nirvana.

Reply: According to the guiding principle of the Prajna-paramita texts, there is not such thing as passion from the ultimate point of view. [109] "Nirvana is attained through abandoning" is not to be claimed. From the ultimate point of view, nirvana is empty of any characteristic of "reality" or "unreality." Because of its unknowability, nirvana does not exist from the point of view of what is ultimate real. [110] If nirvana is a real entity, it is ipso facto indeed be a conditioned entity. Entities come into existence as an amalgam of causes and conditions. The alleged unconditioned nature of nirvana is repudiated in this manner. The entity "nirvana" is not the antidote to conditionedness because it also is conditioned, like a conditioned entity that has ceased to function. [111] If nirvana is a nonexistent entity (i.e., the absence of a real entity), then it depends on things because of its nature as nonexistent, like any absent object. Nirvana cannot be taken as the antidote for it depends on other things, like a destroyed object. [112ab] It also cannot be said that nirvana is unconditioned because the refutation of this has already been explained. If it were a real substance, then there would be self-existence, but since it is conditioned it cannot be unconditioned.

If nirvana is a substantive entity that can be designated, is unproduced, and is perpetual, [112cd] then is there any distinction between this and the liberation of consciousness (i.e., the individual self) as conceived by the Samkhya? [113] The mental afflictions are ignited by the fire starter of mental discriminations and die naturally (once the discriminations are ended). Thus, since nothing is accumulated, by the extinction of what does your release become an extinction? In addition, the mental afflictions are nonexistent in the ultimate sense, and thus there is no accumulation of anything real. Where there is no annihilation, from what is it released? [114] Where nothing real is born, the mental discriminations are also unreal. Thus, bondage and release are the same in this regard (since there is nothing to liberate or to be liberated from). Thus, whether the extinction exists or not, by what extinction can release be spoken of?

Does liberation exist? In the conventional sense it does, but not in the ultimate sense. [115] By realizing that things are empty of self-existence, this knowledge itself ceases. Thus, the true nature of the imperishability of the imperishable is attained by means of nonattainment! That is, the knowledge itself becomes extinct because the yogin does not conceive any self-existence to any phenomenon, including knowledge. The inexhaustible natural condition of phenomena is realized. [116] Thus, those who, seeking refuge, investigate phenomena as they really are do not address the foul smelling words of the disease of faulty views.

Unconditioned Phenomena

[129] Thus, examples of conditioned phenomena with the absence of self-nature have been analyzed. In Vaibhashika Buddhism, there are four unconditioned phenomena: two cessations, empty space, and "suchness" (i.e., the true nature of phenomena). [130] From the ultimate point of view, the cessation that results from the analytical calculation of things is certainly not a real entity because it is like the continually changing form of the child of a barren woman. [131] In addition, this is so because the cessation is unproduced, without cause and without activity (effect), and without the assembling of conditions or its cessation. The nature of an entity is characterized by its production, cause, action, conditions, and cessation. How then could the cessation be an unconditioned entity? Since there is no production and so forth, there is no cessation. Cessation is only possible for a produced thing, not the unproduced. [132] And without a cause, of what is it thought to be the effect? It is like the horn on the head of an elephant because of not having been produced and so forth. [133] Thus, it is determined that an unproduced cause is not approved as an effect. (That is, to be a cause, something must change and thus be an effect.) For example, if a (nonexistent) flower in the sky is the cause, there is no effect like honey.

[134] Thus, from this the intelligent know the refutation of any unconditioned phenomena whatsoever, such as space, suchness, spatial directions, and time.

[135] Those things that are to be known — substance, dominant cause, the empirical person, and the other Samkhya and Vaisheshika categories — are the false imaginings of non-Buddhists. They should be refuted by those who are proficient in reasoning and the tradition's scriptures. [136] The universal self is imagined by the accomplished ones of this and other schools. But the wise, having realized the pure (i.e., what is free of the impurities of mental afflictions), drink the ambrosia of the knowledge of what is real. The yogin should attain the realization that entities are free of self and self-existence according to the above method. He should strive to savor the ambrosia of knowing reality that is attained through nonconceptual knowledge in a manner free of all conscious knowing.

The Non-production of Phenomena from Themselves

[137] The expansion of the net of conceptual constructions that begins with such things as substance and that has as its basis produced entities through its force indeed confuses the unwise whose eye of cognition is closed. [138] When one who knows examines entities as they really are with the lamp of knowledge, (the idea of) "production" is extinguished because he negates it by seeing with his eye of cognition that all entities in their nature are non-produced, like an illusion (not being real and thus not really being "produced"). Thereby, conceptual projection is stilled.

Question: The Samkhya say that entities are produced from themselves. Others say that they are produced by other things. Others say they are produced by both. Others say they are produced without a cause. Others say they are produced by the lord Ishvara, or consciousness, or matter, or time, or the god Narayana.

Reply: [139] First, production from its own self is not reasonable even conventionally because production from oneself is not seen, just as curd already exists as itself (and not in milk). If entities arose from themselves, it would be possible that they could arise without causes and conditions. But even conventionally such things are not seen in the world, let alone from the ultimate point of view. If what already exists, what would be the activity of arising again? It is admissible conventionally that curd is produced from milk. However, it is not admissible that curd is produced from itself. So too, a real entity does not arise from itself because this would be a contradiction implying that the act of arising works on itself.

[140] Moreover, real entities does not arise out of themselves because they already have existence, just as the individual consciousness has in your view (i.e., Samkhya's). What is unproduced has no self (i.e., self-existence) because it is not born, like a (nonexistent) sky-flower. [141] You may think that the meaning of our claim "The sky-flower does not exist" in terms of the "sky" and a "flower" that you think exist, but that is not the point of our example, and so there is no deficiency in this thesis. A "sky-flower" is different from both the "sky" and a "flower" and does not exist, and so the example is apropos.

Samkhya objection: [142] The self-existence of an effect is from its (self-existent) cause. The arising of the effect is from its cause. Real entities are effects (in their cause), and thus birth from themselves is accepted.

Reply: [143ab] But then the cause is not a cause because the effect is not different from the cause, like the self (and its alleged effects). If a cause and effect are different from each other, it is possible to establish the conventional expression "This is the cause, and this is the effect." But when they are identical, even this conventional expression cannot be established. If they were identical, it would also follow that the seed would not be different from the sprout — then the cause would be identical to the self-nature of the effect. The sprout would also not be different from the seed because it would be identical to the self-existent cause.

[143cd] Moreover, since matter and consciousness (according to you) are themselves unproduced, what could be the cause of what? What could be the noncause? Since they are unproduced, there is no distinction of "before" and "after" and so they are not causes.

Samkhya: Some hold the view that the cause is not exactly the same as the effect since the effect exists in the cause in a potential state and is only manifested under certain conditions. But since "potentiality" and "manifestation" do not differ in their nature, arising from the potentiality means arising from itself.

Reply: [144] When the self of an entity is real, it is pointless to conceptualize "a cause" for it. If anything is produced from itself, what begets and what is begotten are one.

Samkhya: They are not identical — when one phenomenon that exists as the substance "milk" ceases, then the other phenomenon "curd" arises. Thus, the conventional expression "cause and effect" is justified.

Reply: [145] If what we said above about "milk" and "curd" does not refute your thesis, then it is refuted by the example that a father is not the child. In fathering a child, the father does not abandon his state and change to the state of the child. (A father causes the son but remains distinct.)

Objection: Your reasons — "because it already exists in itself" (v. 139) and "because they have existence" (v. 140) — cannot establish nonproduction. Those reasons are present for what produced entities, such as jars, but are absent in unproduced things, such as the horns of a rabbit. Thus, those reasons are not present in any of the similar examples for establishing the nonexistence of entities and are only present in dissimilar instances. Those reasons establish the existence of arising, which is the opposite of a self-existent nature. Thus, your thesis is contradicted.

Reply: Our reasons are only conventional. What arises dependent upon them has no self-existence from the ultimate point of view. Since in the ultimate sense there is no arising of anything in any way from itself, from others, from both itself and others, or without a cause, there is dissimilarity. [146] From the absence of dissimilar examples, it would be also not be right to hold that the reason in our argument is contradicted.

[Verses 147-58 cover non-production from other things; verses 192-93 cover non-production from a thing and other things; verses 194-95 cover non-production without a cause.]

Conclusion to the Topic of Production

[247] From the ultimate point of view, there is no self-existence, or existence from another, or from both, or without a cause. Nor is anything real or unreal or otherwise. And nothing arises from itself or is manifested in any way from itself, from anything else, from both, or from nothing at all. [248] Nor does anything caused by Vishnu, the lord Shiva, the self, unevolved matter, particles, and so forth. Nor are there even any real entities whatsoever that are brought forth or driven away. [249] These notions are based on self-existence, actions, things possessing certain defining characteristics, and the characteristics themselves. They are based on oneness and otherness and on the actions of afflictions and their termination. [250] All conceptualizations of these matters also do not arise, just as a stroke of a whip, a painting, or seeds obviously do not appear in the sky.

[251] By getting rid of eye-diseases and having eyes that are pure and clear, one does not see spots, hairs, flies, or double images of the moon. [252] So too, by getting rid of the eye-disease of mental afflictions and knowable objects and having the clear eye complete knowledge, one does not see any objects at all.

[253] One who feels drowsy and falls asleep see young men, women, palaces, and so forth. But when he wakes up, he does not see them. [254] So too, one who has opened the eye of cognition and has awakened from the sleep of ignorance does not see things as they are conventionally.

[255] On a dark night, one sees unreal ghosts, but when the sun arises and he opens his eyes, he does not see them. [256] So too, when an intelligent person has destroyed all traces of ignorance by means of the sun of true knowledge, he does not see the mind or what belongs to the mind as real.

[257] Entities are not self-existent because they do not have self-existence and do not arise from themselves, like enjoyment. Thus, true self-existence of entities is not seen. [258] From a conventional point of view, entities do arise and have a cause, like enjoyment, but the true self-existence of entities is not seen.

[259] The idea that entities do not exist is not considered the way things are because it arises by the obstruction of conceptualizations, like the idea that a post is a man. [260] The incorrect thought that an entity has a self-nature is attained only by an unreal cognition, like the cognition of water in a mirage perceived through ignorance and conceptualizations. [261] But by attending to the real and unreal cognitions, this is warded off. A real cognition free of discrimination is won by developing yogic practices. [262] From the emptiness of all phenomena, the cognition of non-emptiness is not acceptable. That it is acceptable that there is a cognition of the non-empty without conceptualizing was previously refuted. [263] Emptiness is empty of any self-existence — indeed, it is empty of "emptiness." Thus, the wise do not see emptiness as "emptiness." [264] The domain of cognition without conceptualizing is the nature of entities without false appearances. From what has support in what is real, cognitions of the moon are not like the reflected image of the moon in water.

[265] A cognition that has "no discrimination" as its object is false, even though it is nonconceptual, because, like a cognition with discriminations, it is a cognition of "no self" and so forth as self-existent. (That is, one still has concepts in the mind if one notices the absence of concepts.)

[266] No object of knowledge exists at all. Thus, the buddhas who know reality say that the reality that has no parallel is something about which not even a nonconceptual cognition arises. [267] The non-arising of cognition is called "the Buddha" because it is the understanding of this is the primary buddha. It is the understanding that is no understanding and it dispels the sleep of concepts.

8. Examining the Nature of Reality
According to the Vedanta

The Opponent Presents the Case for Vedanta
[1] Vedantins say "Outside our school, it is very difficult to find anyone who knows the self. How could those who dismiss the self, maintaining that all conditioned entities are empty of self-existence and are momentary, attain liberation? [2] An intelligent person surpasses death when he sees (with his eye of cognition) the true self of the individual that is on the other side of the darkness (of this world). The self is radiant like the sun, is the

transcendental self pervading all, and is the great lord of the universe. [3] When one sees the gold-colored lord through the eye of meditation, one will see that the lord is the creator. Having cast off demerit and merit, one will attain supreme identity with the lord. By turning away from all action, one attains the tranquility that is beyond the discrimination of discrete entities.

Question: If the lord is beyond the three realms of the universe (i.e., the realm of desire and the formed and formless realms created by meditation), how could he be an agent within the universe? And if he is so distant as to transcend the three realms, whose lord is he?

Opponent's reply: Despite his distant abode, he indeed is all-pervading. [4] Whatever is past, present, or future is all regarded as the transcendental self. He is within the person and outside the person, far and near, and he is the maker of action.

Question: If the self is one, how is he able to undertake a variety of activities and to remain unaffected (and unchanged)?

Reply: [5] All entities in the universe are born out of the self, like threads coming out of a spider. Wise men merged in the lord through meditation are not reborn again (but remain in the lord after death). Through meditation, one perceives the lord with the eye of insight.

Question: Why can't a yogin attain immortality even if he hasn't seen the lord with his eye of insight?

[6] Reply: What is mortal cannot be regarded as immortal, just as fire cannot be regarded as cold. Thus, it is unreasonable to say that immortality could be attained if one has not become awakened in the immortal self.

[7] Since nothing more excellent or superior or more subtle than the lord is found, he alone upholds the entire universe. The character of one who is one with the lord is [8] endowed with the supernatural powers to shrink himself in size, expand himself, levitate, and reach things beyond his normal grasp; his will is irresistible and he may proceed however he desires (without acquiring karmic demerit). Although he is one, he has the same nature of diversity as the three realms of the universe. [9] For the one who sees the lord, all the elements of the universe and the self itself exist in the lord. He sees as equal the ignorant and the learned, an outcaste and a Brahmin.

Question: This self is said to be all-pervading and from him alone are born the bodies of all kinds of living beings such as gods and humans — why does he not acquire a nature that is not eternal and not all-pervading, like all embodied beings?

Reply: [10] When a pot is produced or destroyed, the space in it is not identical with it (and so the space is not produced or destroyed). When such things as bodies are born or die, they cannot be considered to be identical with the self. [11] If you say "The one self in the diversity of bodies is many, like space in pots," we reply that space is one: it is not made multiple by the breaking of the pots, and it is the same in all pots. Thus, the self does not exist separately in each embodied being. Despite the multiplicity of bodies, the self is the same in them all. [12] Although pots are different, the clay in them all is in no way different. So too, although the bodies are different, the self is not differentiated.

Question: Since the self is all-pervading, when one person is happy shouldn't everyone be happy?

Reply: [13] Space is one, but when the space that is within one pot is covered with dust, smoke, and so on, it is certainly not the case that the space in all pots also becomes similarly affected. So too, when the self of one person has pleasure, it is not the case that all other persons come to possess pleasure.

Question: How does pleasure and suffering arise at all in each of these individual stream of becoming (i.e., the chains of rebirths)?

Answer: [14] Because one does not recognize the lord because of one's own ignorance, one proudly acquires karmic acts and experiences the fruits that are pleasurable or not pleasurable, just as one who dreams imagines himself really to have those dream experiences.

Question: Since the self of the individual person is both the performer of acts and the enjoyer of their karmic effects, he accumulates and enjoys demeritorious acts as well as meritorious acts — so isn't he an evil doer?

Reply: [15] Although the self resides in a body, he is not defiled when he enjoys the karmic fruits since he is not attached to them, just as a king who behaves according to his pleasure remains innocent of demeritorious acts.

[16] When, through the practice meditation, a yogin knows the self is one, all-pervading, eternal, and immortal, then he is not reborn again. [17] That self is permanent, beyond conception, and beyond the scope of speech. Various words — such as "Brahman," "universal self," "individual self," "lord," "great lord," and "the eternal" — are applied to it by those who mind has been led astray by differentiations. The meaning of all such terms is to be understood just like the meaning of the term "universal self."

Bhavya's Critical Examination of the Vedanta's Position

[18] What has been previously said now must be investigated critically by those who do not firmly hold any proposition because a mind that is concealed by attachment to propositions cannot see reality as it truly is.

Refutation of Liberation as the Result of Seeing the Self

[19] The existence of the self has already been refuted by me, and so it cannot be the cause of the world. Thus, a liberation that results from seeing the self is entirely unreal — it has the nature only of a fabrication. [20] The inborn view of the reality of personal identity — i.e., that the five bodily aggregates are the self or belong to the self — that is promoted by you cannot lead to tranquility, even among those with the mind of an animal, since it is the root of all the mental afflictions.

Objection: [21] Liberation for those people who cherish a belief in "I" and "mine," as full of belief in personal identity as they are, arises out of that from which the cycle of rebirths arises — i.e., belief in personal identity.

Reply: The Buddha, the omniscient one, has said that by destroying the views connected to a real self, one sees reality as it truly is. You say that the very thing that increases rebirths is the cause of liberation — this is like someone who tried to put out a fire by pouring more fuel on it!

Objection: What does not cause tranquility, however, by the right means can in fact cause tranquility, just as one who is intoxicated can become sober by means of more liquor. For one who does not know the right means, mental afflictions will arise if he relies on views of the self, but for a yogin meditating on the same view of the self, the afflictions are stilled.

Reply: [22] If tranquility could arise on the basis of seeing the self, then someone suffering from indigestion could recover by eating more, just as a person recovering from intoxication does through more liquor.

[23] Adherents of the Vedanta's teaching maintain that the self appears in two forms: the self that is bound to the body, and the liberated self that rests in the supreme reality. [24] But the cognition that has as its object the self that rests in the supreme state is not real because in such a cognition there is grasping of the self and thus activity in relation to the self occurs, like the idea of a self in relation to the body, the sense-faculties, and sense-objects. (Thus, the completely still tranquility of liberation is not possible through experiences that utilizes the concept of a "self.")

Objection: The self is imagined to be a "self" by the power of the residues of attachment to the self.

Reply: Nothing is established by the imagination.

Refutation of the Self as a Performer of Actions

[25] Even if the self is by nature only imagined, how does that affect your position? A cognition that has form, speech, and so forth as its object is not acceptable. [26] Cognitions that have form and so forth as their object do not arise with the self as the performer, because their arising is dependent on conditions (consciousness, sense-faculties, and sense-objects), just as fire depends on a crystal (to focus sunlight like a magnifying glass). [27] Nor can sound, which has the nature of syllables, be regarded as having the self as a performer, because it is something that must be heard (and thus is dependent on a sense-faculty), or because it is a sound like an echo (which is also dependent on a source). [28] In the same way, all remaining physical activities — e.g., going and coming — accomplished by the movement of the hands and feet are also negated. (Thus, the self is not a performer of acts.)

[29] Perception occurs when one perceives by discriminating entities. Memories occur due to remembering (which arises from conditions). An insight arises from discerning a specific class of things (i.e., discriminating the individual characteristic mark from the general characteristic of phenomena). Feeling arises out of knowledge. Thus, not even the slightest action of a self is apprehended apart from the mind. [30] The proper self-existent nature of the self cannot be determined apart from these (i.e., perception and so forth). Thus, the self's existence cannot be precisely determined (since it does not have the characteristic mark of an action).

Objection: The self does sense, think, and remember because it is the performer. The senses and the mind are its instruments. The instruments do not sense or think — the self does.

Reply: [31] The sense-faculties are deemed "instruments" because it is said that knowledge and so forth require an instrument, and being deemed "a performer" differs from instrumentality, like a man who cuts differs from a sickle. But this is unacceptable. [32] The sense-faculties are not deemed "instruments" since the person arises from conditions. Thus, the reason has either an unestablished meaning or is inconclusive. The eye sees by itself and is not the agent of another. The eye sees, and the self does not.

[33] Indeed, such things as "knowledge as the performer" require a word designating the performer, just as being the performer is seen in the expression "A man cuts."

Objection: A man does not cut — the sword does.

Reply: Action is accomplished here by a combination of both the instrument and the performer. Neither cuts without the other. It is impossible to conceive of either "a performer" or "an instrument" without the other. Things are brought about due to the assembled conditions, not one principal condition alone. Otherwise, an expression is just a way of approaching a subject (that does not designate anything in the world). [34] One may assume the existence of a performer, but such a performer exists only on the basis of a group of completely motionless conditioned entities, just as when we say "The lamp sheds light" even though the lamp is only a means since the light is brought about dependent on the conditions of oil, a wick, a vessel, and fire.

Objection: The self is supreme — all actions proceed dependent on it as the chief performer. But the "lamp" and so forth are only designations, just as a potter is the performer although many conditions are involved.

Reply: [35] In reality, there is no chief performer since one person alone cannot make a pot. Thus, it is not acceptable that a lamp and so forth are a performer merely in a metaphorical sense. The self alone is not the cause of actions because those actions are dependent on a collection of causes and conditions. The eye and the lamp are chief performers, not metaphorical ones, because one chief performer is not established. From the conventional point of view, the collection of conditions is the performer, but in the ultimate sense, it is not established that there is any chief performer.

Refutation of the Self as Either Bound or Liberated

Objection: By the power of past actions, the stream of momentary phenomena cannot be bound or liberated since what ceases in each moment cannot have any activity. Thus, the permanent self must be the basis of continuing rebirth or liberation.

Reply: Although the mind ceases to exist in each moment and is without any independent power or self-existence, it continues like the flow of a river. (There is nothing permanent, but there is a connected flowing.)

[36] The mind is subject to desire and so forth and is attached to the sphere of form and so forth. Thus, it is obstructed from liberation and bound to the prison of the cycle of rebirth since it is without independence and lacks the light of insight. [37] When the aggregate of the hands and so forth is associated with the mind, it is designated "a sentient being." When the intentions of giving arise, the aggregate is called "a giver," and so on.

[38] The bonds of the root-ignorance and the rest of dependent arising are removed the moment knowledge arises. When the stream of the aggregates is free from the bondage of desire and so forth, having traversed the path to liberation by the illumination of insight through hearing, reflecting, and meditating, it is designated "liberated." [39] But because the self is like the sky, all of this thus is very difficult to discuss since the defilements that fill the sky — snow, hail, wind, and so on — are not produced by the sky. So too, even if desire, anger, and pride have arisen, there is no change in the self itself, and thus it cannot be said to be "bound" or "liberated." If you still greatly cherish your self, consider the self as a sky-flower (that also does not exist).

Refutation of Knowledge as the Nature of the Self

[40] If one maintains that the very nature of the self is knowledge, then its "oneness" is not reasonable since knowledge depends on instruments such as the eye and on conditions. In addition, if the self already has the nature of knowledge, then why does it depend on instruments? If you claim that without the sense-faculties knowledge is not apprehended, then since something other than the instruments of knowledge is apprehended its oneness would be lost. This contradicts you own doctrine.

[41] (Morever, to know the self makes the self an "object of knowledge.") If the self were a truly-existing object of knowledge, then knowledge of the self would never cease. (That is, nothing could cause it to stop.) When a lamp accomplishes its purpose, it still relies on its own causes. Likewise, the self could not accomplish its objective without activity. Thus, even if one could see the self with the eye of knowledge, liberation could not occur (since the self is not in fact permanent and unchanging). [42] If knowledge arises with a truly-existing object of knowledge, a new seed will be planted in the consciousness, just as an echo will continue long after a sound. But if the object of knowledge is not truly existing, knowledge cannot arise.

[43] How can the cycle of rebirths exist for one who knows the self, when at the same time this knowledge exists without an instrument of knowledge? In addition, since the self is in every way without distinction, how can bondage and liberation exist in it? [44] Moreover, the self cannot be free from suffering even in the state of liberation: when only the self exists, suffering cannot be different from that self (and suffering still occurs), just as fire cannot be different from heat.

[45] How could a latent and unarisen power of cognition produce knowledge without any instrument of knowledge? It would be just as inconsistent as a woodpecker having the ability to peck without a beak!

Objection: If a fire burns, still it is indicated that the person burns by means of the fire. Likewise, even though it is the cognition that knows, it is said that the person knows, not the cognition itself.

Reply: [46] When it is said that a person burns by means of fire, it is the fire that burns, not the one who makes the fire. The burning occurs within the fire, not in the person who does the burning. So too, when it is said that one knows by means of the mind, it the cognition that knows, not the self.

Objection: Just as a potter is called a "potter" even at times when he is not making pots, and fire is called "the burner" even at times it is not burning fuel, so too the self has the nature of knowledge even when it is not related to an instrument of knowledge.

Reply: [47] The self cannot be established by the analogy to the potter since a potter is not always "a potter" because of self-existence. Nor is the self established by the analogy to fire since without something to be burned, fire does not exist. When the self acts by means of an instrument of knowledge, it is correct to say that it has the nature of knowledge, but apart from then "knowledge" is merely a designation in contrast to what is "nonknowledge," and so it is not established as self-existent since it is dependent upon something else for its existence. (Thus, the self could not have knowledge as its nature. In addition, we cannot be one with the self and still be ignorant of it, but if we cannot know the self it cannot exist.)

[48] In addition, you cannot in any way establish that the self, which is by nature non-knowing, can become a knowing performer and enjoyer of the fruits of action. Moreover, what is the purpose of imagining that the self, like the sky, is beyond all mental discriminations merely on the basis of a tradition's texts? (That is, scripture is not a "means of correct knowledge.")

Objection: Even though the self has the nature of nonknowledge, it has the nature of knowledge when the instruments of knowledge are present.

Reply: Since prior to the rise of the instruments, the self has the nature of nonknowledge, it could not be a performer or an enjoyer. [49] In addition, a self without the nature of either knowledge or nonknowledge has no self-existent nature. And a self without any nature is, like the son of a barren woman, nonexistent.

Refutation of the Identity of the Inner Self and the Universal Self

[50] The universal self is not affected by suffering or pleasure when one is tormented or pleased, and thus it cannot arguably be your inner individual self. Thus, it cannot belong to a single person any more than the sky can. [51] If you maintain that such things as meditative knowledge lead to liberation of the inner self, then it must take effort to negate the self. But how could a mortal self become immortal? [52] If the inner self is different from the universal self, then your assertion "Everything is the self" is unacceptable since the individual self would then be different from the universal self. [53] If the inner self is not different from the universal self, then your assertion "Everything is the self" is again unacceptable: since the universal self does not experience pleasure or suffering, the individual self (which experiences them) could not be the universal self. [54] If the universal self is subtle, it cannot be large; if it is large, there is no subtleness. and the self is neither one. How can the formless self have any property of form? "Subtle" and "large," "one" and "many" all are mental discriminations.

Objection: Those who do not see the self conceive it in many forms: some say it all-pervading; some say that it only extends as far as the body; others say it has the nature of a minute particle. However, like the elephant's nature, it is only one but it is also many, like the limbs of the elephant.

Reply: [55] On the basis of the elephant example, it is not reasonable to conclude that what is one has many forms since a part is not considered the whole. In addition, "oneness" does not apply to the part (but only to the whole). The trunk is only the trunk and not the elephant. The "elephant" itself does not exist, and the trunk and so forth have no single nature.

[56ab] If the self has the color of the sun, how can it also be without color?

Vedanta Response: Like foliage, one thing pervades everything — the foliage exists in the root, trunk, branches, and so forth, and thus also has many forms.

Bhavya's reply: [56cd] On the basis of the foliage example, the multiple forms of the self are not to be accepted. [57] Since the foliage is not one, it always changes its form. In addition, since the parts are not one, they are differentiated by conditions.

[58] In addition, concepts such as "most excellent" and "supreme" are meaningful only in relation to something other. How can the existence of such concepts be accepted when there is only oneness?

Refutation of the Self as a Substance or Material Support

[59] If the self were a substance, it could not be all-pervading because substance is not all-pervading. Like a pot (which is a substance), it would also not be permanent. So how then could the universe be filled by it?

[60] "Being a support" is possible only in relation to a substance, but the self has no relation to a substance. It cannot be a support at all because it is unborn, like a sky-flower. (That is, only something that comes into existence in relation to something else can be called "a support.") [61] How can all the elements (earth, water, fire, and air) be precisely the self of the one who experiences the self? It is unacceptable that what is without self is the self, just as what has the nature of a nonentity is not possible.

Refutation of the Oneness and Existence of Space and of the Self

[62] Thus, the difference of the learned and ignorant on this point is seen. Many errors would flow from the self not being one. [63] The self of one person would be perceived by another person's sense-faculties and vice versa because the embodiment of the two is not different or because the place (where the self is) is not different. [64] One person who is still an enjoyer of happiness and suffering would be liberated when another person is liberated; or, conversely, if one person is in the cycle of rebirths, so is another, or if one person suffers, then another should too.

Objection: As both sides to this argument accept, the space within a pot is one with the space outside of the pot. (See verses 8.10-13.)

Reply: [65] The analogy does not work since the oneness and existence of space are not established. [66] The entity free of any substance that causes resistance is indeed known conventionally as "space." There is a place for movement and room for those needing room. Thus, space exists as a designation. But the example of space in a pot is not permanent, all-pervasive, or one, and so it does not establish the existence of a self. [67] Space is not open (but is devoid of objects or substance and so not experiencable), and it is not an active donor of room (because it is room and so provides room passively). (A self is supposedly experiencable and is also an active performer, and so it cannot be like empty, passive space.) Thus, any reason you give regarding space's existence cannot be accepted as a valid reason. [68] And space cannot be regarded as an entity since it does not arise from a cause. Thus, the self does not exist, any more than does the son of a barren woman.

[69] The clay in the shape of a pot is one since it always remains the same clay. But in other pots there is always a new and different piece of clay. Similarly, the self is not one (but differs from person to person).

[70] When one knows, one cannot regard the state of knowing as a state of imagination of one who does not know since there is no error in a state of actually knowing. So too, when one does not know, one cannot regard the state of not knowing as a state of imagination since there is no error here either.

Refutation of the Self as the Performer and Enjoyer of Actions

[71] Because like space, the self does not change and is not attached, the claim that the self is the performer or the enjoyer (of the fruit of action) is not reasonable. Something that always remains the same cannot act or enjoy and so could not be a performer or enjoyer. [72] If the self is the performer and is not stained (by the merit or demerit of action), how can he produce a result that he wishes for? If there is no later enjoyment of the fruits, all of a performer's actions would be pointless. Because the self does not enjoy the fruits, establishing it to be "a performer" is very difficult. The example of the king (from verse 8.15, who behaves according to his desires but remains untouched by demerit in committing demeritorious acts) is thus not reasonable because the king is evil (and will suffer the repercussions of his acts).

Refutation of the Self as One, All-pervasive, Permanent, Inexpressible, and Inconceivable

[73] It is not reasonable that what is without a second (i.e., the self) is "one" since it is independent of anything external (to compare it to). If it is one from its union with "oneness," then the union is only with itself — there is no other relation. Since the self is everything, what could it have a relation with? There does not exist anything different from the self. It cannot relate to itself just as the finger cannot touch its own finger tip.

[74] The self is conceptualized to be many, but if it is one because of the exclusion of diversity, then oneness could not exist in reality since the conception of "oneness" and so forth is only a conventional truth. [75] If a self were found in reality with the form of "oneness" and "permanence," the cognitions and words "one" and so forth would be well-founded because their referents would exist. (But no such referents exist.) [76] But then since the self is conceptualized to be "one" and so forth, how can the self be

beyond conception? But it is undeniable that words function based on referents, which are the domain of mental discriminations. (If the self is one, then the diversity of referents does not exist.) [77] Thus, how can the self be neither an object of cognition nor of speech (if the self and the knowledge are one)? As discussed, it is false that the self is inexpressible or beyond mental discrimination. (That is, the self is a conceptualized entity and thus not ultimately real since there are no real, discrete entities.)

Refutation of Liberation and Enlightenment as a State of Non-Arising Resulting from Knowing the Self

[78] If liberation comes from seeing the self by means of the mind, how can the two be one? The self and cognition are different, and thus there cannot be oneness. In addition, the liberation would be false because the self would be grasped as an object, like the cognition of diversity. [79] If there is knowledge that sees the sameness of all non-arising, then because there is no difference between the knowledge and the non-arising, how could there be seeing? (For seeing something, things must be distinct.) Liberation would then result from not seeing — otherwise, there would be no liberation for anyone.

[80] If enlightenment results from the arising of seeing, how could all non-arising be the same? If seeing is not a truly existing entity and does not arise, it would be the same as a conceptual construction of "non-arising." (That is, it would not be an experience but another conceptual construct.) [81] "Non-arising" is a phenomenon derived from "arising" — it exists only as the absence of arising. Thus, it is not at all reasonable that non-arising is the same as the self or abides within it.

[82] It is not accepted that difference exists in what is unborn as a potentiality, since in reality "being unborn" is not accepted for what is born or for what is not born. [83] If the self is said to be undifferentiated, then it is not different from a sky-flower. It is a proposition that is not true. But if you say that there is differentiation in what is perfected, then the nonduality of what is real cannot be established. [84] Thus, the self is neither an entity nor its absence, and neither different nor identical. Nor is it either permanent or impermanent. Nor is it an object within the scope of cognition (and thus is not an object of knowledge).

[85] We Buddhists agree with you Vedantins that what is real is ultimately beyond speech and cognition. But our reasoning is different: no object of knowledge can be established in any way; thus, there is no domain

for the mind to operate in. When the domain of cognition has ceased, there is no domain of speech. Conventionally, an object of the six forms of cognition is imagined to exist, but from the point of view of reality, what is imagined or conceptually constructed is completely unestablished. Since cognition does not arise regarding nonexistent objects, there are no objects of knowledge, and thus there is no basis for speech.

Vedanta as a Contradictory and Completely Heterodox School

[86] Being convinced that the Buddha's true system is good and being desirous (of truth), you Vedantins have made this doctrine your own. But this mixture of doctrines is infused with contradictory parts, and thus is a mental construction. [87] Who could have faith in such a system! Parts there are completely incompatible, just as when a jewel is not distinguished from a piece of metal. [88] The Buddhist teaching is also varied, but the doctrine of the "self" and "no-self" is used in accordance with conventional and ultimate truth here for the sake of attracting some and turning the remainder away from grasping. The existence of the self is taught in order to divert those who grasp or advocate nonexistence or whose minds are impaired by the view that denies the causality of the fruit of action. The nonexistence of the self is taught to stop attachment to the self and the grasping by adherents of the doctrine of a self. But to those endowed with the endurance for the deep and profound teaching, the doctrine is ultimately taught that there is no self or non-self. Thus, there is no contradiction in the doctrine.

Non-arising and the Absence of Self-existence as the Self or Nature of all Entities

[89] Indeed, the self-existence of entities does not have a birth because it is not constructed and does not disappear. Self-existent and nonexistent entities do not arise from themselves, from others, from both, or without a cause. Self-existence is also declared to be the self in all things. [90] It is said to be one because of its single form and without differentiations, even though there is a differentiation of entities. It pervades all phenomena, is permanent, and does not disappear. It possesses the property of grasping the true defining characteristic of all phenomena: that they have no defining characteristic. [91] It is unarisen because it is not born. For that reason, it is not subject to old age and death. It is imperishable because it is free of perishing. It is considered unsurpassable because of its excellence. [92] It is

not form, sound, smell, and so forth. It is not earth, water, fire, or air. It is not space, the moon, the sun, and so forth. It does not have the defining characteristic of the mind or knowledge. [93] It is everything because it is the self-existence of all entities. But it is not any particular entity since (being eternal) it is without destruction. Because mental afflictions do not arise in it, it is pure. It is also thoroughly tranquil because it completely transcends all actions. [94] It is expressible only by the imposition of conceptual constructions, but in reality it is inexpressible. Moreover, because it is inexpressible in every way, it is said to be "without embellishments." [95] Certainly, if you accept such a self, then it is without faults and completely fit for its purpose because of the identity of the nature of what goes by many names and so forth. In that way, we are the same: you say "supreme self," and we say "non-arising."

[96] Those who are afraid because of the fear generated by the absence of a self remain exactly where they are, just as those who are afraid of empty space remain exactly where they are — where else could they stand? [97] Feel welcome to quench your thirst! Here no one is hindered from anything. The buddhas, the friends of the world, offer this exquisite ambrosia of reality. [98] Abandon the false clinging to the belief in a self, a performer, an enjoyer, and so forth. It is groundless, and it prevents anyone from seeing the real.

Objection: If our doctrine of the self and your doctrine of the non-self are similar, then our objectives are the same.

Reply: [99] From the point of view of reality, it is understood that entities are unarisen, (not because they are the self, but) because they do not arise through self-existence. Indeed, entities are said to be without self-existence because they do not arise through self-existence. [100] The self is not "the lack of self-existence" or "the lack of a self" since that would be a contradiction. If the lack of a self were the same as being the self, then the absence of a cow would be the same as a cow. [101] How is it plausible that a real performer and enjoyer is without self-existence? It is not by chance that a performer and enjoyer is seen here as being like the son of a barren woman. [102] How can a self-existent self arise? And how could everything dissolve into it? It is implausible to imagine anything arising from, or dissolving into, a sky-flower!

[103] As long as the power of cognition proceeds by having as its object the absence of a self-existent entity, so long will one think of "one" and so forth as the imposition of the conceptual constructs of cognition. [104]

When both conceptual and nonconceptual cognition ceases, the tranquil cessation of all conceptual projection of what is an object of cognition occurs. A "nonconceptual cognition" apprehends what is not the self without any conception of it as either having self-existence or not. (See verse 3.265.) Reality is that in which all entities are completely unsupported (i.e., empty of anything that would provide external support to a cognition of entities) and which is beyond speech and knowledge. Your view of a self that is conceptually constructed is not reality.

* * *

Notes

Verse 1.1. The attribute "not a receptacle storing mental phenomena (*analaya*)" is a rebuttal to the Yogachara idea of a "storehouse-consciousness (*alaya-vijnana*)" that stores karmic seeds and thus explains the continuity in rebirths.

The fundamental realm (*dharma-dhatu*) is the source and substratum of the phenomena of a Buddha (Conze 1967: 144, 225-26). It is the closest the Mahayana come to having a transcendental Absolute (ibid.: 95.) The reference comes in the commentary, and not in the text itself. Thus, this may come from a period long after Bhavya.

Verse 3.1. Note the importance of *vision* for Indian philosophy. "Vision," "illumination," and "insight" are all central terms. Even the name for a philosophical school — "*darshana*" — comes from a root meaning "to see." The "eye of insight (*prajna*)" analyzes phenomena and leads to the wordless "eye of knowledge (*jnana*)" that sees the true nature of things. And erroneous philosophical positions are wrong "views (*drishtis*)."

Verse 3.7cd. See MAS 7-11 and accompanying notes.

Verse 3.23cd. The constituents of the body and consciousness are all ultimately conditioned and not unconditioned.

Verse 3.24. See the commentary on the ambiguity of Bhavya denying what is known.

Verse 3.25-26. The distinction here is between the "gross elements (*bhutas*) and the four traditional elements (earth, water, fire, and air) that, according to the Samkhyas, are emitted out of the gross elements. Because the gross elements are produced they have no self-existence and thus neither does anything that is emitted or produced from them.

Verse 3.26, Bhavya's form of reasoning requires an example (see the Commentary), but most of the times he merely says "like *x*" or "as with *x*"without further explanation as to why the example is apropos. In verse 3.46, he simply uses another sense-faculty as the example for the eye.

Verses 3.31-34. Note that there is a distinction between the four elements and substance (*dravya*). That is, substance is not *matter* in the modern sense. See the note on Aryadeva's HVNP 3ab.

Verse 3.35. "Mind (*manas*)" and "consciousness (*chitta*)" are distinguishable: the former is a sense-faculty like the five senses recognized in the West while the latter is more broadly "mind."

Verses 3.40-47. The "visual sense-faculty" is not the material eye.

Verse 3.70. "Perception (*samjna*)" is one of the bodily aggregates. It is ability to recognize or identify a thing. See the note on Aryadeva's *Four Hundred Verses*, verse 13.22 for the five aggregates. Perception involves *structuring*: we discriminate and see discrete objects. It is not the same as a structureless sensory-sensation. Nor is it reality as it really is.

Verse 3.71. In Buddhist psychology, there are eighteen constituents (*dhatus*) altogether: the six physical sense-organs (the mind [*manas*] being the sixth), the six sense-faculties associated with them, and the six sense-objects. The later two categories together are the sense-fields (*ayatanas*).

Verses 3.77-84. See MK 2. He analyzes all the aspects of "going" because it is the paradigm of activity (*kriya*) and thus is applicable more broadly.

Verse 3.138. In Samkhya metaphysics, "matter (*pradana* or *prakriti*)" is the material out of which the physical universe evolves. It is distinct from the individual center of consciousness that makes up a person (*purusha*).

Verse 3.266. Bhavya later equates reality with the "Dharma-body (*dharma-kaya*)" of the Buddha of which the historical Buddha is only a manifestation — i.e., a transcendental reality comparable to the Brahman of the Upanishads (verse 3.289). In the commentary to verse 1.3, he says that the that-ness (*tattva*) of reality is synonymous with "such-ness (*tathata*)," "emptiness," and the Dharma Body of the Buddha.

Chapter 8. The Prasangas see Bhavya as somewhat of a misfit, in part because of the "sympathies to a certain extent with the monistic illusionism of the early Vedantins" that he displays in this chapter (Gokhale 1972: 45).

Verses 8.1-2. Bhavya uses "the universal self (*atman*)" and "the self of the individual (*purusha*)" interchangeably for the self that transcends the individual, mortal person (see verse 8.17). In Vedanta, the *atman* pervades the entire universe; in Samkhya, there are a plurality of *purushas*, each a core of consciousness, isolated from matter (*prakriti*). Bhavya also uses "lord (*ishvara*)" and "great lord (*maha-ishvara*)" for the self. This shows that at this early stage, the terminology for Vedanta had not been sorted out yet.

Verse 8.3. One attains a unity (*samya*) with the *atman*. This is not the later Advaita Vedantins' view: we are already one with the *brahman/atman*, and so there is no second real thing to unite with that the one reality — only our knowledge of the state of things needs to be corrected.

Verse 8.3-4. The lord is the "*kartri*." This could mean either "creator" of all realms or "the real actor in all deeds" even those for which we think we are the actors. In verse 4, the lord is the "maker of action (*karma-krit*)." This could mean that he is the one that connects action with its karmic effects. That is, he is the enforcer of the law of karma.

Verse. 8.5. The image of beings being born out of the self like threads out of an unchanging spider is in *Brihadaranyaka Upanishad* 2.1.20, *Mundaka Upanishad* 1.7, and *Shvetashvatara Upanishad* 6.10. Such an emergentism does not fit the later Advaita Vedanta's view of oneness.

Verse 8.7. See *Shvetashvatara Upanishad* 3.9.

Verse 8.9. See *Bhagavad-gita* 5.18 and 6.29.

Verse 8.13. Brahman is likened to space, which is extended. Advaita did not see Brahman as in any way an object or extended. It was a nondimensional reality that transcends what we see as the objective universe.

Verse 8.17. The self is "beyond conception (*avikalpa*, i.e., without mental discriminations of distinct entities) and beyond the realm of speech" because it is free of discrete entities that we could experience and conceptualize.

Verse 8.18. Bhavya uses "*paksha*" — "proposition" — here, as Nagarjuna does in the *Jewel Garland of Advice*. It means the same as "thesis (*pratijna*)," which comes up more often in Nagarjuna's works.

Verse 8.19. Mental afflictions do not depend on language. According to Bhavya, animals do not have language but have the mental affliction of the failure to grasp the nature of things (Potter 2003: 391).

Verse 8.25. "*Buddhi*" can mean "cognition (*dhi*)" or the mental power to have cognitions — the "intellect," "intelligence," or the "mind (*mati*)."

Verses 8.41-45. See Nagarjuna's VV on "objects of knowledge" and "instruments of knowledge."

Verses 8.65-68. See Aryadeva's SS chapters 3 and 4.

Verse 8.93. Advaitins also claim that Brahman can be expressed only by the superimposition (*adhyasa*) of concepts onto what is inexpressible.

Verse 8.96. On the fear of emptiness, see R 1.

II. Commentaries

The Death of Aryadeva

Aryadeva's writings do not require commentary beyond the notes added after each text. His main contribution to the Madhyamaka thought was explicitly to criticize both Buddhist and non-Buddhist schools with Nagarjuna's method. (And it must be said that the arguments in his writing are not as rigorous as Nagarjuna's.) However, the legend surrounding his death is worth relating because it highlights the religious nature of Buddhist philosophy.

Aryadeva was a formidable debater, and he died from being stabbed in the stomach by a student of a non-Buddhist teacher he had just defeated in a debate. But Aryadeva was a Mahayana Buddhist to the end. As he lay dying, holding his wound, he forgave his attacker and expressed his sorrow for the karmic demerit the young man had incurred; he told him to take his (Aryadeva's) things and flee. His assailant was moved by Aryadeva's compassion and asked to be taught the Buddhist doctrine. Aryadeva explained the Madhyamaka doctrine that things were empty of self-existence, and the student converted to Buddhism. When Aryadeva's students arrived at the scene and asked who did this, he explained that, since there are no real entities, there was no "friend" and no "enemy," no "murderer" or "one who is murdered," and hence no "murder." Serenely he passed away.

* * *

Buddhapalita's Contribution to Madhyamaka Philosophy

Dependent Designation

Buddhapalita was not a major innovator, but a few point in his philosophy should be emphasized. One is his emphasis on "dependent designation (*upadaya-prajnaptir*)." In MK 24.18, Nagarjuna equates "emptiness" with "dependent arising" (*pratitya-samutpada*) and then says that this indicator (*prajnaptir*) is dependent (*upadaya*) and that comprehending this is the "middle way." In MK 22.11, he also says "'Empty,' 'not empty,' 'both (empty and not empty),' or 'neither (empty nor not empty)' — these should not be said, but they are said only as indicators." The idea is that names and words do not correspond to any reality but are merely social conventions about the constantly changing world. Buddhapalita makes much more use of the idea: whatever entities arise dependent upon other entities are only dependently designated. What is real would not depend in any way on anything, and their designations would reflect that independence. But dependently designated entities arise dependently upon other dependently designated entities — all such designations would only reflect worldly customs. But this means that for the Madhyamikas all alleged realities are really only dependent designations. For example, Buddhapalita says that an agent depends on an action and is designated "an agent" in relation to it; in turn, the action arises dependent on the agent, and is designated "an action" in relation to him; thus, the two are designated in relation to each other and are not established or nonestablished by self-existence; apart from the designation as the "middle way," we see no other defining characteristic of the establishment of the two (MKV 8.12).

This leads Buddhapalita to speak of *dependent designation* where most Madhayamikas would speak of *dependent arising*. For example, MKV 22.16 states that the Buddha is designated in dependence on his aggregates; he is not established by himself and so is without self-existence. Or, the Buddha is designated in dependence on his aggregates and does not exist by self-existence (MKV 22.2). By a designation, something is designated as an "entity" that arose according to causes and conditions, but no entities exist by self-existence (MKV 8.13). The meaning of dependent designation is precisely that an entity that is dependently designated cannot be said to be real or not real because it is completely empty of self-existence (MKV 22.10). Any entity is a dependent designation (MKV 17.33). All conceptual constructions (*kalpanas*), entities, and nonentities (i.e., the absence of real entities) lead to the faults of permanence and annihilation, but what is dependent arisen stands outside the views of real "entities" and "nonentities" and thus is free from the faults of the views of permanence and annihilation (ibid.). This permits the conventional Buddhist and worldly teachings about agent, action, result, experiencer of the result, mental afflictions, and body but without the faults of permanence and annihilation (ibid.).

The Doctrine of Two Truths

The basis for that claim is the doctrine of the "two truths." We do not have Buddhapalita's Commentary on MK 24.18 where Nagarjuna explicitly mentions this doctrine, but he does employ it. What is "dependently designated" is what is real from the conventional point of view (*vyavahara*), but from the point of view of true ontological status (*paramarthatas*) such entities are not real. (Buddhapalita is not adverse to using the word "view (*drishti*)" to refer to the point of view of emptiness [e.g., MKV 18.7cd].) Buddhapalita uses this doctrine of two truths to explain the Buddha apparently claiming "Everything is real" (MKV 18.8ab): according to worldly truth, it is said "The pot exists," and because a pot is impermanent, it is said "The pot is broken," but when one investigates reality (*tattva-cinta*), a "pot" is not possible but is only a dependent designation — how could it be broken? So too, the Buddha is said to be impermanent according to worldly, superficial reality (*lokasamvriti*): "The Buddha is old; the Buddha has passed into nirvana." But when investigated from the point of view of reality (*paramarthatas*), not entity "the Buddha" is possible — how then could his old age and nirvana be possible (MKV 22.16.)?

Words are as empty as any entities. They exist only according to worldly convention (MKV 19.6). But this does not render language useless. In particular, the buddhas affirm "this" or "that" according to worldly usage, but those who wish to see the that-ness of reality must not cling to the words spoken according to worldly conventions but must grasp the reality (MKV 18.8). That is, words do not designate anything real in the world and yet the enlightened buddhas can still have recourse to the linguistic conventions of a society without falling from the state of enlightenment. So too, the unenlightened must get beyond the conventional designations and grasp reality as is truly is. Engaging in conventional activities without attachment to existence and nonexistence, liberation is possible (MKV 15.7).

Knowledge and Liberation

To Buddhapalita, the comprehension of reality is called "liberation" (MKV 18.4, 5). But this is not merely acknowledge the claim that reality is devoid of self-existent entities. Rather, this involves an investigation into reality (*tattva-cinta*) (MKV 10.14). The practitioner must cultivate a realization of this through meditation that leads to *actually seeing* that the world is empty of all self-existence, not merely thinking this is true. The difference is between one who sees that the world is empty of self-existence and one who merely says "The world is empty of self-existence" without seeing that this is true (MKV 18.7). The defining characteristic of reality (*tattva-lakshana*) is knowing its nature directly oneself, not learning it from another (MKV 18.9). Those who see entities (*bhavas*) as "real" and "not real" do not see reality (*tattva*); thus, for them liberation is not possible. For those who see entities and the absence of entities, bondage and liberation are not possible because views of permanence and annihilation follow if there are entities; bondage and liberation are established only for the proponents of dependent arising (MKV 16.10). Only by seeing entities' lack of self-existence will one be liberated (MKV 15.7). Seeing the lack of self-existence in entities is the vision of reality as it really is; it is the middle way, and realizing this is the attainment of reality (MKV 15.11).

Buddhapalita confronts the objection that if there is no self-existence, there is nothing real (i.e., *ontological nihilism*), then no one can have a vision of reality and thus liberation is impossible. He replies: entities' lack of self-existence is reality as it truly is. The Madhyamikas see reality illuminated by the sun of dependent arising. Thus, only they have the vision of reality, and so only for them is liberation possible (MKV 15.6).

Ontology

Ontologically, everything in the phenomenal world is dependently arisen. All entities are established to have the status of a magical illusion, a mirage, the city in the sky of the heavenly musicians, a dream, an echo, or a reflection (MKV 11.8, 18.8cd), since they are dependent for their existence on other entities and thus are not independent and self-existent. Only real things can be identical to or different from other real things (MKV 18.10), and since what is dependently designated is empty of self-existence and thus not real, to what could such an entity be identical and from what could it be different (MKV 21.16, 22.7)? Rather, things are like a seed and a sprout: not identical, but not totally unrelated (MKV 18.10). All other relations exist only as conventional, not as ultimately real — e.g., past, present, and future; best, middling, and worst; beginning, middle, and end; far and near; earlier and later; oneness and otherness; identity and difference; cause and effect; long and short; small and large; self and nonself; conditioned and unconditioned; one, two, and many (MKV 19.4).

As with other Madhayamikas, Buddhapalita rejects both the notion that anything is real (*sat*) — i.e., self-existent and eternal — and that phenomena are unreal (*asat*) — i.e., totally nonexistent, like the horns of a rabbit. Self-existence is the opposite of change — it is unchanging and permanent — but we observe change in entities, and thus self-existence is not possible for entities (MKV 15.8). What is real cannot change and so cannot be a cause or an effect since these involve change; also what is unreal cannot be a cause since it does not exist (MKV 1.7). But we cannot say that what is dependently arisen "exists" or "does not exist" (MKV 17.30) since they have no self-existence. But what is empty is not nothingness — Buddhapalita, like Nagarjuna and Aryadeva before him, is not a nihilist (e.g., MKV 18.7cd). In MKV 20.24, he addressed the charge of advocating nihilism (*na-asti-vada*). He replies that the conceptual construction that things exist by self-existence is simply not possible; things are established only as dependent designations. Elsewhere he states: the Madhyamikas do not say the aggregates, elements, and bases are nonexistent; rather, they reject the doctrine that they are real; both the doctrines of existence and nonexistence have great faults; thus, they teach that because the aggregates, elements, and bases arise dependently, they are free from the faults of existence and nonexistence, not annihilated, not permanent, but they do not say that they are nonexistent (MKV 5.7). Rather, because the aggregates, elements, and sense-bases are dependently arisen, they are free from the faults of existence and nonexistence, not annihilated and not eternal (MKV 5.8). In sum, the Madhyamikas are not denying the phenomenal world in banishing the idea of "self-existent" parts and thus are not ontological nihilists.

More than Nagarjuna, Buddhapalita emphasizes the idea in MK 1.1. that there is no "self-arising (svata-utpatti)." For the Madhyamikas, real arising and ceasing in general is impossible: what is real cannot arise or cease since it is permanent (eternal) and so has no beginning or end; the non-real cannot arise or cease since, being unreal, there is nothing to arise or cease. Either way, there is no arising or ceasing, and the terms are merely worldly conventions. Nor can there be a moment where something is partially arisen and partially unarisen since it would have both of these faults (see SSK 5). Also in general, an effect cannot arise conjoined to the cause because then the two would exist together; nor can they exist disconnected or the cause would not really be a cause. What is dependently arisen cannot be real because it is dependent on causes and conditions and hence is not permanent with an inherent nature but changing. Buddhapalita's basic argument with regard to any arising is to ask whether something exists or does not exist at the time it supposedly arises — if it exists already, then it cannot arise again; and if it does not exist, then how can something that does not exist arise? But self-arising in particular is impossible: nothing can arise from itself since in order to so it would already have to exist, and so the idea of "arising" would be meaningless; or, if it occurs, it would keep on recurring without end.

He gives numerous examples of what is dependently designated being neither real (self-existent) nor unreal (totally nonexistent). For instance, it is not possible to say that the Buddha who is dependently designated either exists or does not exist (MKV 22.11). He rejects the conceptual construction that an actor and his action are really existent (sadbhuta) or really nonexistent; rather, "actor" and "action" are dependent designations; thus, the two are not maintained to be either real or not real (MKV 8.12). So too, action lacks self-existence, and so what could arise? And even if some action did arise, it would not arise with a self-existent nature of action. What does not arise as self-existent action is not action since it does not have the self-existent nature of action (MKV 17.21). So too, no person is found who is established by his own self-existence, and so there is nothing about which one could say "He is this." The designations "real" or "not real" do not apply to that person. Because he is not established by his own self-existence, how can it be said that he exists? But because he is made manifest by vision and the other senses, how can it said that he does not exist? Thus, the conceptualizations "He exists" and "He does not exist" are not possible. The "person" is simply designated, but apart from that, no other establishment of it is possible (MKV 9.12). The causes of the body, action, and defilements are dependently arisen and thus empty of self-existence. It must also be held that effects possess the same nature of the qualities of their causes — thus, if the causes of the body and so forth are empty, how can the body and so forth be self-existent (MKV 17.27)?

"Empty" should not be said, nor "Not empty," nor "Both empty and not empty," nor "Neither empty nor not empty" — but they are said for the sake of exposing the nonreality of conceptualizations (*abhuta-samkalpa*) and for the sake of designating the ultimate nature of reality (*paramartha-tattva*) (MKV 22.11). Such groundless discriminations of objects arise from conceptual projections (*prapancha*) (MKV 18.5). Those who mind adheres to the notion "This is real" concerning phenomena (*dharma*) form discriminations among the phenomena arising from their conceptual projections (MKV 18.5).

Three points on the issue of ontology need to be made. First, Buddhapalita uses the term "*tattva*" extensively. The word literally means "that-ness (*tat-tva*)." In classical Indian philosophy, "truth" and "reality" are not differentiated in the concept "*satya*"— both truth and reality are what is able to accomplish things, i.e., bring things about. But his preference for a term referring to the that-ness of things warrants giving "*tattva*" an ontological, rather than epistemological, reading — i.e., "reality" rather than "truth."

Second, the Madhyamaka idea that what is empty is "unarisen and unceased" needs to be clarified. Since action lacks self-existence, it is unarisen and because it is unarisen it does not disappear; those who do not understand reality have become attached to the word "nondisappearance" as a real entity and utter many worthless statements (MKV 17.21). The Commentary on verse 18.7 states that we see that all entities are unarisen and unceasing because they are empty of self-existence. The Commentary on verse 21.9 states that what does not exist by self-existence cannot arise or cease. What is empty does not exist by self-existence; thus, how could it arise or cease (since there is nothing real that could arise or cease) (MKV 20.18)? In other words, what is empty of self-existence cannot arise or cease. Thus, the empty is unarisen and unceasing. However, being "unarisen and unceasing" may make us think that what is empty is *eternal* since what is eternal never arose and will never cease. But to conclude that is to misconstrue the point: only the self-existent is *real*, and for Buddhapalita only the real could arise or cease. What is empty is not real to begin with and so there is nothing to arise or cease — it is incapable of arising in the first place.

Third, Buddhapalita, like Nagarjuna, does not think of "emptiness" as an ontological reality — e.g., the source of what is empty or any "ultimate reality." In his Commentary on MK 13.8, he explicitly states "There is no entity called 'emptiness.'" He continues by saying that for those who are attached to "emptiness" as an entity, that attachment cannot be removed by anything else — Nagarjuna said here they were incurable. In the Commentary on this verse, Buddhapalita gives this example: if someone is told "There is nothing" and then replies "Give me that nothing!" how can he be made to grasp the notion of nonexistence? Only those who see that "emptiness" is itself an empty concept have achieved emptiness.

The true state of the world for Buddhapalita, as for Nagarjuna, is to be free of our conceptualizations, i.e., the discrimination (*vikalpa*) of independent entities. The phenomenal world free of our projections is how things are "from the highest point of view" and experientially realizing this is liberation. This does not mean that "emptiness" does not label or describe the ultimate nature of things but only that any realization of the truth involves a personal experience and not merely the acceptance of a claim even if that claim is true. To use a Buddhist analogy, the distinction here is between *accepting the claim* "Water quenches thirst" and actually *drinking* water and *knowing* the claim is true. Drinking the water is a nonconceptual event, but it does not change the fact that the claim "Water quenches thirst" is a true statement that reflects reality. To the extent that we think "This is water" or "This is quenching my thirst" as we drink, the experience is arguably not nonconceptual or nonlinguistic, but then again if we were thinking those thoughts we would not be approaching the experience free of conceptions and thus would not be enlightened. Similarly, merely accepting the claim "The world is empty of self-existent entities" is not enlightenment: we must stop thinking in terms of "empty entities" and actually see the world as it truly is.

* * *

Bhavaviveka's Innovations

The Doctrine of Two Truths

Bhavya's major innovation involves his new way of arguing, but before discussing that, another important point should be noted: he utilized the "two truths" more explicitly than does Nagarjuna (see Jones 2010: 147-48) and introduced a new wrinkle. He starts his *Summary of the Meaning of the Middle Way* by distinguishing "ultimate truth (*parama-artha*)" and "conventional truth (*samvrti*)." The first type of truth expresses reality as it truly is — i.e., what in the final analysis is real. Statements made "from the ultimate point of view (*paramarthatas*)" are only about what is truly real. More literally, they are topics of the "ultimate matter" or "ultimate goal." As discussed below, some ultimate truths are statable (MAS 4-6).

Conventional truth expresses the realities of everyday matters in terms of "established uses" — worldly conventions (*loka-vyavahara*) — that "cover" or "obscure" reality as it really is (*tathata*) since it cannot express the ultimate ontological status of what it discusses. Thus, these are "surface" truths that cover how things really are. Entities that arise dependently only exist conventionally — ultimately, there are no entities or "arising" involved in the process of changing phenomena. Of particular concern to Buddhists are the causes and conditions involved in changes. But even the four "noble truths (*arya-satyas*)" involving the end of suffering (*duhkha*) are only conventional truths since they are not about the ultimate ontological nature of things but only about how things are on a conventional level — ultimately, there is no "suffering" and no one who suffers.

Nagarjuna gives conventional truth a role in the Buddha's teaching and argues that without relying upon worldly convention the truth from the highest point of view cannot be taught (MK 24.8, 10). But many Buddhists rejected the doctrine of "two truths" arguing that if the higher variety is true then the lower type is ultimately false (see SS 10.15). However, conventional truths are about something other than ultimate ontological status, and Bhavya apparently was the first Buddhist to defend them as important.

Ultimate truth is of two types: what can be conceptualized or specified in words (*paryaya-paramartha*) and what cannot (*a-paryaya-paramartha*) (MAS 4-6). Thus, some ultimate truths are expressible and some are not. Expressible truths involve the ultimate ontological nature of things in terms of *entities* being empty of self-existence. But how reality is in itself beyond the negation of self-existence is inexpressible. There are "inexpressible *truths*" since the concept "*satya*" does not differentiate "truth" and "reality." That is, Bhavya is saying that there are realities that cannot be reflected in language. That the expressible ultimate truths must rely on conventions (see MK 24.10) does not mean that they are in any sense "conventional truths" — they are still about the ultimate ontological status of things, and thus they are in a different class from conventional truths. In earlier Buddhism, they would be called statements of "final meaning (*nitartha*)," not "provisional meaning (*neyartha*)." Only the conceptualizable is expressible, and so only imagined entities are expressible. But all ultimate truths are free of conceptual projection (*prapancha*), even those that are expressible (MAS 4). Thus, reality as it truly is is free of the conceptual distinctions we project onto it even when we expressing ultimate truths.

Bhavya also distinguishes "true (*tathya*)" and "false (*mithya*)" conventional "truths." Something with causal power — the capacity to perform or to achieve a purpose (*artha-kriya-samartha*) — is what is "genuine conventional truth." What is "true" can achieve something — again, what is "real" and what is "true" are not differentiated in the Indian concept of "*satya*" (MAS 10). The case of the rope that we take to be a snake is a "false conventional truth": although our misreading of the situation may indeed produce an emotional reaction and thus is a truth (*satya*), in reality there is no "snake" there in any way, and so there is nothing that has no power to do anything — it is all a matter of our erroneous subjective reaction. Thus, a "false conventional truth" is still part of the conventional reality (*samvriti*) and thus a "reality/truth (*satya*)" (MAS 3, 9). It is what is thought to be true but in fact has no reality, even conventionally (MAS 4). That is, it is a claim that *appears* true but is false even on the conventional level. "True conventional truths" are the customary truths accepted by most people but free of any ultimate ontological implications. "True conventional truths" are false only when misread as making our discriminated entities into the ultimate features of reality, but they are true if we do not misread them ontologically. False conventionalities are false even without considering the true ontological status of the entities involved. Thus, the "water" in a mirage is a "false conventional truth," while the water in a river is a true conventional truth.

The Two Truths and Metaphysics

But having the enlightening knowledge does not change conventional facts — leaving aside the issue of paranormal powers, a broken arm would still be broken and a poisonous snake bite would still kill despite knowing that ultimately there are no "arms" or "snakes." More generally, Bhavya says that what the world unanimously believes to exist the Madhyamikas admit to exist conventionally. He can both accept Buddhist metaphysics of "dependent arising" (from the conventional point of view) and reject it (from the ultimate point of view). Thus, apparent contradictions of affirming and denying the same thing can be resolved: he can deny something is utterly nonexistent while still claiming it is not a real, self-existent entity in the final analysis, thereby carving out the Madhyamaka "middle way."

Thus, entities arise dependently (from the conventional point of view), and yet there are no real, self-existent entities (from the point of view of ultimate ontological status). That is, there are no real distinct entities in reality existing by their own self-existence (*svabhava*) — such entities are only the product of our ideas. Reality is not made up of a collection of discrete, "self-existent" entities, but there is something there empty of such divisions — reality as it really is (*tathata*). On the basis of ordinary perception, he can admit the conditions of perception really exist *conventionally*, but from the highest point of view — the point of view of the "that-ness (*tattva*)" of reality — all conditioned things including perception are empty of anything giving them an unchanging essence (Potter 2003: 385). Conventionally, things have defining characteristics (*lakshanas*) — indeed, he even says they have self-existence (MHK 3.25) — but ultimately there are none (MHK 8.48). (In the Buddhist metaphysics, there are no such "essences," but it should be noted that in current Western metaphysics and philosophy of mind essences are making a comeback.) He can accept "going" conventionally while claiming that ultimately there is no "goer" (i.e., one who goes) and hence no "going" (MHK 3.81-82). So too, we can conventionally speak of "rebirth" and "release," but ultimately there are no such things and no "person" to be reborn or released (MHK 3.89). Conventionally, Buddhists deny the existence of any real, self-existent "self" in any sense whatsoever, but the ultimate doctrine is that there is no "self" and no "non-self" as a reality either (MHK 8.88).

The doctrine of "two truths" also explains an apparent contradiction in Bhavya's work concerning whether something is *knowable* (*jneya*). Sometimes "what is knowable" is considered not real and sometimes it is considered real (e.g., MHK 3.24, 3.90-91). But the "two truths" approach removes the apparent conflict. From the ultimate point of view, what is knowable is *reality as it really is* without any covering. But if something is knowable conventionally, this means that conventional distinctions are involved and thus what is known is *not real*. Reality is expressible conventionally by the superimposition of conceptual constructions (*kalpana-samaropa*), but from the ultimate point of view reality in fact is inexpressible (MHK 8.94) and thus free of all conceptual projection (*prapancha*). So, if something is knowable or expressible conventionally, it is a distinct object of knowledge and thus not ultimately real. But what is knowable from the ultimate point of view is real and not a distinct "object" at all. Nirvana is unknowable because from the ultimate point of view it is not a distinct object (MHK 3.109). Knowledge of liberation disappears once one realizes that there is no self-existence (MHK 3.115) — thus, the ambrosia of knowing reality that is attained through a nonconceptual cognition (*avikalpa-dhi*) in a manner free of all conscious knowing (MHK 3.136), i.e., a knowledge without mental discriminations. It is a "tranquil" knowledge (*jnana*) that comes about through the inaction of intellectual activity, unlike a cognition (*dhi*) (MHK 1.3), since reality is free of distinctions to be cognized. A nonconceptual cognition is needed, but even if the experiencer is aware that he or she is having a "nonconceptual cognition" then concepts are still operating in his or her mind (see MHK 3.265). Thus, only when both conceptual and nonconceptual cognition ceases does the cessation of all conceptual projection of objects of cognition finally occur (MHK 8.104).

The ontological truth is that reality as it truly is is empty of our conceptual projections (*prapancha-shunya*). We can state what reality is not (e.g. MK 18.9), but no positive depiction is possible because it is free of any structure that could be mirrored in concepts (MAS 7-8). "Emptiness (*shunyata*)" itself is as empty of anything self-existent (*nihsvabhava*) as any convention — it is not some transcendental source out of which phenomena emerge. Reality as it really is is devoid of any type of metaphysical substance, and the wise do not see the emptiness of reality as an entity *"emptiness"* in any sense (see MK 13.8). As Bhavya puts it in MHK 3.263: "Emptiness is empty of any self-existence — indeed, it is empty of 'emptiness.' Thus, the wise do not see emptiness as 'emptiness.'" The necessary knowledge to realize that this is actually true is devoid of any conceptualizations including "emptiness." Without our concepts, we cannot express the nature of reality as it truly is beyond saying that it is free of the permanence of being (*sat*) and the nonexistence of nonbeing (*a-sat*). That is, reality as it truly is does not have what would give permanent existence to individual entities, but it is not completely nonexistent either, as is a rabbit's horn. Beyond that, the bare "such-ness" or "being-ness" of things is ineffable — it is a dimension of things that cannot be expressed without misleading the listener.

New Method of Arguing

Bhavya's major innovation was the claim that the defense of the Madhyamaka position requires a method of argument or reasoning (*yukti*) that involves a positive defense of a claim, not merely the negative *reductio ad absurdum* arguments exemplified by Nagarjuna and Buddhapalita. Later Tibetans credited him with founding a subtradition of Madhyamaka called the "Svatantrika," after the term *"svatantrika-anumana"* for the independent premises and formal reasoning that members of this tradition advocate. The counter subtradition then became known as the "Prasangika," after the method that of drawing out consequences (*prasanga*) that its members believed their opponents would find unacceptable. The later Svatantrika was also known as the Sautranika-Madhyamaka in contrast to a later synthesized tradition — the Yogachara-Madhyamaka. But these labels only arose hundred of years later in Tibet, and whether later Madhyamikas in India (such as Chandrakirti) thought of themselves as belonging to one of two subtraditions is a question raised by historians. (See Dreyfus and McClintock 2003.) In India, the more usual division was between the Madhyamikas who accepted external objects conventionally and the Yogacharas who said that external objects did not exist in any sense; the Madhyamikas also extended the idea that all things are only conventionally real to the mind, while the Yogacharas defended a form of idealism. In particular, Bhavya defends both that what is really there is not merely mental, and that what is conventionally real can be accepted conventionally: we project our conventional constructs on what is really there (*tattva*), but even the constructs — conventional entities — are not totally nonexistent (*asat*). His position apparently dominated later Indian Madhyamaka philosophy. Only Chandrakirti, perhaps a century after Bhavya, began to question whether Bhavya's innovation violated Nagarjuna's intent. Nevertheless, the Prasangika became the dominant tradition in Tibet, where the schools including the Dalai Lama's consider it the highest of the Mahayana schools.

One Buddhist school, started by Dignaga, who lived around the time of Buddhapalita and is associated with the Yogachara tradition, took a serious interest in the nature of reasoning and argument. They developed a formal logical structure for arguments that was adapted from the Hindu school that focused on reasoning, the Nyaya. The Naiyayikas' standard syllogism consisted of five members:

(1) The proposition to be established (e.g., "The house is on fire")
(2) The reason ("Because we see smoke")
(3) An example ("Whatever is smoking is on fire, e.g., a camp fire")
(4) The application ("The house, like a camp fire, has smoke")
(5) The conclusion ("Therefore, the house is on fire")

More than one reason may be given. The examples can be positive (how something is like something else) or negative (how something contrasts with something else); sometimes both types of examples are given.

In order to "modernize" Nagarjuna's thought, Bhavya applied the syllogism-form. The point of employing the syllogism in Indian debates was to convince *others*, not to justify a knowledge-claim to *oneself*, and thus Bhavya adopted a form of premise and syllogism that others would accept. That is, it is an attempt to refute others' positions on grounds that they would accept, and to do this Bhavya needed to employ a form that the opponents would recognize as valid. Nagarjuna and those in the Prasangika school do not adopt such a form but accept that drawing out the negative implications of others' arguments is sufficient.

In the Buddhist adaptation, the syllogism consisted of only the first three members: a proposition (*praksha*), a reason (*hetu*), and an example (*drishtanta*) of the positive variety only. This is called a logical "inference (*anumana*)," but in this form no conclusion is *inferred* from premises: the structure is different — a reason and example are simply given for a claim. For example, from *Verses on the Heart of the Middle Way* 8.26:

(*Proposition*) Cognitions that have form and so forth as their object do not arise with the self as the performer, (*Reason*) because their arising is dependent on conditions, (*Example*) just as fire depends on a light-focusing crystal.

For Bhavya, a proposition about being is always qualified as "from the point of view of what is real" or "from the highest sense" — *paramarthatas*. He argues that without this qualification claims against the reality of "arising" conflict with the established Buddhist doctrine of "dependent arising." Thus, all his premises are qualified — they present how things are from the ultimate ontological point of view.

This is not to say that all of Bhavya's verses are in that form. Nor is it to say that Nagarjuna, Aryadeva, and Buddhapalita do not present *reasons* and *examples* for there claims. But their reasons are for *rejecting self-existence* — e.g., we see change and since the self-existent does not change, the self-existent cannot exist. Their arguments are in the form, for example, "The human body is empty of self-existence, because it arises dependently." In no way do these arguments reject reasoning or logic. Rather, the difference is that these arguments advance no reasons other than criticism of self-existence for why we should accept emptiness, and thus they do not commit the Madhyamikas to holding any counterclaim during these debates. That is, this method negates one proposition without giving the opponents an implied, affirmative counter-proposition to attack.

But Bhavya argues that without a positive reason and example for holding a claim, an argument cannot exclude the opposite thesis and thus does not have full probative force (Ruegg 1981: 64). That is, without a positive reason to hold the Madhyamaka claim, the negative method alone would still permit some counter-claim to be acceptable. Thus, Bhavya argues in his Commentary on MK 1.1 that Buddhapalita's argument against self-causation in his Commentary on the verse — that any arising from what is self-existent and thus already existing would be pointless, and in addition if arising from oneself were possible the arising would go on endlessly — suggests the propositions "arising has a point" and "arising is finite," which is unacceptable to the Madhyamikas. "Emptiness is defined as the absence of all conceptual elaborations [*prapancha*], and thus the total, categorical negation must not leave any conceivable thing remaining" (Dalai Lama 2009: 85).

In sum, Bhavya thinks it is necessary to restate the Madhyamaka arguments in a formal syllogism that defended a proposition and did not merely attack another claim. Whether Bhavya and Buddhapalita differed on more than this point over basic Buddhist doctrines is a matter of debate. (See the articles by William Ames, Tom Tillemans, C. W. Huntington, and Sara McClintock in Dreyfus & McClintock 2003.) But it must be said that Bhavya in responding to Buddhapalita did not think he was creating a new branch of the Madhyamaka tradition — he was criticizing a fellow member of the same tradition and not accusing Buddhapalita of being unorthodox or substantively erroneous, as he argued the Hindus he was criticizing were.

Independent Propositions

This new method may seem innocuous enough, but it introduced an innovation: it made Madhyamaka claims about emptiness into *propositions* (*pakshas*) or *theses* (*pratijnas*) to be defended — this after Nagarjuna explicitly said that he had no thesis to defend (VV 29). Aryadeva follows Nagarjuna: when the objection is raised in the *Four Hundred Verses* that in refuting his opponent's proposition, he established his own proposition and so should approve of positively proving a proposition, he responded: "If what does not exist when thoroughly examined cannot be a proposition, then the three claims (proposition, counter-proposition, and non-proposition) are not tenable propositions at all" (16.4-5; also see 16.8, 19-24 and SS 10.1-4, 12). But Bhavya now argues that, in order to make Madhyamaka claims acceptable to others, it was necessary to present *positive* arguments in favor of the Madhyamaka claims, not merely present the *negative* consequences of holding the opposite view (the *prasanga*-type of arguing). For example, the Commentary to MHK 3.26 states that their proposition is "Everything is empty of self-existence." He defends his move with a simple argument: he is *a commentator* and his role is different from that of those who originally introduced the idea of emptiness. His role is to clarify and defend the idea to non-Buddhists, and this warrants a change in presentation. (In the West, think of the difference in the role and style of *prophets* and of *theologians*, although the role here is not "faith seeking understanding" but attempts to convince other people.)

That is, Nagarjuna merely shows how opponents' theses involving self-existent realities were *wrong* without articulating any positive reasons to accept the alternative position of emptiness. Thereby, he only indirectly establishes by default the Madhyamaka claim that all entities are empty of any reifying self-existent substance. Thus, Nagarjuna knocks down the metaphysics of self-existence and thereby left emptiness as the only position still standing without actually defending emptiness. But Bhavya takes the Madhyamaka claim "All entities are empty of self-existence," not merely as the conclusion to be reached when the thesis of self-existence is refuted, but as a positive thesis that needs defending. This also meant that he could use Madhyamaka claims about emptiness as premises in arguments against his opponents.

Bhavya thinks that independent propositions are implied in Nagarjuna's arguments and that they elucidate his intent (Dreyfus & McClintock 2003: 8). He makes explicit what he thinks is implicit in Nagarjuna's arguments. But it "accepted a degree of 'realism' on the conventional level" (ibid.: 11) that made some Madhyamikas uneasy. Certainly, saying that conventionally entities can be said to be self-existent (MHK 3.25) would raise a red flag. Bhavya's approach to argumentation also raises the issue of whether what is referred to in the premise of the syllogism is established as real in some sense. If a statement is true, isn't what is referred to real in the final analysis (i.e., from an absolute point of view)? Doesn't it ultimately have to exist? He also seems to give the "means of knowledge," the "objects of knowledge," and the form of argumentation more reality than they warranted even on only a conventional level. It also brings up issues Nagarjuna had to address in *Overturning the Objections*: if Madhyamikas utilize experience (seeing change and decay), doesn't that make ordinary empirical observation a valid means of knowing what is in fact *real* in the final analysis? And if such observation is not real in the final sense, how does it invalidate permanence and self-existence?

Types of Negation

Bhavya distinguishes "total negation (*prasaya-pratishedha*)" from "negation with an affirmation (*prayudasa-pratishedha*)." In the case of the latter, saying something is not *x* means it is "not *x* but something similar to *x*." For example, "He is not a Brahmin" means he is not a Brahmin but is a member of another class (MKV 3.26; Iida 1980: 84). A total negation is not qualified, and so negations from the ultimate point of view are absolute — e.g., the denial of self-existence (MHK 3.26). So too, an unqualified negation of one position, Bhavya argues, does not entail the acceptability of the opposite position. We typically think that if something is either *a* or *b* and we show that it is not *a*, then it must be *b* — we need no further positive argument for accepting *b*. But Bhavya's position is that to accept the Madhyamaka claims on emptiness, we need more than merely showing that claims to self-existence are undefendable. (The need for such positive arguments has been raised in modern times: on the foundations of mathematics, the mathematician/philosopher L. E. J. Brouwer argued something similar under the title "intuitionism.") Thus, an unqualified negation of self-existence does not justify an indirect affirmation of emptiness (Ruegg 1981: 65).

Nagarjuna does not distinguish types of negation, but his refutation of self-existence can be interpreted as a matter of "total negation" not permitting an indirect affirmation of any claims about emptiness. Buddhapalita followed Nagarjuna here. But Bhavya thinks that Nagarjuna's work justified a commentator introducing the syllogism. However, again, this made Madhyamaka claims against self-existence have conclusions about emptiness that become *positive propositions to be defended*, and this introduced something new into the tradition. This led the Buddhist scholar Edward Conze to exclaim that Bhavya's system "seems to have held the well-nigh incredible thesis that in Madhyamika logic valid positive statements can be made" (1967: 238-39). But even for Nagarjuna some statements are consistent with how reality ultimately is. (See Jones 2010: 149-53.) This is not to deny that Bhavya admitted that one type of ultimate truths is not expressible (MAS 4-6). Nagarjuna did provide a definition of "reality" (MMK 18.9):

> The defining characteristic of what is actually real (*tattva*) is this: not dependent upon another, peaceful, free of being projected upon by conceptual projections, free of thoughts that make distinctions, and without multiplicity.

But Bhavya says in his Commentary on this verse that this is merely a preliminary definition to help beginners — reality in itself (*tattva*), being nonconceptualizable, cannot be specified. What is real is ultimately beyond speech and cognition (*dhi*) and is not an object of knowledge; anything conceptually constructed is unreal (MHK 8.85). In his Commentary to verse MHK 1.3, he says that the "that-ness (*tat-tva*)" of reality is beyond language since words name entities and there are no real entities to name. So too, there are no defining characteristics (*lakshanas*) or other information about the actual nature of reality in itself to convey. So too, the Buddha is indescribable because he cannot be conceptualized in any way, and words such "the Buddha" are only metaphorical (*upachara*) — here speech comes to an end, and the reality is not accessible to thought; ideas come to an end, and knowledge becomes silent (MHK 3.282-83).

Language

For a syllogism to work, the conventions of language must be accepted. In the Buddhist ontology, words ultimately cannot correspond to reality: reality is made of interrelated, constantly changing phenomena, and thus there are no discrete, independent objects to be referents of our discrete, static words. However, language can be accepted conventionally as a useful fiction for navigating the conventional world. However, conventionally we can accept that there are referents of words in the world — it is only in the ultimate ontological analysis that there are no referents and words are "mere names." (To Sarvastivada Buddhists, entities are the ultimate components of the phenomenal world, and all entities are nameable and thus nothing is ultimately ineffable. Learning the correct names thus is essential to enlightenment.) Language for Nagarjuna is like any other entity: empty of self-existence, but still usable — in fact, only if all things are empty does anything work (see VV 22-23). In his Commentary on MK 1.3, Bhavya says that language, like all that dependently arises, is conventionally real. In MK 24.18, Nagarjuna says: "Whatever is dependently arisen, we call that 'emptiness.' This indicator, once comprehended, is in fact itself the 'middle way.'" By using the word "indicator (*prajnaptir*)," he is saying that "emptiness" is only a convention. He continues: "Without relying upon worldly convention, the truth from the highest point of view cannot be taught. As noted earlier, without reaching the truth from the highest point of view, nirvana cannot be achieved (MK 24.10)." Bhavya is explicit that some truths from the ultimate point of view are statable (MAS 4). Thus, language is not only necessary to navigate the world on the conventional level but can also be used to state some ultimate truths.

The distinction Bhavya draws between expressible and inexpressible truths is not the distinction between *making claims* and *having experiences*: the truth of expressible ultimate truths still must be realized experientially to realize that they are in fact true of reality. Again, expressible ultimate truths are about the ontological nature of things conceptualized in terms of entities. But the ontological nature of reality as it really is beyond our conceptualizations in terms of entities can be stated only negatively as what it is not — not self-existent, not permanent, and so forth. For Bhavya, a yogic nonconceptual knowledge (*jnana*) is still necessary and is acquired through meditative development and discursive insight or discernment (acts of *prajna*). *Prajna* applies not only to alleged entities, but reality as it is (*tat-tva*) (Lindtner 2001a: xvi), and the perfection of *prajna* is *jnana* (ibid.: xvii).

Only the conceptualizable is expressible, and so only imagined entities are expressible (e.g., MHK 3.41). But what is real is devoid of objects and thus beyond discursive knowledge; there is no objects of knowledge, and thus the domain of the discursive mind has ceased; and when the domain of cognition ceases, there is no domain of speech (MHK 8.85). "Here words stop. This (i.e., reality and knowledge) is not the domain of thought (*citta*, i.e., the discursive mind). Conceptions (*samkalpas*) turn back, and the silence of knowledge (*jnana*) is born (MHK 3.283)." Thus, reality as it truly is is not expressible since it has no distinct parts to conceptualize (MHK 8.104). In short, it is not a conceptual object or a collection of such objects. But Bhavya also argues that one type of ultimate truth is expressible — ultimate truths in terms of the emptiness of entities — as are conventional truths (MAS 4-6). Thus, independent propositions are not a matter of conventional truths only. Nor does he introduce any new laws of logic or rules of reasoning for the ultimate truths.

All of this firmly plants language and reasoning within this mystical system. Nevertheless, there remains a class of higher truths for which language and reasoning are not applicable — ultimately, there are no theses or propositions to defend.

Does Bhavya Go Beyond Nagarjuna?

It can be argued that it is only theses connected to the idea of "*self-existence*" that are condemned by Nagarjuna — i.e., any view entailing self-existent entities as part of the ultimate makeup of the universe — and thus that any thesis about emptiness does not fall into the prohibited type of propositions, but Bhavya does not make this argument. Rather, he seems to make precisely the type of independent thesis that Nagarjuna was attacking. Aryadeva and Buddhapalita are more in keeping with Nagarjuna's original method in their way of attacking other systems of metaphysics.

Nagarjuna would agree that there are no conventional truths about the ultimate ontological status of things. But there are also no ultimate truths about the connections and relations within the conventional world, and thus both types of truth are needed. And it must also be concluded that Bhavya validates some reality to the conventional world, even if he agrees that it is empty of distinct, self-existent entities. Nagarjuna emphasizes the ultimate ontological status of things, but for Bhavya the world of appearances is not merely a delusion but real enough not to be ignored. In addition, he goes beyond Nagarjuna: Nagarjuna implicitly admits some ultimate truths can be stated by means of the conventions of language (MK 24.10), but Bhavya argues for statable ultimate truths. This does go beyond the pure, relentless negation of the *prasanga* method, and whether this interferes with the Buddhist soteriological process by creating positive images of reality as it truly is to which the mind may become attached is a real issue.

* * *

References and
Other Works

Ames, William L. "Buddhapālita's Exposition of the Madhyamaka." *Journal of Indian Philosophy* 14 (September 1986): 313-48.

___. (a) "Buddhapālita's Vritti on Nagārjuna's *Mula-madhyamaka-karikas*." In Potter 2003: 286-305.

___. (b) "Bhāvaviveka's Own View of His Differences with Buddhapālita." In Dreyfus & McClintock 2003: 41-66.

Berzin, Alexander. *Four Hundred Verse Treatise on the Actions of a Bodhisattva's Yoga*. hhttp://www.berzinarchives.com/web/x/nav/group.html_71051276.html.

Bhaskar, Bhagchandra. *Acārya Āryadeva's Catuhśatakam: Along with the Candrakīrti Vrtti & Hindī Translation*. Samsthāna : Prāptisthāna, Kāla Prakāśana 2007.

Conze, Edward. "Rahulabhadra, *Hymn to Perfect Wisdom*." In Edward Conze, I. B. Horner, David Snellgrove, and Arthur Waley, eds., *Buddhist Texts Through the Ages*, pp. 147-49. New York: Harper & Row, 1964.

___. *Buddhist Thought in India*. Ann Arbor: University of Michigan Press, 1967.

His Holiness the Fourteenth Dalai Lama (Tenzin Gyatso). *The Middle Way: Faith Grounded in Reason*. Trans. by Thupten Jinpa. Boston: Wisdom Publications, 2009.

Datar, I. "A Study of the First Twenty Chapters of Buddhapalita's *Mulamadhyama-kavrtti*." *Journal of the Royal Asiatic Society of Great Britain and Ireland (Bombay Branch)* 26 (1950-51): 129-39.

Della Santina, Peter. *Madhyamaka Schools in India: A Study of the Madhyamaka Philosophy and of the Division of the System into the Prāsangika and Svātantrika Schools*. New Delhi: Motilal Banarsidass, 1986.

Dreyfus, Georges B. J. and Sara L. McClintock, ed. *The Svātantrika-Prāsangika Distinction: What Difference Does a Difference Make?* Boston: Wisdom Publications, 2003.

Eckel, Malcolm David. *To See the Buddha: A Philosopher's Quest for the Meaning of Emptiness*. Princeton: Princeton University Press, 1992.

___. *Bhāviveka and His Opponents*. Cambridge: Harvard University Press, 2008.

Fehér, Judit. "Buddhapālita's *Mūlamadhyamakavrtti*: Arrival and Spread of Prāsangika-Mādhyamika Literature in Tibet." In Louis Ligeti, ed., *Tibetan and Buddhist Studies: Commemorating the 200ᵗʰ Anniversary of the Birth of Alexander Csoma de Kőrös*, volume 1, pp. 211-40. Budapest: Akadémiai Kiadó, 1984.

Ferrer, Daniel. "Bhāvaviveka's Abridged Meaning of the Middle Position." *The Tibet Journal* 17 (no. 2 1975): 52-55.

Gokhale, V. V. "The Second Chapter of Bhavya's *Madhyamakrhrdaya* (Taking the Vow of an Ascetic)." *Indo-Iranian Journal* 14 (1972): 40-45.

___. "The Vedānta Philosophy Described by Bhavya in his *Madhyamakahrdaya*." *Indo-Iranian Journal* 2 (1958): 165-80.

___ and S. S. Bahulkar. "Madhyamakahrdayakārikā Tarkjvālā — Chapter 1." In Christian Lindtner, ed., *Miscellenea Buddhica*, pp. 76-107. Copenhagen: Akademisk Forlag, 1985.

Goodman, Charles. "Bhāvaviveka's Arguments for Emptiness." *Asian Philosophy* 18 (July 2008): 167-84.

Hitaka, Ryusho, ed. *Suvikrānatavirkrāmi-pariprcchā Prajñāpāramitā-sūtra*. Fukuoka, Japan: Kyushu University, 1958.

Huntington, C. W., Jr. "*Akutobhayā* on Nāgārjuna's *Madhyamakakārikās*." In Potter 1999: 329-32.

Iida, Shotaro. "The Nature of Samvrti and the Relationship of Paramārtha to it in Svātantrika-Mādhyamika." In Mervyn Sprung, ed., *The Problem of Two Truths in Buddhism and Vedānta*, pp. 64-77. Boston: D. Reidel Publishing, 1973.

___. *Reason and Emptiness: A Study of Logic and Mysticism*. Tokyo: Hokuseido Press, 1980.

Jones, Richard H. *Mysticism and Morality: A New Look at Old Questions*. Lanham, Md.: Lexington Books, 2004.

___. *Nagarjuna: Buddhism's Most Important Philosopher*. New York: Jackson Square Books/Createspace, 2010.

Lang, Karen. *Āryadeva's Catuhśataka: On the Bodhisattva's Cultivation of Merit and Knowledge*. Copenhagen: Akademisk Forlag, 1986.

___. (a) "Summary of Aryadeva's *Catuhśataka*." In Potter 1999: 198-215.

___. (b) "Summary of Aryadeva's *Śataka*." In Potter 1999: 215-22.

___. (c) "Summary of Aryadeva's *Aksharashatkaka*." In Potter 1999: 222-28.

Lindtner, Christian. "Buddhapālita on Emptiness: *Buddhapālita-mula-madhyamaka-vritti XVIII*." *Indo-Iranian Journal* 23 (1981): 187-217.

___, ed. (a) *Madhyamakahrdayam of Bhavya*. Chennai, India: Adyar Library and Research Centre, 2001.

___, ed. and trans. (b) *Bhavya on Mīmāmsā: Mīmāmsātattvanirnayāvatārah*. Chennai, India: Adyar Library and Research Centre, 2001.

Nagao, Gadjin. *The Foundational Standpoint of Mādhyamika Philosophy*. Trans. by John P. Keenan. Albany: State University of New York, 1989.

Nakamura, Hajiame. "The Vedāntic Chapter of Bhavya's *Madhyamakahrdaya*." *Adyar Library Bulletin* 39 (1975): 300-29.

Newland, Guy. *Appearance and Reality: The Two Truths in the Four Buddhist Tenet Systems*. Ithaca, N.Y.: Snow Lion Publications, 1999.

___, ed. *Buddhist Philosophy from 350 to 600 A.D. The Encyclopedia of Indian Philosophies*, volume 9. Delhi: Motilal Banarsidass, 2003.

Qvarnström, Olle. *Hindu Philosophy in Buddhist Perspective: The* Vedāntatattvaviniścaya *Chapter of Bhavya's* Madhyamakahrdayakārikā. Lund, Sweden: Plus Ultra, 1989.

Ruegg, David Seyfort. *The Literature of the Madhyamaka School of Philosophy in India.* Wiesbaden: Otto Harrassowitz, 1981.

___. "On the Authorship of Some Works Ascribed to Bhāvaviveka/Bhavya." In David Seyfort Ruegg and Lambert Schmithausen, eds., *Earliest Buddhism and Madhyamaka*, pp. 61-71. New York: E. J. Brill, 1990.

___. *Three Studies in the History of Indian and Tibetan Madhyamaka Philosophy.* Vienna: Wien University, 2000.

___. "The *Svātantrika-Prāsangika* Distinction in the History of Madhyamaka Thought." *Indo-Iranian Journal* 49 (2006): 319-46.

Sastri, Pandit N. Ayyaswami. "Madhyamāsangraha of Bhāvaviveka (Restored from the Tibetan Version with an English Translation)." *Journal of Oriental Research (Madras)* 5 (March 1931): 41-49.

Sonam, Ruth, trans. *Āryadeva's Four Hundred Versions on the Middle Way, with Commentary by Gyel-tsap.* Ithaca: Snow Lion, 2008.

Tachikawa, Musashi, "A Study of Buddhapālita's *Mūlamadhyamakavrtti* (1)." *Journal of the Faculty of Literature* (Nagoya University) 63 (1974): 1-19.

Thomas, F. W. and H. Ui. "'The Hand Treatise,' a Work of Aryadeva." *Journal of the Royal Asiatic Society of Great Britain and Ireland* (April 1918): 267-310.

Tillemans, Tom J. F. *Materials for the Study of Āryadeva, Dharmapāla and Candrakīrti*, volume 1. Vienna: Wien University, 1990.

Tola, Fernando and Carmen Dragonetti. "The Hastavālanāmaprakaranavrtti." *Journal of Religious Studies (Punjabi University)* 8 (Spring 1980): 18-31.

___. *On Voidness: A Study on Buddhist Nihilism.* Delhi: Motilal Banarsidass, 1995.

Tsering, Geshe Tashi. *Relative Truth, Ultimate Truth: The Foundation of Buddhist Thought*, volume 2. Boston: Wisdom Publications, 2008.

___. *Emptiness: The Foundation of Buddhist Thought*, volume 5. Boston: Wisdom Publications, 2009.

Tucci, Giuseppe. "Āryadeva's *Satasāstra*: Translated from the Chinese." *Pre-Dinnaga Buddhist Texts on Logic From Chinese Sources*, Part 1, pp. 1-89 and Notes, pp. 46-58. Baroda: Gaekwad's Oriental Series, 1929.

Vaidya, P. L. *Études sur Āryadeva et son Catuhśataka.* Paris: Librairie Orientaliste, 1923.

Watanabe, Chikafumi, "A Translation of the *Madhyamakahrdayakārikā* with the *Tarkajvālā* III.137-146." *Journal of the International Association of Buddhist Studies* 21 (no. 1 1998): 125-55.

Index

Made in the USA
Lexington, KY
09 May 2013